W9-BZW-748

THE
BEST GREEN
SMOOTHIES
ON THE PLANET

THE
BEST GREEN
SMOOTHIES
ON THE PLANET

JA 19 '15

*The 150 Most Delicious,
Most Nutritious, 100% Vegan
Recipes for the World's
Healthiest Drink*

641.875
RUS

BY
TRACY RUSSELL

BARRINGTON AREA LIBRARY
505 N. NORTHWEST HWY.
BARRINGTON, ILLINOIS 60010

BENBELLA

BENBELLA BOOKS, INC. • DALLAS, TX

Copyright © 2014 by Tracy Russell
A Hollan Publishing, Inc. Concept

All rights reserved. No part of this book may be used or reproduced in any manner whatsoever without written permission except in the case of brief quotations embodied in critical articles or reviews.

Nothing written in this book is intended to serve as a substitute for professional medical advice. A health care professional should be consulted regarding your specific medical situation. The author and publisher specifically disclaim any and all liability arising directly or indirectly from the use of any information contained in this book. Any product mentioned in this book does not imply endorsement of the product by the author or publisher.

BenBella Books, Inc.
10300 N. Central Expressway
Suite #530
Dallas, TX 75231
www.benbellabooks.com
Send feedback to feedback@benbellabooks.com

Printed in the United States of America
10 9 8 7 6 5 4 3 2 1

Library of Congress Cataloging-in-Publication Data
Russell, Tracy, 1981-
The best green smoothies on the planet: the 150 most delicious, most nutritious, 100% vegan recipes for the world's healthiest drink / by Tracy Russell.
pages cm
Includes bibliographical references and index.
ISBN 978-1-940363-27-1 (paperback)—ISBN 978-1-940363-42-4 (electronic) 1. Smoothies (Beverages) 2. Vegetable juices. I. Title.
TX840.J84R87 2014
641.6'5—dc23
2014011565

Editing by Vy Tran
Copyediting by Stacia Seaman
Proofreading by Cape Cod Compositors, Inc. and
Brittany Dowdle
Indexing by Jigsaw Indexing
Cover photos by Allan Penn
Front cover and text design by Bradford Foltz
Full cover design by Sarah Dombrowsky
Text composition by Integra Software Services Pvt. Ltd

Printed by Versa Press
Distributed by Perseus Distribution
www.perseusdistribution.com

To place orders through Perseus Distribution:
Tel: (800) 343-4499
Fax: (800) 351-5073
E-mail: orderentry@perseusbooks.com

Significant discounts for bulk sales are available. Please contact Glenn Yeffeth at glenn@benbellabooks.com or (214) 750-3628.

*To my sister-in-law, Jen,
who introduced me to green smoothies
and forever changed my life.*

Contents

Foreword • xiii

Introduction • xvii

PART ONE
Introduction to Green Smoothies

Chapter One
Why Green Smoothies? • 3

Chapter Two
How to Make the Perfect Green Smoothie • 17

Chapter Three
The Best Green Smoothie Ingredients • 35

PART TWO
Green Smoothie Recipes

Chapter Four
Detox and Cleansing Green Smoothies · 79

Pear-Dandelion · 86

Mean Green Cleansing · 86

Blueberry-Lemonade · 87

Green Apple · 87

Strawberry-Grapefruit · 88

Pineapple-Lime-Cilantro · 88

Berry Cleansing · 89

Lemon-Lime · 89

Grapefruit-Orange · 90

Dandelion-Orange · 90

The Green Machine · 91

Pineapple-Celery · 91

Apple-Mango · 92

Sweet Grapefruit · 92

Green Goodness Detox · 93

Cranberry Cleanse · 93

Orange-Pear · 94

Strawberry-Lemonade · 94

Chapter Five
Weight Loss Green Smoothies · 95

Pineapple-Mango · 101

Strawberry-Orange · 101

Banana-Pineapple · 102

Cherry-Pineapple · 102

Mango-Kiwifruit · 103

Peach-Cherry · 103

Spiced Blueberry and Pear · 104

Healthy Chocolate · 104

Carrot-Papaya · 105

Apple-Broccoli · 105

Watermelon-Mint · 106

Chocolate-Grape-Strawberry · 106

Peach-Strawberry · 107

Coconut-Mango with Lime · 107

Kiwifruit-Broccoli · 108

Apple-Cherimoya · 108

Chocolate-Kiwifruit · 109

Banana-Pineapple with Aloe
and Kale · 109

Chapter Six
Antioxidant Green Smoothies • 111

Very Berry • 115
Cherry-Plum • 115
Blueberry-Persimmon • 116
Frozen Raspberry-Lemonade • 116
Blueberry-Cherry-Pomegranate • 117
Raspberry-Orange-Pomegranate • 117
Plum-Açaí • 118
Mango-Papaya with Blueberries • 118
Pineapple-Plum with Almond
 Milk • 119

Cherry-Pomegranate • 119
Blackberry-Peach • 120
Raspberry-Carrot • 120
Black and Blue • 121
Blackberry-Açaí • 121
Super Antioxidant Blast • 122
Cherry-Vanilla-Peach • 122
Pineapple-Carrot • 123

Chapter Seven
Fitness and Energy Green Smoothies • 125

Apple-Lime • 130
Goji Berry–Maca • 130
Berry–Chia Seed • 131
Chocolate–Peanut Butter • 131
Blueberry-Oat • 132
Berry-Kale • 132
Mango-Avocado • 133
Blueberry-Maca • 133
Peach-Oat • 134

Ginger-Berry-Oat • 134
Chocolate-Cherry • 135
Cherry-Banana • 135
Vanilla-Avocado • 136
Apple-Avocado • 136
Cucumber-Kale • 137
Peanut Butter–Raspberry • 137
Ginger-Citrus with Kale • 138

Chapter Eight
Immune-Boosting Green Smoothies • 139

Orange-Ginger • 143

Papaya-Mint • 143

Lemon-Kiwifruit • 144

Pear-Broccoli • 144

Zucchini-Vanilla • 145

Cinnamon-Strawberry • 145

Vanilla-Cantaloupe • 146

Happy Berry Muffin • 146

Sweet Potato • 147

Cherry–Sweet Potato • 147

Kiwifruit-Grape with Broccoli • 148

Cantaloupe-Papaya • 148

Pear-Kiwifruit • 149

Mango-Lime • 149

Ginger-Carrot • 150

Refreshing Lemon-Cucumber • 150

Pineapple-Ginger • 151

Chapter Nine
Calcium-Rich Green Smoothies • 153

Coconut–Goji Berry • 158

Sweet Potato–Orange • 158

Nectarine-Cherry • 159

Pear-Tangerine • 159

Red Grape–Fig • 160

Banana-Orange • 160

Pistachio-Banana • 161

Coconut-Grapefruit • 161

Peach-Strawberry-Coconut • 162

Super Green and Peach • 162

Pineapple-Citrus • 163

Banana-Cranberry • 163

Ginger-Peach • 164

Pear-Aloe • 164

Coconut-Peach • 165

Pineapple-Orange Tropical • 165

Strawberry-Raspberry
with Avocado • 166

Orange–Sesame Seed • 166

Chapter Ten
Heart-Healthy Green Smoothies • 167

Watermelon-Blueberry • 171
Goji Berry Superfood • 171
Creamy Chocolate and Vanilla • 172
Kiwifruit-Orange • 172
Tropical • 173
Strawberry Goodness • 173
Avocado-Peach • 174
Cantaloupe-Raspberry • 174
Strawberry-Avocado • 175

Coconut-Apple-Ginger • 175
Blackberry-Almond • 176
Chia Seed–Red Grape • 176
Raspberry-Avocado • 177
Avocado-Berry • 177
Blueberry-Flaxseed • 178
Peach-Vanilla • 178
Coconut-Persimmon • 179

Chapter Eleven
Iron-Rich Green Smoothies • 181

Cherry-Kiwifruit • 186
The Veggie • 186
Chocolate-Raspberry • 187
Star Fruit–Peach • 187
Peach-Mango • 188
Refreshing Apple • 188
Mango-Pear • 189
Kale-Parsley • 189
Chocolate-Mango • 190

Chocolate-Açaí • 190
Broccoli-Kale • 191
Parsley-Pear • 191
Cucumber-Parsley • 192
Peach-Pear • 192
Pear-Grape • 193
Nectarine–Goji Berry • 193
Cucumber-Aloe • 194
Ginger-Spinach • 194

Chapter Twelve
Mood-Enhancing Green Smoothies · 195

Strawberry-Banana · 200
Cherry-Apple · 200
Berry-Banana · 201
Spiced Pineapple · 201
Coconut-Vanilla-Peach · 202

Maca-Cacao · 202
Maca-Almond · 203
Mango-Maca · 203
Mesquite Cacao · 204
Chocolate-Kale · 204

Notes · 205
Index · 211
Recipe Index · 219
About the Author · 235

Foreword

How green is your diet? Go on, take a quick inventory of all the green things on your plate, in your bowl, or in your glass over the past few days. This dietary "green inventory" is something you should probably be taking more often.

Why bother with green? Well, healthy green foods like leafy greens, including kale, spinach, chard, collard, arugula, parsley, mâche, and more, are some of the most nutrient-dense foods we can enjoy. They are rich in fiber, vitamins, minerals, and phytonutrients. Other healthy and delicious green foods include avocados, cruciferous veggies like broccoli, superfoods like spirulina, and more. Green foods provide some serious wellness on demand!

But let's face it. We do not always have the time, creativity, and energy to prepare green foods the way we want to. Sitting down to eat a giant bowl of raw leafy greens and other assorted produce may not be on everyone's to-do list during a busy workday. And some people (kids and picky eaters alike) simply do not enjoy traditional raw salads and produce as much as other foods. Well, green smoothies can change all that! Nearly everyone can agree that these blends are dreamy and delicious.

Green smoothies combine the best of all worlds. The convenience you need. The flavor you crave. The nutrition your body thrives on. The raw greens your body loves. And green smoothies encompass more than greens, with the possibility of combining an array of non-green wellness foods like citrus, bananas, and more.

So keep reading! Dive into this book and learn how to make healthy and delicious green blends. Making green smoothies is a lifelong skill that will benefit you and your family for years to come.

Need more convincing? Just think, in one tall and frosty glass you can enjoy the nutrition benefits of a giant bowl of produce—nutrition made easier. Plus, since blending the greens and produce eases up the digestive process (less work for your body!), you will feel the energy from your green smoothie flowing through your body swiftly and steadily.

On my blog, lunchboxbunch.com, I have been posting green smoothie recipes for years, and it always amazes me how many people who are unfamiliar with green smoothies comment on how they think they will taste grassy, bitter, and hard to drink. Picture someone plugging their nose and guzzling away with a cringed look on their face—that is the quickly changing stereotype. The reality of green smoothies is this: You blend them, you take one sip, and you literally cannot stop yourself from taking another sip, and another. Suddenly you are chugging the vibrant green blend as it fills your senses with an energizing array of delicious tangy-sweet flavors, frosty, creamy, or silky textures, and an overall sense of joy and bliss. You are in green heaven!

Too dramatic? No way. Take one sip and you will soon discover for yourself what this amazing book is all about: green smoothie bliss that you will be craving again and again.

The recipes in *The Best Green Smoothies on the Planet* are truly blends that will show you how craveable and delicious green smoothies can be. So if you have never sipped a green blend, or even if you are a green smoothie pro, these drinks will give you reason to stock your kitchen with healthy ingredients and start a green smoothie habit that will change your life. I always say that one of the best things you can do for your wellness is to start a smoothie habit. Well, starting a green smoothie habit is even *better*. So bring on the green and enjoy these creative, delicious, wellness-enhancing blends!

KATHY PATALSKY
Author of *365 Vegan Smoothies*, blogger at Healthy. Happy. Life.
Lunchboxbunch.com
@lunchboxbunch

Introduction

I woke up on the morning of January 1, 2008, with a headache and a general "blah" feeling. It was a new year, but I felt anything but "new." I forced myself out of bed, shuffled to the kitchen, and squinted in the sunlight as I blew the dust off my blender, which was wedged into the deep recesses of my kitchen cupboards—the ones I rarely opened.

Just the night before, I had climbed on the scale and was shocked to see a number I had never seen before in my life. I was officially the heaviest I've ever been. I realized that I was eating antacids with every meal. My skin was broken out. I felt sluggish. I knew I needed to change my diet—and sustain it this time.

I had already tried almost every diet out there, but I was never able to stick to them because I'd feel deprived (or hungry), and I'd fall off the bandwagon after a week. I tried to exercise regularly, but I had no leftover energy after working a full-time job.

I had also tried for years to eat more fruits and vegetables. Eating an apple or banana a day was easy. Chewing a big salad or eating broccoli and asparagus by the forkful was a challenge. Like many people, I was never a big fan of vegetables. They tend to be bitter, mushy, and not exactly the most pleasant things to eat.

But a few weeks before That Night, my sister-in-law had told me about a workshop she had attended at her local food co-op. She told me about green smoothies and how they were made. I was intrigued—and a little disgusted.

"You mean you actually put spinach . . . IN your smoothie?!" I said to her.

Yet after realizing that I needed to change my eating habits, I thought that green smoothies seemed to be the perfect solution to my problem of getting more fruits and vegetables into my diet. I figured that it would be much easier than trying to eat a large salad every single day. If green smoothies did taste as great as they were promoted to, then I thought that it would be the easiest way to make eating more fruits and vegetables a daily dietary habit.

So I made a New Year's resolution to drink a green smoothie every day for a month. I would have my very first green smoothie on the first day of the New Year.

I poured about four ounces of water into my blender, then tossed in a banana, a handful of frozen strawberries, and a large-ish handful of baby spinach. It almost felt like I was about to ruin a perfectly good strawberry-banana smoothie. I hit the "blend" button and watched as the machine whipped up my concoction.

It was green. I mean really green. Greener than anything I had ever considered as food before. I poured it into a glass, closed my eyes, and with a deep breath, took a drink. I already had my excuse as to why green smoothies weren't for me planned out in my head.

The delicious flavors of sweet banana and tart strawberries danced across my tongue. This smoothie was delicious. My eyes sprang open. Yes, the smoothie was still quite green, but no matter how hard I tried, I just couldn't taste a single speck of spinach.

I was ecstatic. With green smoothies I could get more fruits and vegetables into my diet without having to chew monotonous salads. No longer would I have to grin and bear it when I ate vegetables. I could greatly increase my vegetable intake and not taste them at all!

That fateful day kicked off a dramatic change in my life that I was never able to achieve through any fad diet, supplement, or exercise regimen.

Green smoothies helped me lose forty pounds. My cholesterol dropped 50 points (I was on the verge of "higher than normal" cholesterol at age twenty-three, and my family has a history of high cholesterol). My skin cleared up. I also felt a surge of energy that never petered out halfway through the day. I started running and eventually ran a major marathon.

But one of the biggest impacts that green smoothies had on my life was in the way I ate. After a couple months of drinking a green smoothie every morning for breakfast, I started craving healthy foods. I actually craved vegetables!

I began replacing unhealthy, processed foods with healthier, whole food alternatives. Eventually, it became easier for me to forgo the cookie and satisfy my sweet tooth with a deliciously sweet green smoothie.

My friends and family started asking me about my green smoothies, noticing how they were helping me slim down and get a radiant glow—even in the middle of winter. Excited about all the positive changes that green smoothies had helped me achieve, I decided to start up a blog called Incredible Smoothies (www.incrediblesmoothies.com) to share my experiences and some of my green smoothie recipes with the world.

Now I hope to reach even more people through my book.

The Best Green Smoothies on the Planet features 150 of my favorite, most delicious, most raved-about green smoothie recipes. You will also find lots of tips and advice for coming up with your own healthy and delicious green smoothie recipes.

This book is divided into two parts. The first three chapters that compose Part One provide all of the details that you need to make your green smoothie adventure a delicious delight. Chapter One focuses on the health benefits of green smoothies. You'll learn how to incorporate green smoothies into your current diet in order to lose weight and boost your energy levels.

Chapter Two provides an in-depth primer on how to make the perfect green smoothie and how to save a green smoothie that just doesn't taste as good as you hoped (it happens). You'll also learn how to save money on produce, as well as how to prevent produce from going bad before you can use it.

Chapter Three will turn you into a green smoothie connoisseur. You'll discover dozens of delicious fruit and green pairings, and you'll get a *ton* of ideas for ingredients to use in your smoothie recipes and why you should use them. Nutritional highlights help you plan green smoothie recipes that deliver more of what your body needs.

Part Two of this book contains all 150 delicious green smoothie recipes. The recipes are divided by chapters focusing on specific health benefits such as weight loss, detox, fitness, heart health, immune-boosting, and mood elevation. There are also many nutrient-specific blends for increasing one's intake of calcium, iron, and antioxidants.

Get ready to change your life with green smoothies!

PART ONE

INTRODUCTION TO GREEN SMOOTHIES

CHAPTER ONE

WHY GREEN SMOOTHIES?

Green smoothies are essentially a typical fruit smoothie but with the addition of fresh leafy green vegetables like spinach, kale, and chard. In addition to leafy greens, green smoothies may also be made using vegetables like celery, cucumbers, and even broccoli.

Because of the sweet fruits that make up the base for a green smoothie, even the flavor of added bitter greens such as kale or dandelion is completely hidden. Instead of tasting spinach or kale, you'll taste the sweet fruit in the recipe—like bananas and strawberries!

Unlike typical fruit smoothies that often use frozen chunks of fruit, green smoothies call for fresh whole fruits and vegetables. Typically, green smoothies are not made with dairy milk or yogurt. Creamy textured fruits, and sometimes nut milks, give them all of the creamy goodness they need. There are thousands of variations on the green smoothie, so your options for delicious and nutritious flavors are endless!

There are many reasons to drink green smoothies on a daily basis. However, the most popular include:

1. Easily get five or more servings of fruits and vegetables every single day—without tasting the vegetables.

A banana, an apple, and two large handfuls of fresh baby spinach are all you need to get your recommended five servings of fruits and vegetables every day.

If you are not a salad person, or you dread the thought of noshing on food like asparagus, green smoothies provide a way to get your vegetables, especially your greens, without tasting them or dealing with their textures.

2. Replace unhealthy meals and snacks with fruits and vegetables.

Green smoothies can replace less healthy mid-afternoon snacks. They can also replace a particular meal, like breakfast or lunch. Any one of my weight loss green smoothie recipes is a hearty enough breakfast to keep me full and satisfied until lunch, and they are a much healthier alternative to sugary cereal, muffins, or fast food.

3. Green smoothies are convenient, go-anywhere food.

Green smoothies only take a few minutes to make, and you can take them anywhere. Blend them the night before and grab them from the refrigerator on your way out the door to work the next morning. You can even store green smoothies in a sealed container and have them for lunch on the go.

4. Satisfy your sweet tooth with sweet fruits that are rich in vitamins, minerals, fiber, and antioxidants.

Green smoothies are sweet—but they are the good type of sweet. The natural sugars in fruits are delivered alongside fiber, vitamins, minerals, and antioxidants to nourish your body and feed your cells. They are nothing like the "empty calorie" sweets and soft drinks that provide no nutritional benefit.

Fruits like bananas, mangoes, and peaches that make up the base for green smoothies satisfy my sweet tooth and keep me from eating sugary snacks like cookies and caving into other cravings.

Green Smoothie Health Benefits

In addition to the reasons above, green smoothies also have a lot of health benefits. The top benefit is weight loss, which I will discuss in depth in Chapter Five.

I have interviewed countless readers on my website, Incredible Smoothies, who have lost anywhere from twenty to more than a hundred pounds thanks to green smoothies and a whole foods diet. In every weight-loss story I heard, green smoothies were the catalyst that kicked off a sustainable change leading to successful weight loss.

Another benefit of green smoothies is their ability to support your body's natural detoxification processes, so Chapters Four and Six are all about detox, cleansing, and antioxidants. Green smoothies are made with the most cleansing foods on the planet—fresh, water-rich fruits and vegetables that are loaded with vitamins, minerals, antioxidants, and fiber.

Speaking of fiber, green smoothies are loaded with it. The average American does not consume sufficient fiber in their diet. In fact, there is a whole industry addressing the fiber deficiency in the American diet by selling fiber supplements!

However, the average meal-replacement green smoothie recipe provides almost a day's worth of fiber. Sufficient dietary fiber is thought to reduce the risk of colon cancer.[1] Fiber also slows down the absorption of sugars, making fruit one of the best, non-fattening sources of carbohydrates.[2] Blending fruits and dark, leafy greens into a creamy smoothie breaks down the food, making digestion easier.

Consuming more fruits and vegetables in one's diet may also keep a variety of chronic health conditions at bay, including Alzheimer's,[3] type 2 diabetes,[4–9] high blood pressure,[10–11] high cholesterol,[12–13] heart disease,[14] COPD,[15–17] anxiety and depression,[18–19] Parkinson's,[20] stroke,[21–22] macular degeneration,[23] and several types of cancers.[24–36] The overwhelming scientific consensus is that people who consume more servings of fruits and vegetables each day have a lower risk of developing diseases or illnesses. Specific foods have been studied and found to provide therapeutic benefits for certain medical conditions, but overall, increased fruit and vegetable consumption correlates with a lower incidence of most chronic health problems.

While green smoothies are not a cure for any disease, nor do they take the place of prescription medications and proven treatments, green smoothies provide optimum nutrition to give your body the best chance of reducing the risk of disease, while potentially providing some therapeutic benefit.

Increased energy is also among the top health benefits attributed to green smoothies. Green smoothies provide the sugar (glucose) that feeds every cell in your body. The healthy carbohydrates in sweet fruit also help fuel your body, whether you are powering through a workout or just going through your day and checking things off your to-do list.

The energy boosts from consuming green smoothies often give people the motivation and stamina to not only begin a workout routine but stick with regular exercise over the long term (as long as they are drinking green smoothies consistently). As a result, green smoothies may help facilitate weight loss through their energy-lifting properties.

What Is the Green Smoothie Diet All About?

I just want to be crystal clear: I do not promote or advocate a green smoothie–only diet. This book isn't about drinking nothing but green smoothies for a period of time in order to lose weight quickly or detox.

Short-term crash diets, cleanses, or fasts lead only to short-term results. There is no point to losing twenty pounds in two weeks if you will only gain it all back within a couple months of going off the diet. And there is no point in punishing your body with a crash diet if the results won't last for the rest of your life.

Instead, green smoothies are most effective when incorporated into a plant-based, whole food diet. In fact, simply adding green smoothies to your existing diet, whatever that might be right now, may kick-start an eventual shift in your diet and lifestyle that will propel you toward making healthier choices. Whether you simply add a green smoothie component to your existing diet or you dramatically transform your diet into a strictly whole food, plant-based lifestyle, these changes are sustainable over the long term.

You can drink a green smoothie for breakfast every morning for the rest of your life. You can eat a whole food, plant-based diet for life without feeling deprived or struggling with hunger and all the other drawbacks of short-term diets.

Because these changes are sustainable over the long term, the weight loss and other health benefits will likely last as long as you continue to eat a healthy diet that your body was meant to eat.

Green Smoothies: Fact vs. Fiction

Despite all of the health benefits, there are some myths circulating on the Internet about green smoothies, and you're bound to run into one or two of them. So I'd like to take this opportunity to address some of them.

True or False: Green Smoothies Contain Too Much Sugar

False! Yes, green smoothies are made with sweet fruit, which contains sugar. However, the sugars that are naturally found in fruit are not anywhere in the same league as pure, isolated table sugar, high fructose corn syrup, or other concentrated sweeteners.

Sweet fruit contains both glucose and fructose. Glucose is essential for cell function. Your body needs glucose (sugar) in order to function! As for fructose, while some studies have shown a correlation between fructose consumption and obesity, these studies were performed using isolated fructose. There are no known studies showing a link between fresh fruit consumption and obesity or other metabolic diseases, because consuming fructose-containing fruits does not have the same effect as chugging a soda containing a concentrated source of unhealthy sugars. In fact, studies consistently show that those who consume more fruits and vegetables in their diets tend to have lower body weights.

It is even possible to reduce your overall dietary sugar intake by replacing foods high in added sugar with green smoothies. For example, an average candy bar contains between 40 to 60 grams of sugar, and 20 ounces of soda (e.g., Coca-Cola) contain 65 grams. A green smoothie, on the other hand, made with one banana, one apple, and two handfuls of fresh baby spinach only has 34 grams of sugar.

And remember that green smoothies and fruit are not just "sugar." Instead, they are whole foods rich in vitamins, minerals, antioxidants, fiber, protein, energy-giving carbohydrates, and omega-3 fatty acids.

I always challenge my readers to go beyond "isolated nutrient thinking" and consider the whole food. When you eat whole foods, you are consuming nutrients in balanced amounts. Unless you have an existing medical condition that requires careful monitoring of particular nutrients, it is completely unnecessary to worry about anti-nutrient, sugar, or carbohydrate amounts in any whole food.

In the same vein, a large green smoothie meal that contains 50 grams of sugar might match the sugar content of a candy bar, but it will not have the same effect on your body as a candy bar due to all of the other nutrients. Chocolate bars and soda pop are unhealthy primarily because they are processed foods devoid of any nutritional quality. They do not fill you up, and they do not nourish your body. They only provide excess sugar, calories, and fat. Also, remember that a green smoothie meal *is* your meal, but a candy bar or a soda is 50 to 60+ grams of added sugar (not to mention the extra calories) *in addition to* your meals.

True or False: Green Smoothies Are Too High in Carbohydrates for Weight Loss

False! I regularly hear from people who want to lose weight but are afraid to add green smoothies to their diet because of the carbohydrate content of the sweet fruits in my recipes. Well, rest assured, because there is a *huge* difference between a sugary donut and a fruit-and-vegetable green smoothie! Green smoothies nourish and fuel your body. Donuts just dump excess carbohydrates, sugar, and fat into your diet.

I'm sure you've heard the terms "bad carbs" and "good carbs." While the donut example is full of "bad carbs," fresh fruit and green smoothies are firmly in the "good carbs" camp. So while low-carb diets are all the rage right now, it is not necessary to eliminate all carbohydrates, or even to do a low-carb diet, to lose weight. You can lose weight on a high-carb, low-fat diet if your carbohydrates primarily come from fresh fruits and green smoothies.

The only carbohydrates I worry about are from breads, pasta, and other processed foods.

True or False: The Fructose Content of Green Smoothies (and Fresh Fruit) Causes Weight Gain

False! All of the studies that I have read on fructose deal with isolated, crystalline fructose or fructose-sweetened beverages. I have not seen a single scientific study showing any link between fruit consumption and obesity.

I don't doubt that concentrated sweeteners like high fructose corn syrup, sweetened beverages, and processed foods lead to obesity and weight gain. The evidence shows that these unhealthy foods certainly contribute to the so-called "obesity epidemic."

However, evidence suggests that fruit, while also containing fructose, does not lead to obesity because it contains less fructose than fructose-containing junk foods, and in lower concentrations. The vitamins, minerals, antioxidants, and fiber also mitigate the potential negative effects of fructose. So when it comes to fresh fruits and green smoothies, fructose is simply a non-issue for me.

Fruit doesn't make you gain weight, and I'd argue that neither does fructose per se. What can make you gain weight is a sustained overabundance of calories, excessive amounts of concentrated sugars, a diet rich in processed foods lacking in nutritional quality, and a sedentary lifestyle.

Fresh fruits and green smoothies are less calorie-dense, and contain less sugar, than most other sweetened foods out there. They also fuel your body and provide energy that motivates many green smoothie enthusiasts to exercise, so they're actually great foods for people who are trying to lose weight or maintain a healthy one. Of course, if you're trying to do either, it's a good idea to keep track of your total daily calories. If your daily goal is to consume 1,600 calories, then fruit and green smoothies must fit within that calorie allotment.

True or False: Blending Fruits with Greens, or Melons with Other Fruits, Is Improper Food Combining, Which Will Lead to Health Problems

False! Every time I post a green smoothie recipe on my website that contains melon, I get at least one comment about how melons should be eaten by themselves. Without fail, every time I post a green smoothie recipe that includes a carrot or a stalk of celery or piece of cucumber, I'll get comments from concerned people who've heard that one should never mix fruits and vegetables—or some fruits with other fruits, like how bananas should never, ever meet oranges. It's "bad food combining," they say.

Over and over again, my response is that the food-combining hypothesis was thoroughly debunked almost eighty years ago, there is absolutely zero scientific evidence to support it, and no credible scientists or doctors support "improper food combining" today.

Food combining is a central tenet of the Natural Hygiene philosophy, which was founded by Sylvester Graham in the 1830s and was brought into the twentieth century by Herbert M. Shelton. Elements of Natural Hygiene are particularly popular in the modern raw food movement, and "proper food combining" is often discussed on raw food message boards and websites.

The food combining hypothesis states that certain food combinations should never be consumed since such combinations will disrupt the body's balance, cause digestion problems, and lead to poor health and "toxic buildup." The idea is that certain foods digest using different enzymes, and improper food combining confuses the body, thereby producing health-damaging side effects from digestion.

Food combining "no-nos" include mixing protein with fat or protein with carbohydrate. Food combining theorists believe that certain types of fruit should not be mixed—for example, "acid fruits" like oranges with "sweet fruits" like bananas. In fact, they claim that fruits should always be eaten separately, especially melons.

Many of my green smoothie recipes are at odds with food combining since I routinely blend pineapples with bananas (gasp!) and I also commit the unforgivable sin of blending melons with just about every fruit and vegetable you can think of.

Do I care that I break just about every single food-combining rule every day? No! I don't care because there is absolutely no reason why I should. The food-combining hypothesis is not grounded in science, and it is also not supported by my personal experience or observation.

True or False: Blending Destroys Fiber

False! I've heard some people tell me that putting fruit in a blender "destroys fiber."

The act of blending does not destroy fiber. It may break it down, but you are still getting the same amount of fiber. All blending does is replicate thorough chewing. You wouldn't worry about destroying the fiber in an apple by chewing it, even if you chewed it very well, would you?

You are consuming the same amount of dietary fiber whether you eat an apple whole or you blend it up first. The health benefits are the same, and to my knowledge there are no peer-reviewed scientific studies that indicate that blending inhibits the effectiveness of dietary fiber. Also, keep in mind that most major fiber supplements that are recommended by doctors are in powdered form, which is broken down even more than fruit fiber is when blended.

Green Smoothie Precautions

Certain individuals may need to make changes to the recommendations and recipes in this book to fit their unique medical requirements.

The following suggestions are not comprehensive, but highlight the most common problems that individuals with medical conditions might face when incorporating green smoothies into their diet.

Before you start making green smoothies or any change in your diet or exercise routine, check with your doctor. Be sure to check with your doctor or pharmacist about any complications or interactions that certain foods might have with your medical condition or prescription medications that you might be taking.

Grapefruit and Prescription Drugs

Grapefruits are known to interact with at least eighty-five different prescription medications. Therefore, if you take any medications, ask your doctor or pharmacist about potential side effects of having grapefruit with your medication.

Also be cautious of other citrus fruits that are hybrids of grapefruit, such as pomelo and oro blanco.

Cruciferous Vegetables and Hypothyroidism

Cruciferous vegetables, such as kale, bok choy, turnip, collards, broccoli, and cabbage, contain goitrogenic glucosinolates, which produce thiocyanates that compete with iodine for absorption by the thyroid gland.

In persons with a healthy thyroid, there is sufficient thyroid hormone production that consuming goitrogenic foods in normal amounts poses no harm unless one's diet is deficient in iodine.

However, for those with hypothyroidism, consuming large amounts of cruciferous vegetables can further reduce thyroid function or lower the effectiveness of replacement thyroid hormone medication. So while those with hypothyroidism may not need to completely abstain from cruciferous vegetables, I recommend checking with your doctor to determine a safe amount for you to consume.

Alternative leafy greens that do not contain goitrogens are green leaf and romaine lettuces.

Spinach, Oxalates, and Kidney Stones

If you have had or are susceptible to kidney stones, your doctor may place you on a low-oxalate diet.

If you do not have an increased risk for developing kidney stones, there is no need to eliminate or avoid foods that contain oxalates, since these foods do not cause kidney stones in healthy individuals.

Green smoothie foods that are **high in oxalates** include: nuts and nut milks, beets, spinach, chard, sesame seeds, sweet potato, apricots, kiwifruit, figs, soy products (e.g., soy milk, soy protein powder), and chocolate (raw cacao).

Green smoothie foods that are **low in oxalates** include: coconut, flaxseeds, pumpkin, avocado, broccoli, cucumber, bell pepper, and most fruits, with the exception of apricot, fig, kiwifruit, citrus fruits (oranges, lemons, etc.), blueberries, blackberries, strawberries, and mangoes.[37]

Vitamin K in Leafy Greens and Blood-Thinning Drugs

Dark, leafy green vegetables such as kale, spinach, and collard greens are extremely rich in vitamin K. One of the things that vitamin K does is help blood to clot. Therefore, people who take blood thinners such as Warfarin

(Coumadin) should consult with their doctor or pharmacist about how much dietary vitamin K they should consume, since too much vitamin K in the diet could counteract the effectiveness of blood-thinning medications.

Large amounts of dietary vitamin K pose no health risk for individuals who are not on blood-thinning medications.

Fruit Sugar and Diabetes

There is a lot of controversy about fruit sugar and diabetes on the Internet. I've addressed the fruit sugar controversy earlier in this chapter, but if you are diabetic, you may need to limit your intake of carbohydrates or sugar-containing foods.

This, of course, doesn't mean that you can't have any fresh fruits or green smoothies. The American Diabetes Association does not advocate fruit avoidance. In fact, many of my readers on Incredible Smoothies who have type-2 diabetes have been helped immensely by green smoothies, a whole foods diet, and exercise. To learn more about their stories, check out the Testimonials section on my website, Incredible Smoothies, and hear directly from diabetics who were able to get off diabetes medications, as well as lower their blood sugar and triglyceride levels.

If you are diabetic, it is important to closely monitor your blood sugar levels and to know how your body reacts to certain fruits or to serving sizes of fruits and green smoothies. You may not be able to handle large green smoothie meals or you may need to limit your use of bananas, mangoes, and grapes, which are three fruits with the highest sugar content.

CHAPTER TWO

HOW TO MAKE THE PERFECT GREEN SMOOTHIE

Now that you know why green smoothies are so good for you, it's time to learn how to turn fresh fruits and dark leafy greens into delicious, weight loss–inducing, life-enhancing nourishment.

In this chapter, I will show you how to make a perfectly delicious green smoothie with a creamy texture—even without yogurt or dairy milk. I will also show you how to save a green smoothie that comes out wrong. It happens, but instead of dumping expensive produce after making a smoothie that tastes like vomit, you'll learn how to turn it into something special.

Another topic that I cover in this chapter is how to purchase the freshest fruits and vegetables for your smoothies and how to store them. I will also talk about the importance of buying organic, as well as provide proven tips to save money, even while buying lots of fresh, organic fruits and vegetables.

If you have food allergies (bananas, mangoes, pineapple, kiwifruit, and citrus are common fruit allergens) or simply dislike the taste of certain fruits, this chapter will also show you how to substitute key ingredients in a smoothie recipe.

Green Smoothie Tools: What You Need to Get Started

Most people already have the tools they need to start making green smoothies right now. A simple cutting board, sharp knife, and any old blender will get you started.

However, once green smoothies become a daily habit, other tools (or upgraded tools) can make your morning blending routine much more efficient.

Here are a few things that will make your green smoothie adventure more satisfying and easier to stick to.

A high-speed blender: The most important part of your green smoothie, other than the fruits and greens you use, is the blender that you use to mix them.

The blender I use, love, and recommend to everybody is the Vitamix blender (www.incrediblesmoothies.com/vitamix). It's a fantastic, high-speed (2 horsepower) blender that makes the process of blending incredibly delicious green smoothies an absolute breeze! The Vitamix isn't a cheap blender, but it truly is worth every penny and it will pay for itself over time.

Similar in quality to the Vitamix is the Blendtec (www.incrediblesmoothies.com/blendtec). I recommend the Designer Series, which has a modern touch interface and sleek, upscale design. If you absolutely can't afford a Vitamix or Blendtec blender, then another one I've used and recommend is the JTC OmniBlend V (www.incrediblesmoothies.com/omniblend). This blender costs about half what the Vitamix costs and is almost as powerful. It's a huge step up from anything you'd get in a department or big-box store. However, the OmniBlend is not a "less expensive Vitamix" (though it is still a fantastic blender), and for that reason I always recommend the Vitamix or Blendtec first, then the OmniBlend for those who are budget-constrained.

The only other blender I've heard enough about to feel comfortable discussing here is the Ninja blender. It is around the $100 mark, but it is not in the same league as a Vitamix, Blendtec, or OmniBlend. I've heard good things about it, but the general consensus from my readers and fans on Facebook is that the Ninja is just "okay" for green smoothies.

Essentially, just about any blender will make a green smoothie. Higher-end blenders like the Vitamix, Blendtec, and OmniBlend do, indeed, make creamier smoothies. But if you cannot afford a high-end machine, it's better to use what you have than to put off a healthy green smoothie habit until you can afford a good blender. Look for blenders that have at least a 500-watt motor and get the absolute best one you can for what you can afford.

Mason jars: I find that the one-quart mason jars are ideal green smoothie drinking containers—especially for the larger meal-replacement smoothies that I drink every day for breakfast. What's even better is that they double as an airtight storage container to keep leftovers in. They are also portable, so you can take your green smoothies with you on your commute to work.

Knife: Since you will be cutting and peeling lots of different fruits and vegetables every day, a good knife makes things a lot easier and efficient.

My favorite knives to use for green smoothie preparation are the 5-inch or 7-inch Santoku-type knives. These sizes are comfortable to hold, and they are versatile whether you are peeling an apple or cutting into a pineapple or pumpkin.

A weighted meat cleaver is essential for opening young coconuts.

Cutting board: A good cutting board is a must. I prefer bamboo cutting boards because they are easier to clean, don't scratch as much as wood, and are better for you and the environment than plastic.

Glass straw: While not a necessity, an eco-friendly, reusable glass straw (I use Glass Dharma straws, see www.glassdharma.com) makes the smoothie drinking process easier.

I find that using a straw is less messy and more convenient than drinking directly from a container. It also helps protect your teeth by minimizing the amount of fruit sugars that come in contact with your teeth. I have been drinking green smoothies with a glass straw for a few years now and I prefer it to drinking straight from a glass or mason jar.

Nut milk bag: If you decide to make your own nut milks using your blender, then a nut milk straining bag is an inexpensive investment. Nut milk bags make it easy to separate the liquid nut milk from the pulp.

Compost bin: A compost bin is a great investment if you have a garden. You will accumulate a *ton* of fruit and vegetable waste through making daily green smoothies, so there will be no shortage of raw material for making healthy soil for your garden.

Calorie/nutrition-calculating program: And finally, a good calorie- and/or nutrition–tracking software or app is essential if you want to lose weight or ensure that you are getting your recommended allotment of nutrients. You can also find out the complete nutrition facts for every green smoothie recipe you make.

There are quite a few nutrition-tracking programs on the Internet, but the one I use and recommend is CRON-o-Meter (www.incrediblesmoothies. com/tools/Cron-o-Meter.html). Initially created for people who follow a calorie restriction diet (which I do not personally recommend), CRON-o-Meter is easy to use with any diet. To use CRON-o-Meter, simply log into the website (free) or download the app for your mobile phone or tablet device.

How to Make the Best Green Smoothies on the Planet

Making a delicious smoothie with a thick, creamy texture is an art. Fortunately, it's an art that anybody can learn. Once you know the basics, you can make your own creations and never have to get tired of using the same recipes day after day.

Step 1: Add a Liquid

Liquid is necessary to help your blender mix the ingredients. It's impossible for most low-end blenders to make a smoothie without some added liquid. Not adding enough liquid might make the smoothie too thick. Too much liquid, however, will make the smoothie too thin and cause separation when it sits for more than a few minutes.

The amount of liquid you need to add will vary depending on your blender's make and model. I have found that high-powered blenders like the Vitamix, Blendtec, or OmniBlend need slightly more liquid than lower-end models. This is because a high-powered blender does a better job at puréeing fruits and greens, so it needs more liquid to thoroughly mix them. A low-end blender doesn't blend as thoroughly and may produce a slightly chunky smoothie where separation occurs. For example, I used to only add about 4 ounces of liquid per smoothie to my old blender, but my new Vitamix needs 6 ounces since it blends much more thoroughly.

Recipe Tip: Start with about 4 to 6 ounces of a liquid. If you are using water-rich fruits like citrus or grapes, you can use less liquid. If you are using a lot of base fruits (banana or mango), you can use 8 to 10 ounces of liquid, depending on your blender.

What Liquids to Use

Filtered water: I usually use filtered water when I make a green smoothie because it doesn't affect the flavor.

Coconut water: If you want to give your smoothie a tropical tone, use young (green or "Thai") coconut water straight from the coconut itself. You can find young coconuts at Asian markets or at health food stores. Each coconut contains about 16 ounces of delicious, sweet water and the meat is soft like hard-boiled egg whites. The meat from young coconuts can also help improve the texture of your smoothie.

Fruit juices: I don't recommend using commercial fruit juices in your green smoothie because bottled juices are never fresh. Additionally, bottled juices almost always have added sugar, colorings, and preservatives that your body doesn't need.

You can, however, use your own, freshly squeezed fruit juice. Oranges, tangerines, grapefruits, and other juicy fruits are perfect. Use the same principle of flavor combining as you would with flavor fruits. Juicy fruits will complement the other fruit you put into your smoothie.

Milks: My personal philosophy steers me away from using animal milk as a liquid. If you are tempted to add dairy milk in order to boost the calcium content of your smoothie, remember that many fruits and vegetables, especially greens, are already rich in calcium. It's actually quite easy to make a smoothie with more calcium than a glass of milk!

If you want to use milk as a liquid, I recommend trying plant-based milks made from hemp, almond or other nuts, oats, or rice. You can find certain brands that are fortified with calcium and vitamin D. You can also make your own almond milk (page 64) too!

Step 2: Pick Your "Base" Fruit

Base fruits give your smoothie a *creamy* texture. Without a base fruit, your smoothie will be too runny or you will end up with pulpy fruit juice (like if you blended oranges and grapes together). For a perfectly smooth texture, use "creamy" fruits like bananas, mangoes, pears, peaches, plums, papayas, durians, or even apples as your base fruit. Do not rely on water-rich fruits like watermelons, grapes, and oranges. You can still use them in a smoothie, just not as your "base fruit."

If you want to make a smoothie using more than one fruit, like a banana plus strawberries, use slightly more banana than you would strawberry. For example, two bananas to one cup of strawberries would provide a nice flavor combo while preserving the creamy smoothie texture.

Avocado and coconut meat can also help thicken your smoothie while adding more calories and healthy fat for a meal-replacement shake. I typically use no more than a quarter of an avocado in any smoothie recipe I make.

Greens will help thicken a smoothie as well, so the more greens you add, the less base fruit you will need. However, you shouldn't rely on greens for a base since they are too fibrous.

Recipe Tip: Start with one of the following: one banana, one apple, one pear, or one large mango, to make the base for your green smoothie. That should provide enough base fruit to give you the rich, creamy smoothie texture you want.

Step 3: Mixing Flavors

Flavor fruits are optional. They enhance the flavor of your smoothies as well as boost the overall nutrition. I like to use berries, citrus fruits, pineapples, or other strongly flavored fruits. You can experiment to find flavor fruits that will complement the base fruits that you are using.

It's easy to come up with ideas for flavor combinations by looking at the fruit juice aisle or the yogurt section in the supermarket. Millions of dollars in product research have done the legwork for you, so just look at what popular flavors of juices and fruit-flavored prepared snacks are there and make your own smoothies based on those combinations.

I have even found inspiration for smoothie ideas while looking at scented candles. Wonderfully fragranced candles such as peach-ginger and citrus-cilantro stirred up my curiosity and gave me ideas for new smoothies to try. Just use your taste buds as a guide and don't be afraid to let your whimsical side take over when you are at your blender.

My favorite flavor combos are:

Banana (base fruit) with strawberry (flavor fruit)
Mango (base fruit) with pineapple (flavor fruit)
Pear (base fruit) with orange (flavor fruit)
Apple (base fruit) with blueberry (flavor fruit)

In addition, you can get creative with your smoothies by flavoring them with spices like vanilla bean, clove, cinnamon, or even cayenne pepper (great with chocolaty smoothies made with raw cacao). Flavored protein powders will also change the overall smoothie flavor, so keep this in mind when mixing fruits.

Recipe Tip: Use half the amount of flavor fruit as you do base fruit. For example, if you use one banana, use half a cup of pineapple.

Step 4: Add Your Greens!

> ### Hit the "Pulse" Button Now
>
> Now would be a good time to blend your fruit and liquid together. Just hold down the "pulse" button on your blender until the ingredients are lightly mixed into a sludge. Doing this before adding the greens will make it easier for you and your blender. (You can skip this step if you own a Blendtec WildSide blender or a Vitamix.)

If you have never had a green smoothie before, you might wrinkle your nose at the notion of drinking spinach. Let me tell you that when blended in a green smoothie, the fruit masks the flavor of most vegetables you put in. I'm serious! Give it a try. It's a perfect way to get your greens without tasting them. This is also a great way to sneak them into your kids' diet too! Fresh baby spinach has a mild flavor, so start with that and gradually increase the amount you use to a large handful or two in each smoothie. Your body will thank you for it! I started off with fresh baby spinach and now I use primarily dandelion greens, romaine lettuce (I stuff the entire head in my blender!), kale, chard, parsley, and any other organic leafy green I can find.

The recommended ratio of greens to use in a green smoothie is 40 percent greens to 60 percent fruits/vegetables (by volume). Start at a lower percentage and work your way up as you get used to it, and don't be afraid to boost your greens to 50 or even 60 percent by volume.

Don't Forget to Rotate Your Greens!

Leafy greens contain small amounts of toxins as a defense mechanism to protect a plant from predation. For example, glucosinolates in cruciferous vegetables like kale, turnip, and cabbage, as well as oxalic acid in spinach and beet greens, may provide some health benefits in small amounts, but in large amounts can be toxic to humans and other animals.

Eating up to four cups of leafy greens each day is perfectly safe (unless a preexisting health condition makes you more susceptible to the anti-nutrients in leafy greens), but to prevent a *potential* for a buildup or overdose of toxic elements in a certain species of plant, it's best to rotate every few weeks. For example, I might eat dandelion greens and romaine lettuce every day for a week, and then I'll switch to beet greens and kale for a couple of weeks. Then I might do leaf lettuce and spinach for a few days.

It is important to rotate greens among different plant families. Swapping one cruciferous vegetable like kale for another crucifer like bok choy isn't a good rotation because you are still getting the anti-nutrients that are in all cruciferous vegetables. A better rotation for kale would be a non-crucifer like beet greens, lettuce, or chard.

Here's a chart showing the plant families of common vegetable greens:

PLANT FAMILY	VEGETABLE GREENS
Brassicaceae / Cruciferae	Kale, collard, arugula, turnip, cabbage, bok choy, radish greens, mustard greens, broccoli
Amaranthaceae / Chenopodiaceae	Spinach, chard, beet, lambsquarters
Asteraceae	Dandelion, leaf lettuce, romaine lettuce
Apiaceae	Parsley, cilantro

Recipe Tip: Start by adding two or three cups or handfuls of your favorite leafy green. If you are new to this, stick with two cups of fresh baby spinach or a small head of butter lettuce. As you get more into green smoothies, try kale, dandelion, chard, and other leafy greens. I regularly put an entire head of romaine lettuce in my smoothie or I'll use up to four cups of chopped kale or dandelion.

Step 5: Now Blend It Up!

Unless you have a high-end blender, you might need to chop up your greens rather than adding whole leaves or large bunches. If you have large chunks of fruit that won't blend, try cutting smaller pieces and leaving out tough bits like cores.

Now, depending on your blender, you might need to hit the "pulse" button a few times to mix the greens before hitting any pre-set "smoothie" buttons. Otherwise, blend on high for anywhere from thirty to sixty seconds or until all ingredients are whirling away and your smoothie is creamy.

Look for a texture that is thick and smooth, but try not to over-blend your smoothie. Don't leave your blender whirling the ingredients for more than a minute, to reduce oxidation and nutrient loss. It might take a few times to get the hang of it, but once you do, aim for blending your smoothie enough to drink through a straw, but not so that it's completely liquid.

Liquid: Start with about 4 to 6 ounces of a liquid. If you are using water-rich fruits like citrus or grapes, you can use less liquid. If you are using a lot of base fruits like bananas or mangoes, you can use 8 to 10 ounces, depending on your blender.

Base Fruit: Start with one banana, apple, pear, or large mango. That should provide enough base fruit to give you the rich, creamy smoothie texture you want.

Flavor Fruit: Use half the amount of flavor fruit as you do base fruit. For example, if you use two bananas, use one cup of pineapple.

Making the Recipe (The 30-Second Recap)

The ratio of fruits to greens in a green smoothie that works best for most people is 60 percent sweet fruits to 40 percent leafy greens by volume. This ratio calls for sufficient sweet fruits to hide the bitter taste of greens like kale and dandelion. To many people, including me, green smoothies that fit this ratio are the most delicious and most balanced. Green smoothies that contain more non-sweet fruit or leafy greens than sweet fruit tend to be less tasty, and they do not make good meal replacements because they have too few calories.

Greens: Start by adding two or three cups or handfuls of your favorite leafy green. If you are new to this, stick with two cups of baby spinach or a small head of butter lettuce. As you get more into green smoothies, try kale, dandelion, chard, and other leafy greens.

Vegetables: Feel free to experiment by adding vegetables to your green smoothies. Toss in a whole carrot or a couple of cherry or grape tomatoes. A stalk or two of celery is also nice and adds more minerals.

Using Ice or Frozen Fruit

I prefer my green smoothies at room temperature, so most of the recipes in this book do not contain frozen ingredients or ice. However, if you prefer your smoothies cold, simply add two or three ice cubes or freeze some of the fruit before adding it to your smoothie.

Adding frozen ingredients will slightly change the consistency of your smoothie. For example, using frozen banana instead of fresh banana will give you the consistency of a smoothie made with ice cream or frozen yogurt.

You can also add frozen greens, such as spinach or kale. I recommend buying these greens fresh and then freezing them instead of going to the freezer aisle and buying the frozen packages that are meant to be cooked.

I don't recommend making a smoothie with only frozen ingredients. Your smoothie will come out extremely thick and you will need to eat it with a spoon. Instead, only add one frozen ingredient and keep the rest of the ingredients fresh.

How to Fix a Green Smoothie Disaster

Hey, it happens. More than once, I've blended a mix of otherwise delicious fruits and greens together only to get a concoction that tasted like vomit. If you don't believe me, try mixing frozen blueberries with dandelion greens.

Sometimes, you can simply hold your nose and chug it down. Other times, it's just so nasty that you're left with no recourse other than to dump $10 worth of expensive, organic produce (and all those nutrients) down the drain.

Instead of wasting your money, however, I'm telling you there are a few tricks you can do to save a nasty concoction.

If Your Smoothie Is Not Sweet Enough

Use a very ripe banana or other very ripe, sweet fruit (pineapple, strawberry, peach, kiwifruit, grapes) to sweeten. Or toss in a couple of dates for added sweetness without the extra volume that additional banana provides.

I try to avoid any concentrated sweetener like agave nectar, honey, maple syrup, and especially table sugar. Stevia might be something to try when you are starting out or to save a smoothie that is too bitter. However, I recommend that you drink green smoothies without added sweetener so that your taste buds adjust to the real flavors of whole foods.

If Your Smoothie Is Bitter or Tastes "Funky"

Use pineapple, citrus fruits, or strawberries to cover up funky flavors. Keep in mind that not all berries will mask a bitter taste. Blackberries and blueberries may only enhance the bitter flavor.

From my experience, I don't recommend using green bell peppers, asparagus, or cauliflower in green smoothies. Use broccoli sparingly. I have also found that some fruits taste great in a freshly made smoothie, but if the smoothie sits in the fridge for a few hours, it can turn funky. I've experienced this with blackberries. And I've found it best to always drink a smoothie made with kale right away.

If Your Smoothie Is Too Runny

Banana makes a great thickener, as do other base fruits like mango and durian. Just a quarter of an avocado thickens up a smoothie nicely without adding too much fat.

Try to avoid using too many water-rich fruits so that separation doesn't occur while you are drinking it.

If Your Smoothie Is Too Thick

I've made smoothies that I had to eat with a spoon. It's actually not really a problem. A coconut-cacao blend might be just as appealing as a pudding than as a smoothie. But if you really want a smoothie and want to drink it through a straw without giving yourself a headache, be cautious of the amount of base fruit you use. Also be sure to add enough liquid—and add more if needed.

Avoid using more than a quarter of an avocado in a green smoothie. I once blended an entire avocado with pineapple, banana, and fresh baby spinach. What I ended up with was pineapple-flavored, blended guacamole. It wasn't exactly what I was going for, and the only way to eat my mistake was to spoon it out of the blender pitcher.

If you add too much ice or frozen fruit to your smoothies, you always run the risk of turning it into ice cream. For this reason, I never use more than one serving of a frozen ingredient. For example, if I make a green smoothie with a frozen banana, I won't use any other frozen ingredients. If your green smoothie turns out like ice cream or sorbet, try adding some room-temperature water and blend again.

Storing a Green Smoothie

I prefer to drink my green smoothies immediately after making them, since that is when they are at their most nutritious. However, life can be busy and mornings are hectic enough, so it's sometimes necessary to make a smoothie in advance or store leftovers in the refrigerator.

Because there are no preservatives in green smoothies that you make yourself, they are highly perishable, so be sure to always store them in an airtight container in the refrigerator. Glass mason jars are great for this purpose, and an insulated travel mug with a sealed top is also perfect for taking your green smoothie to work or when you're on the go.

Green smoothies can be kept fresh in the refrigerator for up to twenty-four hours. While some people suggest that a smoothie can be kept in the refrigerator for up to three days, I feel that the quality, taste, and nutrition degrade when it is stored for that long.

Separation can also occur when a green smoothie sits for a few hours. This happens quickly when water-rich fruits like oranges or watermelon are used. Don't be discouraged by the look of it: Simply shake your smoothie well before drinking.

Can You Freeze a Green Smoothie?

I get asked frequently about freezing green smoothies. For me, I want my food fresh and as close to its natural state as possible. However, not everyone has the time I have in the morning. If you are really tight on time, you can make smoothies four to five days in advance and freeze them until you can drink them.

Simply blend your smoothie and store it in a glass jar in the freezer. The night before you want to drink it put it in the refrigerator to help it thaw. This method might reduce the amount of nutrients in your smoothie, however.

Another option is to chop all the ingredients and put them into a freezer bag or container. When you are ready to make your smoothie, remove the ingredients from the freezer and run them under hot water for about thirty seconds to thaw, then blend them in your blender with liquid until smooth.

How to Store Fresh Produce and Keep It Fresh Longer

Fresh produce doesn't last forever. In fact, it might only last a few days—especially if it was fully ripe when you purchased it. However, you don't need to run to the grocery store or farmers' market every few days to keep fresh fruits and vegetables in the house.

Here are some things that you can do to prevent wasting money on fruits and vegetables that spoil too quickly.

Buy the Best—Avoid Less Than Perfect Produce

First of all, buy the best quality produce that you can. Avoid yellowing or wilted greens. Skip over any fruits that are bruised, too soft, overly ripe, or punctured, or that do not have an appropriately bright, fresh color.

Plan Your Fruit/Vegetable Consumption

When you buy fruits and vegetables, think about how you will use them.

For example, I don't buy two weeks' worth of bananas all at once. I buy enough for about five days and then restock later in the week. Unripe mangoes can take up to five days or so to ripen, so I will eat more perishable fruits like peaches and plums first.

Apples and oranges keep well in the refrigerator and will last up to three weeks (if necessary) if kept in the crisper bins. A package of avocados that are unripe can be distributed out over time. Simply take out one or two that you want to ripen and keep the rest in the refrigerator until you are ready to have them ripen. Allow up to three days for an avocado to ripen at room temperature.

If a fruit is getting too ripe, place it in the refrigerator and use it up within a couple of days. If it looks like you can't use the fruit in that time frame, cut it up and freeze it.

On the occasions when my bananas ripen too fast, I simply peel them and freeze them (no need to chop them up, just lay them in a freezer-safe bag or container). If I find an incredible deal on ripe, in-season strawberries at a local market, I usually freeze more than half of them, since they'd otherwise go bad before I am able to eat them all.

How to Wash and Store Fresh Greens

I am frequently asked about the proper way to wash and store fresh leafy greens. As you probably know, greens love to wilt and spoil before you have a chance to use them.

After years of eating a *ton* of leafy greens (I usually buy about twelve bunches at a time), I have learned a few tricks for keeping leafy greens fresh for as long as possible.

Soon after I get home from the grocery store, I transfer my leafy greens from the produce bags into plastic tubs. I reuse the same one-pound plastic tubs that baby spinach or mixed greens often come in. You can also buy produce tubs at kitchen and home stores. Never store leafy greens in produce bags, since they will rapidly wilt, yellow, and get slimy.

To regulate moisture in the plastic tub, I tear a paper towel in half and line the bottom. Then I add the greens and cover them with the other half of the paper towel before putting the lid on. I might add a layer of paper towel between bunches of greens if they are particularly wet from the misters in the produce displays. (An eco-friendly and affordable alternative to paper towels are reusable cloth "paper" towels. They are the perfect size and texture for this purpose. You can find them online at www.etsy.com.)

Storage times for greens may vary. If you buy them really fresh, they'll last longer than if you buy them when they are just starting to wilt. Kale and chard will last longer than dandelion greens and spinach, so use those first and save the heartier greens for later in the week.

Kale and collards last the longest and may keep for up to ten days using my tub storage method. Dandelion greens and most lettuces generally last about three to five days if kept relatively dry. Chard may last up to four to five days. Baby spinach and mixed greens that you buy in bulk may last three to four days, depending on their freshness and moisture levels.

I do not pre-wash leafy greens. I usually cut the ends of the stems off, usually just above or below where the twist tie bundles them together. When placing them in the refrigerator, I always make sure the stem side faces the back of the fridge. Delicate greens may freeze if the leafy tips are up against the back of the fridge where it is coldest.

As far as washing leafy greens, all I do is run them under tap water to remove any dirt or debris. I don't use a veggie wash and I don't use any disinfectant (as long as I am not traveling outside the United States). I wash my greens just prior to using.

CHAPTER THREE

THE BEST GREEN SMOOTHIE INGREDIENTS

Before I get to the green smoothie recipes in this book, I want to discuss the many different ingredients I use in the recipes and why I use them.

This chapter will introduce you to all of my favorite fruits, vegetables, nuts, and seeds that I regularly use in my own green smoothie creations. I will discuss optimal flavor pairings, including tips about which green goes best with which fruit and which fruits blend best together. I will also share my favorite "green smoothie boosters," such as superfood supplements, protein powders, and other nutrient-boosting foods.

Another thing that you will learn in this chapter is why I use certain fruits and vegetables from a nutrition standpoint. Whether you are trying to get more calcium, vitamin B6, or potassium, you'll see which fruits and greens provide the nutrients you need.

It is easy to get stuck in a rut of using the same fruits and vegetables over and over again. To prevent boredom and discover unlimited options for flavor combinations in your green smoothies, peruse the foods in this chapter for tips and ideas—soon you'll be using fruits, greens, seeds, and superfoods in new and delicious combinations!

Fruits for Green Smoothies

A green smoothie is only as good as the fruits you add to it. Below is a summary of my favorite green smoothie fruits, why they work well, and how they work with other fruits and greens.

Be sure to refer to the seasonal availability chart in this book so that you can buy the freshest, tastiest fruits and vegetables.

Base Fruits

Base fruits are the most important part of your smoothie because they create a thick, creamy texture.

Apple: Apples add a lot of fiber and are more water-rich than other base fruits. They blend well with coconut, pear, and most berries. Cinnamon adds a nice flavor to apple smoothies as well.

Pectin, a dietary fiber in apples, binds to cholesterol in the digestive tract and slows down glucose absorption.[38]

Avocado: Avocado is great for thickening up your smoothie, adding calories, and boosting the healthy fat content. I use a quarter of an avocado in a smoothie recipe. You can add it to just about any smoothie, but I try not to use avocado with a lot of other fatty fruits like durian and coconut or with other fats like chia or flaxseed. Add extra water if you use avocado because it will make your smoothie quite thick.

Avocado is a good source of vitamins B5, C, and E. Because avocados contain healthy fats, they aid in the absorption of antioxidant carotenoids such as beta-carotene (which your body converts to vitamin A), lutein, and lycopene. These carotenoids are abundant in leafy greens and other green smoothie ingredients, so adding a little avocado to your smoothie can help your body get the most from them.

Banana: Bananas are *the* perfect smoothie base fruit. You can use banana with any fruit since most things taste good with banana and most flavors will easily mask the banana's as well. Really ripe bananas also help sweeten a bitter smoothie and mask bitter greens such as dandelion and kale.

Bananas are full of minerals (magnesium, manganese, copper, and potassium). They are also one of the richest fruit sources of vitamin B6.

Durian: Durian is a fatty fruit from Asia. If you've never had durian before, don't let the foul smell fool you. This fruit is notorious for its unpleasant odor but revered for its wonderful, almond custard–like flavor. Use durian with coconut, banana, and cacao, or spice it with ginger, cinnamon, and nutmeg. Avoid blending durian with fruity flavors like berries and other tropical fruits.

Durian is a potent source of B vitamins, especially vitamins B1, B2, and B6, as well as B3 and folate. Durian also contains good levels of vitamin C and minerals such as copper, potassium, magnesium, and manganese.

Fig: Fresh figs make a tasty and creamy base fruit. I typically use three to five figs with one banana. Then I'll add red grapes, peaches, or plums to create a deliciously complex flavor. Use mild-flavored greens with simple banana-fig smoothies or experiment with bitter greens in fig smoothies accented with more flavorful fruits like pineapple and oranges.

Figs are a good source of all B vitamins (except B12). They also contain many essential minerals and are among the richest fruit sources of calcium and iron.

Mango: Mangoes are one of my favorite base fruits. They create the perfect smoothie base while giving a wonderful tropical flavor. Blend with other base fruits like banana, coconut, peach, and papaya or with flavor fruits like kiwi, strawberry, raspberry, orange, and pineapple. Ripe mangoes are flavorful enough to blend with bitter greens like kale, collards, and dandelion. Orange fruits and vegetables pair nicely together with mangoes too. For example, if you are adding mangoes to a smoothie, try adding carrots and/or oranges as well. Also try using a bit of fresh ginger in your mango smoothies.

Mangoes are a nutritional superfruit. They are a good source of all B vitamins (except B12), and they are particularly rich in vitamins A (as beta-carotene), C, and E. One mango can contain up to 11 percent of your recommended daily value of omega-3 fatty acids.

Nectarine: Use nectarines interchangeably with peaches (see entry on peaches, below), as their flavor, texture, and nutritional profile are similar.

Papaya: Papayas' delicate flavor means you can complement them with other base fruits like mangoes or peaches. Papayas blend well with other flavor fruits like strawberries, coconut, and pineapple. Use mild greens in a papaya smoothie, unless you are also blending sweet fruits like pineapple or banana.

Papayas are an excellent source of vitamins A (as beta-carotene) and C, and they are a good source of folate. Papayas also contain an enzyme called papain, which may help facilitate digestion.

Peach: Peaches are one of my favorite fruits to use in smoothies. I like to either use peaches by themselves or combine them with plums, apricots, or oranges. They blend well with bananas and cacao. Depending on how ripe, large, and juicy your peaches are, you might need to use less water or combine them with another non-watery base fruit like banana. Peaches do a good job of masking the flavor of bitter greens like kale.

Peaches are a good source of vitamin A (as beta-carotene) as well as vitamin C.

Pear: Pears are "creamier" than apples. Their delicate flavor makes them a nice base fruit to use with flavorful complementary fruits like berries, pineapple, and banana. Fresh Italian parsley also complements the flavor of pear quite nicely! If pear is the dominant ingredient used in your smoothie, avoid bitter greens like kale and dandelion. Instead, opt for mild greens like fresh baby spinach or green leaf lettuce.

Like most fruits, pears are a good source of vitamin C and the mineral copper.

Pumpkin: Raw pumpkin can be blended with banana, apple, or pear and spiced with cinnamon, nutmeg, clove, or pumpkin pie spice to make a delicious fall smoothie. Raw pumpkin can be a little starchy, so soak it in water with a squeeze of lemon juice overnight to reduce the starchiness. As a shortcut, you can use baked (then chilled) pumpkin or even canned pumpkin pie mix for an easy and quick pumpkin pie smoothie.

Pumpkin is especially rich in vitamin A (as beta-carotene). It is also a good source of vitamins B2, B5, and vitamin E. As for minerals, pumpkin is a good source of copper, iron, phosphorus, and potassium.

Sapote (Mamey, Sapodilla): Depending on where you live, you might have access to fresh sapote fruit. With a flavor reminiscent of brown sugar and apple, sapotes make a perfect base and sweetener in a smoothie recipe. Sapotes blend well with just about any flavor fruit you add. Use mild-flavored greens to preserve the flavor of sapote or use sapote to sweeten a smoothie using bitter greens.

Mamey sapotes have a creamy pumpkin-like flavor. They are hard to find outside of the area where they grow, but if you can get your hands on one, you'll be holding on to one of the richest fruit sources of dietary iron (4.4 mg per fruit). Mamey is also a good source of manganese, potassium, and zinc. As for vitamins, mamey provides vitamin A (as beta-carotene), all B vitamins (except B12), and vitamin E (78 percent of recommended daily value per fruit).

Sweet Potato: Okay, it's not a fruit, but a sweet potato can be a delicious addition to a smoothie recipe. You can blend it up raw or cook it and cool it before blending. Blend sweet potatoes with cinnamon, nutmeg, and other spices. They also go well with citrus fruits.

Sweet potatoes are especially rich in vitamin A (as beta-carotene). They are also a good source of all B vitamins (except B12) and vitamins C and E. As for minerals, sweet potatoes provide a good source of calcium, copper, iron, magnesium, manganese, potassium, and phosphorus.

Flavor Fruits

Flavor fruits, as their name suggests, add flavor to your smoothie while complementing the base fruit.

Açaí Berry: Açaí (pronounced *ah-sigh-ee*) berries have a distinctive "dark chocolate and red wine" flavor that makes a wonderful accent to many smoothie recipes. Use banana, apple, pear, or even mango for a base fruit and complement açaí with pomegranate, cranberry, or other berries. Açaí can also stand on its own as a dominant flavor or mix well with cacao or coconut. I highly recommend finding a quality frozen açaí purée for best results rather than more readily available juices and powders. I use the Amafruits brand açaí berry purée (amafruits.com).

Açaí tops the charts for antioxidant activity, measured by its Oxygen Radical Absorbance Capacity, or ORAC, value. Açaí is loaded with vitamins and minerals and is a good source of plant-based omega-3 fatty acids.

Acerola: Acerolas have a tart, citrus-like flavor. You can use them in place of any citrus fruit (orange, lemon, lime, tangerine, etc.) or pineapple in a green smoothie recipe. Blend acerolas with other sweet fruits like banana, pear, apple, or coconut. The citrus-like flavor of acerolas is accented nicely with cacao or even vanilla.

Outside of the local regions where they grow (the tropics), acerolas are available as a frozen purée. I buy mine from a company called Amafruits (amafruits.com).

Acerolas are billed as "nature's most potent source of vitamin C," containing almost thirty times more vitamin C per serving than an orange.

Apricot: Apricots are delicious on their own (with banana as the base fruit) as the dominant flavor or blended with peaches, nectarines, or even plums. Apricots work well with base fruits like bananas, mangoes, apples, or pears. You'll need to use quite a few apricots to get a dominant apricot flavor. I typically add four or so to a smoothie recipe and blend with non-bitter greens.

Apricots are an exceptionally rich source of vitamin A (as beta-carotene).

Blackberry: Use blackberries as you would raspberries (see entry on raspberry, page 48). My experience with blackberries is that they tend to make the smoothie flavor a bit funky after it sits for a few hours. Only use blackberries when you plan to drink your smoothie right away.

Blackberries are a good source of iron, manganese, and copper, as well as vitamins C, E, and K.

Blueberry: Blueberries are a great addition to any green smoothie. When they are in season, I buy them fresh and blend them with delicately flavored base fruits so that blueberry is the dominant flavor. During the rest of the year, I add frozen blueberries to many smoothie recipes to chill and boost the antioxidants. If you buy frozen, look for wild blueberries, which are more nutritious. Use with mild-flavored greens like spinach and lettuce. Wild frozen blueberries do not mix well with dandelion greens but can be added to a kale smoothie with coconut or citrus fruit.

Blueberries are one of the antioxidant superstars. They are also an excellent source of vitamin K.

Cactus Pear: Cactus pear is the fruit of the prickly pear cactus or nopal. Cactus pears are rich in antioxidants and add a bright, deep reddish color to your smoothie. As with guavas, they are filled with hard seeds that do not blend up well, even in a high-speed blender. For this reason, I recommend mashing them through a metal strainer to separate the seeds from the pulp and collect the juice in your blender.

Cactus pears are excellent with bananas as a base fruit and complement many other base and flavor fruits nicely. Blend with berries, grapes, and figs for some wonderful combinations.

Cactus pears are a good source of vitamin C and magnesium. They are also one of a handful of calcium-rich fruits with 6 percent recommended daily value per 42 calories.

Cherimoya: Cherimoyas have a delicate flavor, so I blend them with other delicately or complementary flavored fruits when I use them in a smoothie. They blend up best with bananas, apples, pears, peaches, bananas, papayas, and strawberries. As for greens, stick with mild greens like fresh baby spinach, leaf lettuce, or romaine.

Cherimoyas are an excellent source of vitamin C and all B vitamins, with the exception of vitamin B12. They're also a good source of minerals. One cherimoya contains 23 percent of your recommended daily value of omega-3 fatty acids.

Cherry: I love using cherries in green smoothies, but it's too bad they need to be pitted one at a time if you want to use fresh ones! You can get frozen pitted cherries at most grocery stores, though. Cherries blend well with banana, coconut, and pear for base fruits. I like to mix them with açaí berries, strawberries, or raspberries. Cherries also blend well with a little cacao for a chocolate-covered-cherry flavor. If cherries are your dominant flavor fruit, use mild greens like lettuce, spinach, or chard.

The primary nutritional benefits in cherries are from the generous amount of antioxidants they contain.

Coconut: Coconuts are both flavorful and a great complement to any base fruit. I use young (green or Thai) coconuts and add the meat and liquid to smoothies with a tropical base fruit such as a mango, banana, or durian. Coconuts also work well with non-tropical fruits like peaches, pears, and even apples. Cacao and just about any flavor fruit like citrus fruits and berries are excellent with coconut. Coconut can help sweeten a grapefruit smoothie and can also help sweeten a kale or dandelion green smoothie.

Young Thai coconut is an excellent source of calcium (up to 17 percent of your recommended daily value) in a green smoothie. Coconut water is an excellent source of electrolytes and one of my favorite ingredients for a post-workout green smoothie.

Cranberry: In the fall and early winter, fresh cranberries are readily available and I add them to smoothies by the handful. Cranberries are very tart, so blending them with a sweet fruit like banana can moderate their flavor. They are particularly delicious when mixed with pomegranate, red grapes, strawberries, or blueberries.

Cranberries are famous for their protective effects against urinary tract infections (UTIs). Raw cranberries are not necessarily consumed for their nutritional value, since they are not as potent in amounts that you would typically be able to eat raw (they are quite tart!). However, their potent antioxidant and health-supporting compounds make them an excellent addition to a green smoothie.

Cupuacu: Available outside of their native region as a frozen purée, cupuacus have a complex and distinctive flavor. You might not care for the flavor on its own, but blended in a green smoothie with sweet fruits such as oranges, pineapples, or bananas, it is quite delicious. Cupuacus add just the slightest hint of bitterness, reminiscent of grapefruit but not as strong.

Cupuacu is related to cacao (chocolate). Unlike chocolate, it does not contain caffeine and theobromine. Instead, it contains theacrines, which provide a similar boost in mood and energy but without the jitters of caffeine. My husband, who is hypersensitive to caffeine and large amounts of raw cacao, can tolerate a 100-gram portion of cupuacu purée in his green smoothie with no ill effects.

Guava: Guavas are one of my favorite flavor fruits, although it can be a little tricky using them in a green smoothie. Since guavas have hard seeds, even a high-speed blender can have trouble pulverizing them. What happens is that you end up with very sharp shards of seed floating around in your smoothie. The solution is to use the outer flesh of the guava and discard the inner seeded portion. I usually add about four or five guavas to a recipe.

Guavas blend well with other tropical fruits like bananas, mangoes, coconuts, pineapples, papayas, and kiwis. You can also use guavas with apples or pears, but let them be the dominant flavor and avoid blending them with berries.

Guavas are exceptionally rich in vitamin C. They are also a good source of vitamin A (as beta-carotene), as well as folate and vitamin B5. Like most fruits, guavas are rich in copper and potassium.

Jackfruit: Jackfruits are best used as a base fruit in green smoothies, where they can provide a creamy texture. They are best blended with another base fruit such as banana or mango. Pineapples and strawberries are particularly delicious as complementary flavor fruits in a jackfruit green smoothie blend. Young Thai coconut is also delicious blended with jackfruits, and coconut water makes an excellent smoothie liquid.

Since jackfruits have a delicate flavor, keep your jackfruit smoothie recipes simple to preserve the flavor. I recommend blending just two or three ingredients. Avoid bitter greens such as kale or dandelion and instead choose mild greens such as fresh baby spinach or leaf lettuce.

Jackfruits are a good source of B vitamins, particularly vitamins B1, B6, and folate. They are also a good source of magnesium, copper, and potassium, as well as omega-3 fatty acids.

Kiwifruit: Kiwifruit, also called simply "kiwis," add a little tartness to your smoothie, work well with banana, mango, and peach base fruits, and complement pineapple and strawberry flavor fruits. Use one to two kiwis for best results. Ripe kiwis do a good job at masking bitter greens like kale or dandelion greens.

Kiwifruit are especially rich in vitamin C and provide a good source of vitamin K. One fruit provides 7 percent of your recommended daily value of vitamin E. As for minerals, they are an excellent source of copper.

Lychee: Lychees are small, so I usually use nine in a typical smoothie recipe. Even so, they are a low-calorie fruit, so I don't recommend using them in a meal-replacement green smoothie since you will overpower their delicate flavor too easily. Lychees have a mild flavor that is best accented with other tropical fruits like bananas, a small amount of pineapple, passion fruits, citrus, coconuts, or even mint. Use mild greens like fresh baby spinach and avoid bitter greens like dandelion and kale.

Lychees are a good source of vitamin C.

Passion Fruit: Use passion fruits as a flavor fruit and blend them with creamy base fruits like bananas or mangoes. Passion fruits blend well with other tropical flavor fruits like pineapples, lychees, and many berries. Young green or Thai coconut water or meat in a passion fruit green smoothie provides a wonderful tropical flavor note.

Passion fruits are very tart, so I recommend that you do not blend them with lemon, lime, or other tart fruits. I like to add up to three of them in a green smoothie to get the flavor.

Besides providing vitamins A and C, passion fruits aren't a nutritional powerhouse in your green smoothie recipes, but they do provide a delicious tropical flavor and a good amount of antioxidants.

Persimmon: There are two common types of persimmons, astringent and non-astringent. Astringent persimmons are inedible until they are fully ripened and soft due to the high tannin content. By that time, the flesh should be very soft and the peel might begin to look like the fruit is past its prime. Astringent persimmons are generally elongated, shaped more like a heart or acorn. I generally scoop the flesh out of the cut fruit and eat it as is or add it to smoothies. I generally do not eat the peel of astringent persimmons.

Non-astringent persimmons, commonly sold as "fuyu," may be eaten while still firm (although you should be sure they are ripe). Fuyu persimmons are squat and shaped more like a flattened pumpkin, and these are the ones I use most often in green smoothies. I cut non-astringent persimmons in sections (removing the green top) and add them, peel and all, to my smoothies.

Besides vitamin C, persimmons are also a good source of plant-based iron with 0.6 mg per fruit.

Pineapple: Fresh pineapples are my favorite flavor fruit. They go best with other tropical base fruits like mangoes, papayas, coconuts, and bananas. I typically do not mix pineapples with berries because the flavors fight with each other. Fully ripe, sweet pineapples blend very well with kiwifruit! Fully ripe pineapples are also perfect for masking bitter greens like kale, dandelion, collards, or even parsley.

Pineapples are an excellent source of vitamin C. They also contain all B vitamins (except B12) and are an especially good source of vitamins B1 and B6. As for minerals, pineapples are an excellent source of manganese and copper. In addition, pineapples contain an enzyme called bromelain, which works similarly to papain (an enzyme in papaya) to break down protein.

Plum: Plums make a great dominant flavor when blended with bananas, or you can blend them with peaches, nectarines, or apricots. Since plums are small, use up to four of them per smoothie. You can also use plums as a base fruit; just add a tiny bit of water and lots of greens like baby spinach.

A delicious variation of the plum is the pluot, a hybrid blend of plum and apricot.

Plums may not be the most nutritionally potent of fruits, but they do provide some vitamins A (as beta-carotene) and C to your green smoothie.

Pomegranate: Pomegranates are delicious, but they can be tricky. If you have a high-speed blender, you can cut them in half and scrape the pith and seeds into your smoothie and blend. Otherwise, juice them (or mash them into a metal mesh strainer) and use the liquid. Pomegranates blend well with bananas, apples, and pears and can be complemented with blueberries, strawberries, or raspberries. Açaí berries and cranberries also go well with pomegranate.

Pomegranates are another nutritional "superfruit." With the exception of B12, they contain all B vitamins, especially folate. They are also a good source of vitamins E and K. In addition, pomegranates are a good source of most essential minerals, and one of the few fruits that are a good source of zinc (9 percent of your recommended daily value in one fruit).

Raspberry: I like to make raspberry a dominant flavor, so I choose delicate base fruits like pear or banana to complement it. If I combine flavor fruits, I usually pair raspberries with strawberries, blackberries, or blueberries. Use one cup for dominant flavor, half a cup otherwise. Use with mild or bitter greens.

Raspberries are a good source of vitamins C, E, and K. One cup of raspberries provides up to 10 percent of your recommended daily value of omega-3 fatty acids.

Strawberry: Strawberries are my favorite berries to use with green smoothies. They blend well with bananas, peaches, and pears, complement oranges, and stand well on their own as a dominant flavor. They mix well with coconut or cacao too. I usually use one cup of whole strawberries in a smoothie. They also freeze well for later use. Use mild greens with strawberries to help preserve the flavor.

Strawberries are a rich source of vitamin C, and they are a good source of folate. As far as minerals go, strawberries provide a decent source of iron (0.7 mg in one cup), as well as manganese.

Water-Rich Flavor Fruits

These flavor fruits have high water content, so I recommend using only one of these fruits per recipe, combined with enough of a base fruit to yield a creamy, smooth texture. You might need to use a little less liquid as well.

Grapefruit/Oro Blanco/Pomelo: Use them interchangeably with oranges for a more tart smoothie. To sweeten, blend with sweet pineapple and use banana as the base fruit. You can also blend with strawberries and coconut milk. I would recommend using mild greens with grapefruit.

Not surprisingly, grapefruit is rich in vitamin C. Pink grapefruit is a good source of vitamin A due to the high levels of beta-carotene that provide its rosy color.

Grapefruit is notoriously problematic for people who are on prescription drugs, so it is best avoided if you take medications. Check with your doctor or pharmacist to see if there are any interactions associated with your medicines.

Grapes: Grapes blend well with bananas, figs, and many base fruits. Accent grapes with strawberries, raspberries, blackberries, cranberries, pomegranates, açaí berries, or cacao. Grapes are flavorful and sweet enough to help mask bitter greens.

Grapes are a good source of vitamins B1, B2, and K. They also provide copper and iron. Red grapes are highest in antioxidants. The most important health-promoting antioxidant in red grapes is resveratrol, which has been, and continues to be, the subject of numerous studies on potential therapeutic benefits.

Lemon/Lime: Lemon and lime add a bit of tartness to your smoothie. I recommend only adding half of either a lemon or lime at most and using it with delicately flavored base fruits. You can either use chunks of the fruit or simply juice it into your blender. Avoid mixing with berries, pineapple, or other sour fruits.

Lemons and limes are rich in vitamin C, but for the purposes of a green smoothie, you are only using enough to flavor the smoothie and not for the nutritional benefits.

Melon (Cantaloupe/Honey Dew): Melons blend best with other mild fruits like papayas and bananas. Accent the flavor of melons with kiwis, strawberries, or citrus fruits. Contrary to belief (and warnings on natural health websites), there are no digestion or health consequences from eating melons with other fruits.

Melons contain small amounts of all B vitamins (except B12). As with most other fruits, they are a rich source of vitamins A and C.

Minneola/Tangelo: Use as you would oranges.

Orange: I add an orange to my morning smoothie every day during the winter. Cut off only the outer, colored part of the peel and leave as much of the white pith attached as possible, since it is rich in nutrients like calcium and fiber. Make sure you take the seeds out. I don't need to reduce the normal amount of liquid I use in a smoothie with oranges, provided I have a good base fruit like banana or mango. Oranges and other citrus fruits mask the flavor of bitter greens beautifully. Blending just oranges, bananas, and kale together makes a wonderful, frothy orange juice with no bitterness.

Oranges are famous for their vitamin C content, but they also provide all B vitamins (except B12). They are also a great source of calcium, with 5 percent of your recommended daily value per fruit.

Tangerine/Clementine: Use as you would oranges. Use two smaller tangerines or clementines in place of one orange. Always remove tangerine seeds, since they contain toxic compounds that give your smoothie a bitter flavor.

While tangerines have less vitamin C than oranges (they are smaller, after all), each tangerine does contain more vitamin A than one orange (20 percent of your recommended daily value per fruit).

Ugli Fruit: Ugli fruit is a citrus that is very similar to oranges and can be used interchangeably. It is, in fact, a cross between a tangerine and a grapefruit. Since ugli fruits are much larger than oranges, one fruit would be equal to about two small or medium oranges. I have also seen ugli fruit sold as "uniq" fruit, perhaps a more appetizing name.

Watermelon: Watermelons are delicious in a smoothie and best left as a dominant flavor. Blend with banana, apple, or mango as a base fruit and complement it with a couple of strawberries, half a peach, or a whole plum. Use with mild greens.

Watermelons are a good source of vitamin A, thanks to the carotenoid compounds that give them their color. Watermelons also contain vitamin C, as well as the amino acid arginine, which helps improve blood flow.

Greens for Green Smoothies

The following is a guide to the most popular smoothie greens.

Aloe Vera: While not technically a leafy green, aloe vera is a green plant that I sometimes use in my green smoothie recipes. You can find aloe leaves at some health food stores or ethnic markets. When using it in a green smoothie, simply cut a one- to two-inch slice near the wide base. Then cut the spines off each side and slice it down the middle. Grab a spoon and scoop out the gel. It's the aloe gel that you use, discarding the outer green skin. Aloe vera gel blends with most fruits and doesn't add much flavor on its own.

While a host of health benefits are attributed to aloe vera, these claims are often over-hyped to sell aloe-derived health products. However, one of the main benefits of using aloe vera gel is its anti-inflammatory properties, which may help those with inflammatory diseases such as asthma and rheumatoid arthritis.

Arugula: As with other herbs, arugula is not a primary green in my smoothies. It is not as nutritious as other leafy greens that I prefer, but it does provide small amounts of vitamins A (as beta-carotene) and K.

Arugula is very bitter so, like dandelion greens, it is best used with pineapple, citrus, berries, and highly flavorful sweet fruits. Combine with fresh baby spinach or leaf lettuce if you wish.

Beet Greens: These are similar in texture to spinach and Swiss chard. Beet greens are easily masked by fruit in a green smoothie and can be used in any recipe where you'd use greens.

Beet greens are a good source of calcium and iron as well as other minerals. As with most leafy greens, they are rich in beta-carotene and vitamin K.

Bok Choy (Pak Choi/Chinese Spinach): I love adding baby bok choy to my green smoothies. Two heads of baby bok choy are a good source of calcium, iron, and many vitamins and minerals to my smoothie.

Bok choy can be a bit bitter, so mix it with sweet flavor fruits like pineapples, strawberries, bananas, and mangoes. Baby bok choy is milder and its flavor is easily masked by fruit.

Cabbage: This isn't something you would generally think of putting in your smoothie, but it's actually quite good for you and works well in some recipes.

Raw cabbage is a rich source of vitamins C and K. Unlike other leafy greens, it is not high in beta-carotene. Cabbage also provides good levels of some important minerals, including calcium.

Blended cabbage might smell funky in your smoothie, but the flavor is easily masked with flavorful fruits such as pineapples. It might be difficult to blend, especially in a cheap blender. You will want to shred or chop cabbage and add a little bit at a time.

Cilantro (Coriander): Cilantro is becoming one of my favorite herbs, but it might not be for everyone when it comes to blending it in a smoothie.

It has a very distinct flavor and works best in delicately flavored smoothies with pears, coconuts, avocados, apples, or peaches. Cilantro is also good with citrus fruits like orange and lemon.

Collard Greens: Collards can be a bit tough and bitter. They are, however, surprisingly easy to mask with most fruits, so they can usually be hidden in delicately flavored fruit smoothies. Try them with pineapples, berries, and citrus fruits.

Collards are an excellent source of beta-carotene and vitamin K, as well as vitamin C and folate.

Dandelion Greens: These are my favorite greens to use in a smoothie because of their overall nutrient content.

Dandelion greens are exceptionally rich in calcium, with one cup having 100 mg (10 percent of the recommended daily allowance, or RDA). They are also a good source of iron, beta-carotene, and vitamins E and K. Many natural health experts recommend dandelion greens for their detoxifying properties, which may help cleanse the liver.

Start out using dandelion greens with bananas, mangoes, pineapples, citrus fruits, and berries. If you are new to adding dandelion greens to smoothies, start with one to two cups. Try to work your way up to adding four to five cups after you are used to the flavor.

Dill Weed: Dill is a great herb that you wouldn't think would be very good in a fruit smoothie, but you might be pleasantly surprised.

Dill isn't necessarily a nutritional powerhouse when compared to kale, dandelion, or leaf lettuce, but it has some unique phytonutrients that make it worthwhile as an occasional addition to your smoothies.

Use only a little bit of fresh dill. Five to ten sprigs will go nicely in most smoothie recipes. It works best with citrus fruits or pineapples. Combine with other greens such as baby spinach, romaine, or leaf lettuce.

Kale: This is the next step up from baby spinach. Kale has a stronger, bitter flavor, so you might want to start using it with pineapples, citrus fruits, and berries. As you get used to it, try it with ripe mangoes and other fruits. Blending ripe bananas or citrus fruits with kale also masks the bitterness.

Kale, like all leafy greens, is an excellent source of beta-carotene and vitamin K. Kale is also an excellent source of calcium and iron.

I recommend that you use kale in a smoothie that you plan to drink right away. My experience is that kale will cause a smoothie to gel when left in the fridge for too long.

Lambsquarters: This is a wild green that grows abundantly in vacant lots, parks, and the woods. Most people have no idea just how nutritious this "weed" really is! Lambsquarters is rich in beta-carotene and vitamin C but also has good levels of riboflavin (vitamin B2). The calcium content in lambsquarters is high and it also has good levels of iron and copper.

Lambsquarters is similar in taste to spinach and can be added to just about any sweet smoothie recipe.

Lettuce, Butterhead: Butterhead lettuce, as well as other types of lettuces like Boston or especially iceberg, is not anywhere as nutrient-dense as other leafy greens. When it comes to using lettuce in green smoothies, I prefer romaine or green/red leaf lettuce. However, butterhead lettuce is a mild green similar to spinach and is great for people just starting out with green smoothies.

Lettuce, Green and Red Leaf: There are two types of common leaf lettuce: green leaf and red leaf. Both have a similar flavor and blend well in most smoothie recipes. Green leaf lettuce, however, has a slightly higher amount of nutrients than red lettuce.

Lettuce in general has a lower concentration of nutrients per cup when compared to kale and dandelion. I recommend using an entire head of lettuce in a smoothie instead of just two cups, as you would with dark greens, if your goal is to maximize nutrition.

Lettuce provides a lot of calcium, iron, and other vitamins and minerals. It also doesn't have an appreciable amount of oxalic acid (like spinach, beet, and chard). I use lettuce frequently to rotate my greens.

You can use it with most fruits. The more lettuce you add to your smoothie (such as an entire head), the more flavorful fruit you might want to add to offset any "salad" or "lettuce" taste.

Lettuce, Romaine: Romaine has become one of my favorite greens to use in a smoothie. It has a subtle flavor that is easy to mask and is super high in calcium and iron when you blend up an entire head of it. An entire head of romaine provides over 200 mg of calcium. Just one half of a head provides more than 100 percent of your recommended daily value of folate.

Romaine has a delicate flavor, so you can easily mask it with just about anything.

Nopal (Cactus): Nopal is the edible "leaf" of the prickly pear cactus. It is often eaten and juiced in Latin America and makes a delicious green smoothie.

It's hard to describe the flavor of nopal. It has a fresh "green" flavor that complements other tropical flavors, like pineapple, citrus, mango, banana, and coconut.

Unlike most smoothie greens, nopal isn't particularly rich in vitamins A and C, but it does provide calcium, magnesium, and manganese.

Parsley: There are two common types of parsley—Italian (flat leaf) and curly parsley (typically used as a garnish). I prefer to use flat-leaf parsley because it tends to blend up the easiest in less powerful blenders. Curly leaf parsley is slightly tougher, and some blenders may leave bits of it unblended in the smoothie.

I use fresh parsley in smoothies all the time because it is really high in iron, with 3.7 mg per cup (chopped). Parsley is also a good source of calcium.

Use no more than half of a bunch or one cup of chopped fresh parsley, otherwise you might not like the flavor. It has a distinct flavor and goes well with flavorful fruits like pineapples and oranges. You can also combine parsley with other greens, preferably baby spinach or lettuce to start. Once you are used to parsley, you can mix it with pineapples, mangoes, and dandelion greens for an iron-rich smoothie.

Radish Greens: Don't discard radish greens! They are actually quite high in calcium and other nutrients. They also blend very well in most smoothie recipes. They are not too bitter, so bananas, pineapples, and other sweet fruits easily mask their flavor.

I usually blend an entire bunch of radish greens in a smoothie. Be sure to wash them thoroughly first.

Spinach: When you are new to making green smoothies, I highly recommend using fresh baby spinach because it has a mild flavor, blends up easily in most blenders, and provides a lot of nutrients without a bitter flavor that other greens can add.

I recommend using two to three cups (or handfuls) of baby spinach per smoothie. If I am making an entire blender pitcher full, I'll use four to five handfuls, or I'll aim to fill the pitcher at least 40 percent of the way with spinach.

Spinach provides you with more than a full day's worth of vitamin A in the form of beta-carotene. It is an excellent source of folate, vitamin K, iron, and manganese.

Swiss Chard: Swiss chard comes in several varieties—red, white, yellow, or "rainbow." The texture of chard is more like spinach and will blend up easily. Use with sweet fruits since the natural sodium in chard will lessen the sweetness.

Chard is a great source of beta-carotene and vitamin K. It is also a good source of natural sodium.

Turnip Greens: These have a tougher texture, similar to collards and kale. Turnip greens are especially rich in beta-carotene and vitamin K. They are also an excellent source of folate, vitamin B6, and vitamin E. Calcium, copper, and manganese are plentiful as well. Blend them with sweet fruits like pineapple and citrus to offset the bitterness.

Vegetables for Green Smoothies

Bell Pepper: Red bell peppers are sweeter than green bell peppers and blend well with red grapes. Experiment and try small amounts of red, orange, or yellow bell peppers in various smoothies and see what combinations you like. I like to make a non-sweet smoothie with red bell pepper, cucumber, celery, spinach, and a banana for the base.

The main nutritional benefit to bell peppers is their high vitamin C content, as well as high beta-carotene content in red and orange bell peppers.

Broccoli: If you have a high-speed blender, use frozen broccoli florets in a green smoothie. Frozen broccoli is almost as nutritious as fresh, but it doesn't have the potent flavor that fresh, raw broccoli has. Adding fresh, raw broccoli to a green smoothie, even if you use a high-speed blender, may render the smoothie undrinkable. Use no more than one cup of florets.

In any other kind of blender, broccoli florets may not blend thoroughly, giving you little green bits that will get stuck between your teeth. If you are not using a high-speed blender, let the frozen broccoli thaw a little before adding it to your smoothie.

Broccoli is a good source of vitamins and minerals across the board, but it is especially rich in vitamins A, C, and K.

Cauliflower: I get asked about using cauliflower in green smoothies quite often. I do not recommend it. Cauliflower just does not have a flavor that works with any fruit I've ever tried. Instead of using cauliflower, use frozen broccoli florets.

Carrot: Carrots can be hidden in any smoothie. Despite their hard, fibrous texture, they purée quite well and their flavor disappears when you add flavorful fruits to the mix. Carrots are especially delicious blended with apples or citrus fruits and accented with ginger and/or cilantro. As I mentioned before, you can add carrots to any smoothie with orange-colored fruit like mangoes, peaches, or oranges.

Carrots are notorious for their beta-carotene content. Carotenoids like beta-carotene not only convert to vitamin A in your body, they are known to protect vision and promote eye health.

Celery: Smoothies are a great way to sneak celery into your diet if you don't like the taste or stringiness. Add one to two stalks to any smoothie recipe. You might taste the celery if you add more than two stalks. I like celery, so I usually add four or so. The natural sodium in celery cuts the sweetness of a fruit smoothie, which I like. It won't make your smoothie "salty."

Celery also increases the overall calcium content of your green smoothie. Each medium-sized stalk contains 16 mg of calcium. Two to three stalks of celery in a green smoothie can increase the calcium content by up to 4 percent of your recommended daily value.

Cucumber: Cucumbers blend well with sweet fruits like pineapple or citrus. If you've never had cucumber in a smoothie before, start with a quarter of a cucumber or a half and use it with a fruity base like mangoes, melons, or pears. You can also make savory vegetable smoothies by blending cucumber with red, orange, or yellow bell peppers and a tomato.

Cucumbers are an excellent source of vitamin K, as well as minerals like iron.

Sprouts: Green smoothies are a great way to eat sprouts. Add any type of sprouts like alfalfa, clover, and even sunflower sprouts by the handful. Keep in mind, however, you really can't hide the flavor of sprouts, so try not to add too much.

While sprouts and "micro greens" are often touted as being "superfoods," the truth is that in the small amounts often consumed, they simply do not provide anywhere near the level of nutrition that a full serving of broccoli or leafy greens provides. If you like the taste of sprouts, you can add them to your smoothie. However, I prefer to add them to wraps and sandwiches and leave them out of my smoothies.

Tomato: Tomatoes also "disappear" in a green smoothie. Their delicate flavor is easily masked by fruit, so try mixing them with very flavorful fruits like pineapples and oranges. Just drop in a plum tomato or a handful of cherry or grape tomatoes for some valuable lycopene. They also provide a good source of folate and beta-carotene.

Zucchini/Yellow Squash: Zucchini and yellow squash make an excellent base in a non-sweet, savory smoothie blended with other vegetables like carrots and tomatoes. You can also add chopped zucchini to a sweet, fruit-based smoothie for extra minerals like calcium, copper, iron, phosphorus, potassium, manganese, magnesium, and zinc.

Zucchini is also a particularly good source of B vitamins, as well as vitamins A, C, and K. Yellow squash contains these nutrients as well but in lower amounts compared to zucchini.

Superfoods for Green Smoothies

There are a few reasons I use superfoods in my smoothies. Sometimes I need a little extra energy. Sometimes I just want a tasty indulgence. They can also be helpful to prevent deficiencies or protect against disease.

Superfoods are versatile, tasty, and easy to add to just about any smoothie recipe. You can enhance the flavor (chocolate!) and get a boost of nutrients at the same time.

Here are a few superfoods that I sometimes use in my green smoothies:

Chocolate (Raw Cacao): Raw chocolate from the cacao bean is a decadent indulgence and great for an occasional dessert smoothie. Cacao is rich in vitamins, minerals, amino acids, omega-6 essential fatty acids, and two mood-enhancing phytochemicals, which will totally bliss you out after a stressful day! Another benefit with cacao is its high antioxidant capacity.

Cacao can be purchased as whole beans, nibs (broken pieces), or fine powder. Whole beans and nibs will need to be ground up in a food processor or coffee grinder before adding to your smoothies. Powder is easier to work with, but look for a *raw* cacao powder, since many nutrients are lost or greatly reduced when cacao is heated, which most powders have been. I prefer to purchase either the nibs or whole beans because I prefer to get food as close to its original, whole form as possible, which is when it has maximum nutrients due to minimum processing.

Cacao does have stimulating properties, and for this reason I do not use it daily anymore. It is helpful if you are transitioning away from coffee.

Cacao can be used with any smoothie, but pairing it with banana, durian, pear, peach, coconut, strawberry, and cherry is the tastiest. I've also blended cacao with mango, orange, pineapple, and berries with good results.

Cacao is bitter because it's dark chocolate in its purest form. For that reason, I'd stick with using greens that are mild, like fresh baby spinach, lettuce, beet greens, and parsley. Dandelion, collards, and kale can be used with cacao but may make your smoothie slightly bitter. Use fresh, ripe pineapple or extra bananas to sweeten if needed.

Goji Berry: Goji berries are grown in China and are widely touted as an antioxidant-rich superfood. You will typically find them at health food stores in dried form, but sometimes I see them as juices or powders in the supplement section.

Goji berries are a rich source of vitamin A (as beta-carotene) and rich in antioxidants. They add protein and a variety of other nutrients to your smoothie.

Use dried berries and either grind them into a powder with a food processor or hydrate them by soaking in water for an hour or so before blending them (be sure to use the soak water too!). I usually add just two tablespoons, since they are high in calories.

I like to blend goji berries with bananas, mangoes, and pears. They also mix well with cacao and young coconut. Mix with blueberries, strawberries, raspberries, blackberries, cranberries, or cherries for the ultimate antioxidant power boost.

Maca: If you are looking for more energy, stamina, and perhaps improved libido, then raw maca powder is for you! I don't use maca anymore, but when I did, I'd put about a tablespoon in my green smoothie every morning and it woke me right up and gave me sustained energy without the crash or jitters that I used to get from coffee.

Maca has a distinct butterscotch aroma and flavor. It smells more like butterscotch than it tastes, however, and the flavor can "funk" things up if you add too much. You will have to find out for yourself which fruit pairings you like and dislike. I find that maca blends well in smoothies with bananas, mangoes, pears, and apples, but too much of it can add a weird taste to citrus fruits or pineapples.

Avoid using cruciferous leafy greens like kale in green smoothies that contain maca. When these two ingredients are blended in a smoothie, certain compounds react and make an irritating sensation in the throat when you are drinking. I prefer to use lettuce, spinach, dandelion, and other noncruciferous greens in my smoothies with maca.

Sea Vegetables: I regularly add a tablespoon of dulse flakes in my green smoothies. Dulse is a sea vegetable particularly rich in iodine, which makes it an important part of my vegan diet. Kelp is also a great source of iodine. You can use kelp powder or dried kelp in a smoothie, as well as other sea vegetables like dulse, wakame, kombu, and hijiki. Prior to blending, be sure to rehydrate sea vegetables by soaking them in water for ten minutes. This will make it easier for your blender to fully pulverize them, and you're less likely to get unblended chunks of kelp. It is not necessary to rehydrate sea vegetables in flake or powder form.

Sea vegetables have plenty of natural sodium, so they help cut the sweetness of a smoothie without making it salty. However, I recommend blending a small amount of sea vegetables with sweet base fruits like bananas or mangoes, or using them to flavor savory smoothies featuring zucchini or cucumber. I don't use nori sheets in smoothies because they don't blend particularly well and they don't have the level of nutrition that other sea vegetables have.

I highly recommend seeking out a quality, organic source of sea vegetables, since they are easily contaminated by heavy metals if harvested in polluted waters.

Spirulina: This is a type of blue-green algae that has had a long history of being cultivated for food and is now used for nutritional supplements. While spirulina is said to be rich in protein, it is not a sufficient source in the amounts you typically would use.

It's a rich source of omega-3 fatty acids and is particularly valuable as a vegan source of EPA and DHA omega-3 fatty acids, which are typically found in fish oils (fish get their omega-3 fatty acids from the algae and plankton they eat and it moves up the food chain).

Spirulina contains vitamins B1, B2, B3, B6, B9, C, D, and E. There is debate about whether spirulina is a reliable source of vitamin B12 for humans. The very few plant sources of B12 contain an analogue form of B12 that is not bio-available to humans. While there is rampant speculation about this online, I recommend that you do not rely solely on spirulina, or any plant sources, for this important vitamin. You should use B12 supplements if you are vegan.

Spirulina typically comes in powdered or tablet form. Simply add the powder to any fruit or green smoothie. It does not interfere with the fruit flavors in your smoothie. I blend it with young coconut, pineapple, mango, banana, pear, or whatever I have on hand.

Seeds for Green Smoothies

Chia Seeds: Chia seeds provide even more omega-3 fatty acids and calcium than flaxseeds. Chia seeds are becoming more and more popular. You can find them in most health food stores and even in some grocery stores.

Chia seeds do not impact the flavor of a green smoothie. However, you need to either grind them up in a coffee grinder or soak them in water for about ten minutes prior to blending them. Soaked chia seeds will absorb water and become gelatinous, which then helps them blend well in a high-speed blender and improves nutrition and protein absorption.

One or two tablespoons of soaked or freshly ground chia seeds is a good serving size for a smoothie. Soaking the chia seeds makes them soft so they will blend up easily. I recommend soaking them in a ratio of 1 part seeds to 3 parts water.

Flaxseeds: Just one tablespoon of flaxseeds will provide 173 percent of your recommended daily value of alpha-linoleic acid, an essential omega-3 fatty acid. This same amount of flaxseeds added to your green smoothie will provide about 30 mg (3 percent RDA) of calcium, 14 percent RDA of copper, 0.6 mg of iron, 10 percent RDA of magnesium, 11 percent RDA of manganese, and 9 percent RDA of phosphorus. You'll also get some selenium and zinc with only 55 calories in a tablespoon of flaxseeds.

Purchase whole flaxseeds and store them in the refrigerator. Grind the seeds up in a coffee grinder before adding to your blender. Avoid purchasing ground flax (flax meal), since the shelf life and nutrients are decreased and the oils are prone to oxidization and rancidity.

Flaxseeds can be added to any smoothie recipe without negatively affecting the flavors. You might detect a hint of subtle nuttiness, but in general, one tablespoon of the ground seeds blends well and won't make your smoothie gritty.

Hemp Seeds: Hemp seeds are a great source of omega-3 fatty acids as well as protein. Shelled hemp seeds are available at certain health food stores or online. Simply add a tablespoon or two to any smoothie recipe. If you are not using a high-speed blender, grind them up first in a coffee grinder. Hemp seeds will lend a slight nutty flavor to your smoothie.

Sesame Seeds: Sesame has a distinct flavor that can come through some flavor combinations. However, you can use a tablespoon of freshly ground sesame in a sweet smoothie that uses bananas or mangoes with berries, pineapples, or kiwifruit. Sesame seeds add calcium and iron to your smoothie. As with all seeds, grind them up in a coffee grinder before adding them to a smoothie.

Spices for Green Smoothies

Cinnamon: Cinnamon can be used with apples, pears, and durians. Blend up a couple of crisp fall apples with a dash of ground cinnamon and you've got a thirty-second apple cider smoothie!

Dill/Oregano/Parsley: See Greens for Green Smoothies section (page 51).

Garlic: Garlic isn't anything you'd want to add to a fruit smoothie, although I've heard of somebody blending it with pineapple. I like to drop a clove of freshly minced garlic to a savory vegetable smoothie.

Ginger: Ginger is a tasty addition to a green smoothie. Either grate it into a smoothie before blending or toss in a small chunk if you have a high-powered blender. Ginger definitely adds a small kick to your smoothie, so add just a little bit until you know how much you want.

Ginger blends well with citrus (oranges, grapefruits), as well as apple, pear, peach, pineapple, banana, and even coconut. One of my favorite ginger smoothies is apple, carrot, ginger, and coconut milk.

Ginger stimulates the digestive tract and may alleviate nausea for some people.

Mint: A few sprigs of fresh mint can add a touch of flavor to a cacao smoothie. Use mint with pear, banana, sapote, or coconut and avoid using flavorful fruits like berries and pineapple, which will mask the mint flavor.

Nutmeg, Clove, and Other Baking Spices: Ground nutmeg, clove, all-spice, and pumpkin pie spice can help you create a pumpkin pie smoothie or come up with other smoothie creations that suggest baked goodies. These spices are best used with banana or durian base fruits and complemented with apples, pears, or sapotes.

Vanilla: Use whole vanilla beans (discard the peel and use only the scrapings from the inside) and blend them with banana, coconut, cacao, durian, or even pineapple. You can also use pure vanilla extract.

Liquids for Green Smoothies

Almond Milk: Almond milk has a subtle almond flavor that adds a slight "nuttiness" to your smoothie. It's great used with bananas, durians, apples, pears, or other fruit combinations where a slight nutty flavor would be desired.

Homemade Almond Milk

Ingredients

1 cup almonds

4 to 5 cups water

2 dates, soaked for 10 minutes
(optional)

1/2 teaspoon vanilla extract
(optional)

Step 1: Place the almonds in a large bowl and fill the bowl with water until the almonds are covered. Cover with a towel and let sit in a cool place for about 24 hours. You can soak them in the refrigerator to avoid risk of fermentation.

After the almonds are done soaking, they should be plump. Drain and rinse the almonds with fresh water. Drain again.

Step 2: Place the almonds in your blender with 4 to 5 cups of water. Add the vanilla and dates if you are using them. Blend on high for about 30 seconds or until you don't have any more large date or almond pieces.

Step 3: Strain the almond milk through a bag strainer or a fine sieve into a large bowl. A nut milk bag will allow you to get more of the milk, but it may be slightly messier. If you use a sieve, use a spoon to scrape the bottom of the sieve to remove built-up almond pulp. You can also use a large spoon to press the almond pulp into the sieve and get more of the milk.

Yields 4 to 5 cups of almond milk.

Almond milk is also fairly easy to make yourself! I make almond milk once or twice a week, and I've included a recipe here for your reference. Note that I only make it to use in smoothies, so I don't add any of the optional ingredients. If you are making it to drink on its own, however, the dates and vanilla extract help to make it a little sweeter.

Coconut Milk: Coconut milk is made from the meat and water of coconut. Instead of using canned coconut milk that you use for cooking, look for coconut milk where other nut milks (like almond milk) are sold. You can also make your own coconut milk by blending the meat and water from a young Thai coconut.

Coconut milk ties together the flavors of other tropical fruits like mangoes, pineapples, and guavas.

Coconut Water: Coconut water comes from young Thai coconuts, which are usually sold in Asian or Mexican markets. Unlike the mature (brown and "hairy") coconuts, young coconuts are filled with up to 20 ounces of electrolyte-rich, coconut-flavored water.

Coffee: While not necessarily for everyone, coffee can work well with certain green smoothie ingredients. A shot of espresso can turn a pumpkin spice green smoothie into a mineral-rich pumpkin spice latte smoothie.

When using coffee, avoid strong fruit flavors.

Fruit Juices: I don't recommend using commercial fruit juices in green smoothies, mainly because fruit juices are a concentrated source of sugar and many commercial juices have additives and sweeteners.

However, squeezing your own citrus juice for a green smoothie is a healthy and delicious way to enhance the citrus flavor of your smoothie. My favorite is tangerine juice!

Hemp Milk: Hemp milk (made from hemp seeds) is increasing in popularity and can be found at some mainstream grocery stores. It's richer and thicker than soy and rice milk. It usually comes in plain, vanilla, and chocolate and is naturally a good source of omega-3 and omega-6 fatty acids.

Oat Milk: Oat milk has a neutral flavor. It's not sweet on its own so it won't make your fruit smoothie too sweet, nor will it interfere with the flavors.

Rice Milk: Rice milk is slightly sweet with a light, crisp texture. It's a great addition to green smoothies, but the brands I am familiar with are not fortified with calcium and vitamins like hemp, almond, and soy milks are. Rice milk tends to be higher in calories and carbohydrates, so it's good if you're active or making a meal-replacement smoothie and need the extra calories. One cup of the original classic Rice Dream brand rice milk has 120 calories, versus almond or hemp milk, which may have as little as 60 calories per cup.

Soy Milk: Personally, I steer clear of soy milk except for rare occasions due to the health controversy surrounding processed soy products. Nevertheless, soy milk is readily available everywhere and comes in many flavors. Many brands are fortified with vitamins and minerals.

Tea: You can use just about any chilled tea in a green smoothie.

Water: I prefer to use filtered tap water or pure spring water in my green smoothies.

Fats for Green Smoothies

Coconut Oil/Butter: While some people use coconut oil or coconut butter in green smoothies, I don't like to. The main reason is that coconut oil/butter is solid at room temperature. When it is in a green smoothie, you'll end up with tiny globs of solidified coconut fat.

Nut Butters: Nut butters like peanut butter and almond butter can be used in small amounts in a green smoothie. One to two tablespoons of nut butter blend deliciously with raw cacao, as well as fruits like apples and pears.

Be sure to choose all-natural, unsweetened, and unsalted nut butters.

Nuts: Nuts can be blended up in a green smoothie provided you have a high-powered blender like a Vitamix or Blendtec. It's best to soak nuts overnight to soften them up and remove the enzyme inhibitors concentrated in the outer skin.

When using nuts in a green smoothie, I recommend using no more than a small handful. Too many nuts may cause digestive difficulty or detract from the texture of the smoothie.

Plant Oils: I generally do not recommend adding refined plant oils to your green smoothie; however, some people enjoy adding a liquid omega-3 oil supplement to their blends. Coconut oil is also a popular one that people add to green smoothies, but it can solidify in the smoothie, making it feel greasy (see entry above on coconut oil/butter). Olive oil has a distinctive flavor that may interfere with the overall flavor of the recipe. Flaxseed oil can be used in small amounts.

If you're using a plant oil, I do not recommend adding more than two tablespoons to a green smoothie. In general, my preference is for fats from whole foods like avocados, durians, or nut butters.

Protein Powders for Green Smoothies

You probably do not need to add a protein powder supplement to your smoothie, even if you are a vegetarian. It is easy to get adequate amounts of protein from your diet.

If you feel the need to supplement your protein intake, however, you will quickly find that you have a lot of options to choose from. Just browsing the supplement section of your local health food store or vitamin shop is enough to make your head spin.

Here is a basic breakdown of current options available.

Egg Protein Powder: Egg protein is made from powdered egg whites. It is a complete protein high in amino acids and each serving is roughly the equivalent of eating six or so egg whites. Because it is made from eggs, it is not recommended for vegans or those with an egg allergy.

I do not currently know of any egg white protein powders made from cage-free eggs, so if you are concerned about the ethical implications of consuming commercial egg protein supplements, make sure you carefully research the brands and products available before making your purchase.

Hemp Protein Powder: Hemp protein has become very popular among health food enthusiasts and much easier to find (and cheaper) at health food stores or online.

Hemp protein powder is derived from hemp seeds and is a complete protein rich with amino acids and omega-3 and omega-6 fatty acids.

Rice Protein Powder: Most people consider brown rice as a carbohydrate rather than a quality source of protein, but it is. Rice protein powder is a complete, low-carbohydrate protein rich with amino acids. It is easily digestible and perfect for those with food allergies, since pure rice protein powder does not contain gluten, dairy, egg, soy, or many of the common food allergens. Rice protein comes in vanilla, chocolate, berry, and plain flavors. Plain rice protein powder adds a mild brown rice flavor to smoothies, which I find appealing.

Rice protein powder is not too expensive and can be found at health food stores and online.

Soy Protein Powder: Soy protein is one of the most readily available protein powders on the market. You can usually find it at any supermarket. Soy protein is affordable and comes in a variety of flavors such as chocolate, vanilla, and strawberry.

However, I do not use soy protein for several reasons. First of all, most soy products come from GMO soy crops. Unless the soy ingredients are from certified organic soybeans, it is most likely GMO. Secondly, there are some controversies about the health benefits (and risks) of consuming soy products, particularly highly processed soy products like isolated soy protein. It is worth your while to research the health benefits and risks yourself and make your own decision. Personally, I would recommend trying rice or hemp protein instead.

Obviously, those with soy allergies should not use soy protein.

Sprouted Protein Powder: Sprouted proteins are a fairly new arrival in the world of protein powders. Usually made from sprouted brown rice or legumes (e.g., peas, beans), these powders are usually raw and appeal to vegans and those following a raw food diet.

I currently use and recommend Epic Protein by Sprouted Living. It is an organic, raw, vegan sprouted protein that has up to 23 grams of protein per serving, depending on which product you get.

Epic Protein is also gluten-free and GMO-free and does not contain pesticides, herbicides, and PCBs. It contains all of the essential and non-essential amino acids as well as glutamic acid. I like the plain flavor since it doesn't really change the flavor of green smoothies. They also have vanilla-lucuma and chocolate-maca varieties.

A single serving does not make my smoothie chalky and the subtle flavor can be easily masked by adding a few additional berries, such as strawberries, if desired. You can find Epic Protein in select health food stores or you can purchase it online.

Whey Protein: Whey protein powder is made from the by-product of turning milk into cheese. Whey is the preferred protein supplement among body builders. It is a complete protein and easily digestible.

Whey protein concentrate is more readily available and less expensive, containing approximately 30 to 85 percent protein. Whey protein isolate is a purer form with at least 90 percent protein and is, therefore, more expensive. Because it comes from dairy, whey is not suitable for vegans or those who are lactose intolerant.

Any protein powder should work in a smoothie, although some types or brands might be chalkier than others.

Substitutions for Green Smoothies

It's bound to happen. Some people don't like certain fruits or, worse, they are allergic to them. I get e-mails all the time from people who are allergic to bananas and mangoes.

So here's a quick and dirty cheat sheet for substituting one fruit for another and still coming up with a great recipe.

When making any sort of substitution in a green smoothie recipe, always replace fruits with others that have a similar texture. For example, swapping out a banana in a recipe for papaya is a good substitution, but replacing a banana with an orange is not, because the orange is too watery.

The chart below contains approximate size/amounts of fruits that are equivalent. There may be some calorie variation between different fruits, even if the smoothie is the same size after the substitution is made.

BASE FRUIT SUBSTITUTIONS	FLAVOR FRUIT SUBSTITUTIONS	WATER-RICH FRUIT SUBSTITUTIONS	BERRIES AND POMEGRANATE SUBSTITUTIONS
1 medium banana	1 cup pineapple	1 cup grapes	1 cup blackberries
1 mango	1 orange	2 cups watermelon	1 cup blueberries
2 small peaches	1 small grapefruit	1 orange	1 cup cherries
2 cups papaya	3 kiwifruit	1 small/medium grapefruit	1/4 cup goji berries
1/2 avocado	1 small pomelo	1/2 cantaloupe	1 pomegranate
2 small pears	2 tangerines		1 cup raspberries
1 medium/large pear	1 cup grapes		1 cup strawberries
1 large apple	1 cup watermelon		1 pouch (100 grams) frozen açaí purée
1 cup durian			
6 small apricots			
1 cherimoya			
4 large figs			
3 persimmons			
2 large plums/pluots			

Tips for Saving Money on Expensive Fruits and Vegetables

Produce isn't cheap. Eating healthy has a reputation (undeservedly, if you ask me) of being expensive.

However, there are a few strategies you can use to dramatically increase your fresh fruit and vegetable intake without dramatically increasing your grocery bill.

Get a Warehouse Club Membership

Warehouse clubs like Costco, BJ's, and Sam's Club help me save a lot of money on fresh produce.

I get mangoes, huge pineapples, tubs of organic spinach and baby greens, ten-pound bags of organic carrots, organic strawberries, organic raspberries, melons, kiwis, oranges, dates, tomatoes, avocados, chia seeds, wild frozen blueberries, and more at Costco and BJ's (I've never had a Sam's Club membership).

The prices I pay for these bulk items are lower than any of our local supermarkets. I am able to get more produce for the same price and save a considerable amount of money on things that I'd pay more for elsewhere. The annual membership fee pays for itself just about every week!

Buy In Season or On Sale and Freeze

Another way to save money is to purchase produce when it is in season and on sale. When strawberries go on sale during the summer months, I buy lots of them to freeze and use during the winter months when fresh produce tends to be more expensive.

Frozen fruits and berries are almost as nutritious as fresh and last a lot longer. Just be sure to thoroughly wash and dry produce before you freeze it.

Almost all fruits and berries can be frozen. I do not recommend freezing water-rich fruits like oranges or grapes.

Leafy greens, with the exception of lettuce and spring mix, can be frozen as well. I regularly buy tubs of organic, pre-washed kale and spinach and place them right in the freezer for later use.

When leafy greens are on sale, I buy double or triple the amount I usually buy. Then I wash, dry, and place them in freezer bags. While doing this makes for a larger grocery bill during the week I buy them, it equates to savings when I do not have to purchase greens at the non-sale price in later weeks, since I can use the less expensive frozen ones I've already bought.

Grow Your Own Food

If you have a garden or a backyard, consider planting some food crops. It's pretty easy to grow your own tomatoes, cucumbers, zucchini, squash, herbs, and anything else you want. Your plants or seed packets will produce a bounty of veggies for pennies!

You can also set up an indoor herb garden as well as a sprouting station for alfalfa, sunflower, beans, and lentils.

You Don't Need Exotic "Superfoods"

It's easy to get caught up in the hype about exotic powdered superfood supplements like raw cacao, maca, spirulina, etc. However, you do not need to stock your pantry full of these food items.

You can get all the nutrition you need from fresh, organic fruits, greens, nuts, seeds, and sprouts. If you wish to use superfoods, use them sparingly or see if you really need them at all.

If you're taking maca every day, go off it for a week and see how you feel. Don't get caught up in the superfood craze and stock your cupboards with eight or so different "must-have" potions and powders. Use one or two at a time and rotate them. Or simply do without because your fresh, organic fruits and vegetables *are* superfoods!

Save Money (and Stay Healthy) by NOT Buying Organic

Wait, did I say NOT to buy organic? Well, what I mean is that you don't *have* to buy absolutely everything organic for health reasons. Avocados, pineapples, and mangoes are among the fruits lowest in pesticide residues. You also typically peel these foods before eating them. So you can save a bit of money by purchasing certain conventionally grown foods that are low in pesticide residue.

How can you find out which ones are okay to buy non-organic and which ones to always buy organic? Check out the "Dirty Dozen List" by the Environmental Working Group (www.ewg.org).

Seek Out Fruit and Vegetable Markets in Your Neighborhood

A cheaper alternative to your supermarket's limited produce section might be a neighborhood fruit and vegetable market. These markets are usually found in cities and sometimes suburbs. Prices are often much lower than at grocery stores.

Buy Young Coconuts at Asian Markets Rather Than at Health Food Stores

If you routinely buy young Thai coconuts from a health food store, you should seek out a local Asian market. My experience has been that Asian markets typically sell coconuts for up to half what a health store chain would sell them for. Plus, they are often better-quality coconuts with fewer bad and fermented ones.

How to Avoid Genetically Modified (GMO) Produce

Genetically modified organisms, commonly referred to as "GMOs," are plants and animals that have been modified through bioengineering, which is the process of combining DNA molecules from different species in order to alter the genes of an organism. Usually, DNA for a genetically modified organism does not come from closely related species. Bioengineering is a strictly human-driven process and cannot occur naturally or without human intervention.

There is a lot of heated debate about whether or not GMOs are harmful for humans, animals, and the environment. Corporations that produce GMO crops assert that they are safe, and the general scientific consensus tends to agree.

However, many people prefer to not use GMO foods.

GMOs are pretty much everywhere in the modern diet. The vast majority of soy and corn grown in the United States is genetically modified. Processed, packaged foods are very likely to contain GMO products—especially if they have corn and soy ingredients.

Two ways that GMO ingredients might sneak into your green smoothie are in soy milk and soy protein powder. Unless the packaging for these products is labeled organic or explicitly labeled "GMO free," they are most likely made from GM soybeans.

In contrast, most produce is not GMO right now. However, there are a few exceptions:

Hawaiian papayas are one example, created in response to the papaya ring spot virus that has plagued the Hawaiian papaya crop. DNA from the virus was mixed with the DNA of the papaya, producing virus-resistant fruits. Up to 80 percent of Hawaiian papayas are genetically modified.

About 13 percent of zucchini on the market is GMO, and a variety of non-browning apple is awaiting approval to go on the market. Corn and soy are the most abundantly available GMO foods on the market.

As genetically modified foods continue to show commercial viability, I expect to see more and more showing up in supermarkets. And I do not expect any of them to be labeled as GMO since there are currently no labeling requirements, and there is major resistance by food industry leaders to labeling.

Choosing organic produce is the best way to avoid GMO foods, since GMO produce cannot be labeled "organic."

PART TWO

GREEN SMOOTHIE RECIPES

The green smoothie recipes in this section are organized by category so you can easily find them. Each green smoothie recipe includes its nutritional information, as well as a brief description and any flavor variations that can be made.

Each green smoothie is around 20 ounces. To make any of the smoothies, simply add the liquid to your blender, followed by the soft fruit and remaining ingredients. Add the greens to your blender last.

If the recipe calls for "2 cups greens, chopped," this means that you will measure out two cups of greens (just cram them in the measuring cup) and then chop them with a knife so that they blend up easier in your blender.

Blend on high for 30–45 seconds (depending on your blender) or until the smoothie is creamy.

CHAPTER FOUR

DETOX AND CLEANSING GREEN SMOOTHIES

Pear-Dandelion Green Smoothie • 86
Mean Green Cleansing Smoothie • 86
Blueberry-Lemonade Smoothie • 87
Green Apple Smoothie • 87
Strawberry-Grapefruit Green Smoothie • 88
Pineapple-Lime-Cilantro Smoothie • 88
Berry Cleansing Smoothie • 89
Lemon-Lime Green Smoothie • 89
Grapefruit-Orange Smoothie • 90

Dandelion-Orange Smoothie • 90
The Green Machine • 91
Pineapple-Celery Green Smoothie • 91
Apple-Mango Green Smoothie • 92
Sweet Grapefruit Smoothie • 92
Green Goodness Detox Smoothie • 93
Cranberry Cleanse Smoothie • 93
Orange-Pear Smoothie • 94
Strawberry-Lemonade Smoothie • 94

Detoxification is one of the biggest purported health benefits that draw people to green smoothies. The idea that a delicious green smoothie can clean out your insides and "undo" years of abuse from an unhealthy diet, lack of exercise, and exposure to toxic substances is an exciting one.

However, the general concept of "detoxification" as defined in the natural health movement is misleading. While many natural health experts recommend regular fasts and strict cleansing regimens, I'll show you, in this chapter, how to support your body's natural "detox organs" and how to facilitate cleansing on a long-term daily basis with no need for fasts or restrictive regimens.

But first, let's make sure we're on the same page when it comes to the concept of detox and cleansing.

In the natural health and raw food movements, the concept of detox refers to the process your body goes through when it expels toxins once you are no longer bombarding your system with toxic substances. Toxic substances may include certain food ingredients (e.g., refined sugar, refined wheat, alcohol, caffeine) and chemicals (e.g., pesticides, fungicides, food colorings, MSG, and ingredients in everyday household cleaners and hygiene products).

You've probably read from multiple sources on the Internet that your body accumulates toxins over time, and these accumulated toxins lead to disease. The solution is often a cleanse (e.g., juice fast, 100 percent raw vegan diet), an expensive detox product, or even colonic hydrotherapy.

The idea behind a cleanse (short-term juice fast or strict diet regimen) is that it gives your body a break so that it can expel toxins that have built up over time. This sudden detox is said to cause a host of unpleasant "detox symptoms" that might include skin breakouts, gas and bloating, body aches, brain fog, fatigue, low energy, headaches, irritability, extreme cravings (for sweet, salty, or other unhealthy foods), constipation, and diarrhea.

However, the idea that your body has accumulated toxins from everyday life, and that these toxins have built up over time and need to be purged through a drastic cleanse regimen, is misleading because your body is always in a state of detox. Whether you eat the purest of pure diets, or you live on pizza, beer, and ice cream, your body never stops detoxifying. As long as you have a functioning liver, kidney, and colon, your body is removing toxins on a daily basis.

When I refer to detox in this book, I am specifically referring to *reducing* the consumption and exposure to toxic or unhealthy substances through a change in diet, recognizing that you aren't necessarily "starting up detoxification"; rather you are supporting it, making the process more efficient.

I believe that simply drinking green smoothies on a daily basis and embracing a whole foods, fitness-oriented lifestyle is the best way to support overall health, as well as your body's ability to fight disease and eliminate everyday toxins and waste.

There is absolutely no need to avoid solid foods for a week, or to drink nothing but green smoothies. I encourage you to forgo the strict cleanse regimens and just focus on eating a diet that is as natural as possible, and make green smoothies a daily habit.

Key Ingredients for a Cleansing Green Smoothie

So now that we are clear about the concept of detox and cleansing with green smoothies, I want to discuss which ingredients you can use in your smoothies that have the best cleansing properties.

Why Organic Fruits Help with Detoxification

Fruits are naturally water-rich and full of nutrients, particularly vitamin C. They have a high fiber content, lots of antioxidants, and are super easy to digest. Both water and fiber facilitate movement in your bowels and excretion of post-digestive waste, dead cells, and toxic substances.

Given the criteria above, citrus fruits should be a go-to smoothie ingredient when you are feeling a little sluggish. Oranges, grapefruit, lemons, and limes have exceptionally high vitamin C content, and lots of fiber, and they are among the most water-rich fruits that we eat.

Why Organic Greens Help with Detoxification

Leafy greens are rich in chlorophyll, a plant compound in all green vegetables that some natural health experts believe purifies the blood and cleanses the body. While there is limited science behind purported claims about the cleansing properties of chlorophyll, there's no debate that greens are rich in vitamins, minerals, and fiber—all of which support optimum functioning of your body's digestive system.

When you combine the purifying power of greens with the cleansing power of citrus fruit in a green smoothie, you've got a natural cleansing shake that will support your body's natural detoxifying organs better than any high-priced detox system on the market.

You're probably wondering which leafy green is best at supporting your body's natural cleansing ability. Most experts recommend dandelion greens for their ability to cleanse the liver and support kidney function.

What Else Can You Add to a Cleansing Green Smoothie?

Garlic is often promoted as a detox food. If it seems a bit weird for you to blend garlic into a green smoothie, you can add it to freshly made blender soups or to savory smoothies. While I've never done it, I've heard that garlic and pineapple are delicious together in a smoothie. Honestly, I can't bring myself to mix these two foods.

Ginger is also a known detoxifying ingredient. Fresh ginger stimulates your digestive tract and speeds up digestion, which helps move waste and toxins out of your body. Fresh ginger can be grated into a green smoothie or added to fresh juices.

Ingredients to Avoid Using in Detox Green Smoothies

Powdered superfoods and supplements: This might seem counterintuitive, but even powdered superfoods have had their water removed, thus decreasing the overall water content of your green smoothie and making it less effective. While they are generally okay, avoid powdered and highly processed ingredients in a green smoothie where the goal is hydration.

Protein powders: While many people use protein powders, myself included, I recommend avoiding them when making a green smoothie specifically for cleansing. Powders make a smoothie less hydrating, and some protein powders have additives that may sabotage your desire to produce a pure, hydrating smoothie.

If you absolutely must use a protein powder in a green smoothie, and your goal is a hydrating, fiber-rich shake, then use a high-quality vegan rice, hemp, or sprouted protein, and be sure to use water-rich citrus fruits, watermelon, and plenty of leafy greens.

Fats: Because fats like nuts, seeds, avocados, coconuts, and refined oils (e.g., flaxseed oil) digest slower than fresh fruits and greens, I recommend that you leave them out of green smoothies made specifically for cleansing. While not necessarily detrimental to your health, adding too much fat to a green smoothie might cause gas and bloating, making you feel anything but "clean" inside.

Nonorganic fruits and vegetables: This is a no-brainer. You want to detox, so don't add produce that has been sprayed and treated with pesticides, fungicides, waxes, and preservatives. Stick with organic as much as possible.

Liquids other than fresh water: Water is the key to cleansing. You can juice your own fruits or greens, but don't use commercial fruit juices as they might have added sugar, flavorings, and preservatives. The same thing goes for nut milks and dairy. I recommend making homemade nut milks (see the homemade almond milk recipe in this book) and avoid store-bought nut milks that may have additives, not to mention potential chemicals leached from the packages. I also prefer to skip dairy such as milk and yogurt in my green smoothie.

When it comes to green smoothie detox, keep it simple—fresh fruits and leafy greens blended with water or coconut water if you want the most cleansing green smoothie on the planet.

About These Recipes

While most detox green smoothie recipes out there can be considered exceptionally cleansing, depending on the ingredients you use, not all of them are delicious and tasty. For this chapter, I will focus on smoothie ingredients that help support your body's natural detoxification processes while also tasting great—even to green smoothie beginners!

PEAR-DANDELION GREEN SMOOTHIE

This smoothie might seem pretty basic, but it is loaded with nutrients. Just two cups of dandelion greens provide up to 17 percent of your recommended daily value of calcium, 3.4 mg of iron, and 3 grams of protein.

INGREDIENTS

2 large pears, cored

2 cups dandelion greens, chopped

4 ounces coconut milk

NUTRITION INFO

*Calories: 227 • Fat: 4g • Protein: 5g
Carbs: 65g • Calcium: 24%
Iron: 4.4mg • Vitamin A: 91%
Vitamin C: 72%*

MEAN GREEN CLEANSING SMOOTHIE

The mint in this green smoothie provides a refreshing flavor, while the kale and parsley boost the vitamin and mineral contents.

The orange in this smoothie is also great for detox since oranges are hydrating and fiber-rich, which helps support colon function. Just one orange contains 5 percent of your recommended daily value of calcium and more than 100 percent of your recommended daily value of vitamin C.

INGREDIENTS

1/2 mango, peeled and pitted

1 medium celery stalk, chopped

1 orange, peeled

1 cup fresh curly kale, stems removed

1/4 cup flat-leaf parsley, chopped

10–15 fresh mint leaves

4 ounces filtered water

NUTRITION INFO

*Calories: 188 • Fat: 2g • Protein: 6g
Carbs: 44g • Calcium: 18%
Iron: 2.4mg • Vitamin A: 70%
Vitamin C: 306%*

BLUEBERRY-LEMONADE SMOOTHIE

As with oranges, the fiber in lemons helps support colon function. They are also a great source of vitamin C.

I used a frozen banana in this recipe to give the smoothie a creamy milkshake consistency. To freeze bananas, simply peel them and then place in a freezer-safe bag in your freezer.

Chia seeds help to give this smoothie some heart-healthy fats and a boost of protein.

INGREDIENTS

1 cup fresh blueberries

1 small frozen banana

1/2 lemon, peeled

1/4 teaspoon grated ginger

1 tablespoon chia seeds, soaked
    for 5 minutes

4 ounces homemade almond milk
    (page 64)

NUTRITION INFO

*Calories: 215 • Fat: 2g • Protein: 4g
Carbs: 49g • Calcium: 3%
Iron: 1.1mg • Vitamin A: 1%
Vitamin C: 51%*

GREEN APPLE SMOOTHIE

Apples are great for cleansing since they are loaded with fiber. It is important to get enough fiber in your diet, which has been linked to a reduced risk of colon cancer. Just one medium apple contains 17 percent of your recommended daily value of fiber.

Hemp seeds are a great source of healthy fats as well as protein. You can find them at most health food stores or online.

INGREDIENTS

1 medium green apple

1/2 tablespoon hemp seeds

8 fresh mint leaves

2 cups green leaf lettuce, torn

1 cup green grapes

4 ounces filtered water

NUTRITION INFO

*Calories: 242 • Fat: 3g • Protein: 4g
Carbs: 55g • Calcium: 5%
Iron: 1.6mg • Vitamin A: 39%
Vitamin C: 27%*

STRAWBERRY-GRAPEFRUIT GREEN SMOOTHIE

While grapefruit can be very bitter, it is great for cleansing. I love adding mint to grapefruit smoothies—I think this is a great combination.

Not only do strawberries help to sweeten the grapefruit but they add 94 percent of your recommended daily value of vitamin C and 10 percent of your recommended daily value of fiber. Make sure you use very ripe strawberries.

INGREDIENTS

1/2 grapefruit, peeled

10 medium strawberries

1 small banana, peeled

10 fresh mint leaves

1 cup fresh baby spinach

4 ounces orange juice

NUTRITION INFO

Calories: 243 • Fat: 1g • Protein: 5g
Carbs: 59g • Calcium: 8%
Iron: 1.9mg • Vitamin A: 33%
Vitamin C: 251%

If you are on medication, please check with your doctor before consuming grapefruit, as it can have a negative reaction that can be fatal.

PINEAPPLE-LIME-CILANTRO SMOOTHIE

While cilantro doesn't have a lot of nutritional value in the amounts you would use in a green smoothie, it provides a unique flavor that is complemented by the pineapple and ginger in this recipe.

Cucumber is a great water-rich food and pineapple is a great source of fiber. Consuming a diet that is both hydrating and fiber-rich is key to making sure your body can expel waste efficiently.

INGREDIENTS

1 cup cubed pineapple

1 small banana, peeled

1/2 small cucumber, chopped

1/2 cup cilantro

1/4 teaspoon grated ginger

1/2 small lime, peeled

4 ounces filtered water

NUTRITION INFO

Calories: 185 • Fat: 1g • Protein: 3g
Carbs: 49g • Calcium: 4%
Iron: 1.1mg • Vitamin A: 5%
Vitamin C: 133%

BERRY CLEANSING SMOOTHIE

If you can, use fresh blueberries instead of frozen wild blueberries in this smoothie. In my opinion, frozen blueberries do not taste very good with dandelion greens, which are a great source of protein, calcium, and fiber. Fresh blueberries and dandelion greens, however, taste great together.

Chia seeds are great for an extra boost of protein and to give the smoothie some heart-healthy fats. Just one tablespoon of chia seeds contains 49 percent of your recommended daily value of omega-3 fatty acids.

INGREDIENTS

5 large strawberries

1/2 cup blueberries

1 cup dandelion greens, chopped

1 tablespoon chia seeds, soaked
    for 5 minutes

4 ounces unsweetened coconut
    milk

NUTRITION INFO

*Calories: 135 • Fat: 4g • Protein: 4g
Carbs: 25g • Calcium: 16%
Iron: 2.9mg • Vitamin A: 51%
Vitamin C: 106%*

LEMON-LIME GREEN SMOOTHIE

This smoothie is a little tart because of the lemon and lime, but it's well worth trying. The grapes and banana help to sweeten it a little.

This smoothie might be small, but it's loaded with nutrients. Just one cup of kale adds 8 percent of your recommended daily value of calcium, 10 percent of your recommended daily value of fiber, and 3 grams of protein. Most of the nutrients in the smoothie come from the kale.

INGREDIENTS

1/4 lemon, peeled

1/4 lime, peeled

1 small frozen banana, peeled

1/2 cup green grapes

1 cup fresh curly kale, stems
    removed

4 ounces filtered water

NUTRITION INFO

*Calories: 132 • Fat: 1g • Protein: 4g
Carbs: 32g • Calcium: 10%
Iron: 1.4mg • Vitamin A: 48%
Vitamin C: 136%*

GRAPEFRUIT-ORANGE SMOOTHIE

A grapefruit smoothie might be too bitter for some people, but when grapefruit is blended with sweet banana, orange, and creamy almond milk, it makes for a pleasant mingling of flavors.

INGREDIENTS

1/2 grapefruit, peeled and seeded

1 orange, peeled

1 small banana, peeled

2 cups fresh baby spinach

4 ounces homemade almond milk
  (page 64)

NUTRITION INFO

*Calories: 242 • Fat: 1g • Protein: 6g
Carbs: 56g • Calcium: 13%
Iron: 2.2mg • Vitamin A: 53%
Vitamin C: 196%*

If you are on medication, please check with your doctor before consuming grapefruit, as it can have a negative reaction that can be fatal.

DANDELION-ORANGE SMOOTHIE

Avocado is a great alternative to bananas for making a smoothie creamy. It's also loaded with heart-healthy fats. Just a quarter of an avocado has 4 percent of your recommended daily value of omega-3 fatty acids and 6 percent of your recommended daily value of omega-6 fatty acids. It also contains 11 percent of your recommended daily value of fiber.

INGREDIENTS

2 oranges, peeled

1/4 avocado, peeled and pitted

1 cup dandelion greens

4 ounces filtered water

NUTRITION INFO

*Calories: 242 • Fat: 8g • Protein: 5g
Carbs: 45g • Calcium: 19%
Iron: 2.3mg • Vitamin A: 45%
Vitamin C: 253%*

THE GREEN MACHINE

Parsley is another powerhouse green. It's loaded with iron and vitamins C and K. Just half a cup of parsley contains 1.9 mg of iron. Parsley is great for detoxifying your liver and kidneys. It has a distinctive flavor, however, so I recommend using a small amount. This recipe only calls for half a cup, but I have used one cup in some green smoothie recipes. I would not recommend using any more than one cup of parsley in a green smoothie.

INGREDIENTS

1/2 cup green grapes

1 small banana

1/2 cup flat-leaf parsley

1 cup fresh curly kale, stems
removed

1 teaspoon ground flaxseeds

6 ounces filtered water

NUTRITION INFO

*Calories: 180 • Fat: 3g • Protein: 8g
Carbs: 38g • Calcium: 21%
Iron: 4.2mg • Vitamin A: 114%
Vitamin C: 279%*

PINEAPPLE-CELERY GREEN SMOOTHIE

This is a variation of one of my favorite green smoothies that I make on a regular basis. It's loaded with minerals from the celery, spinach, and parsley, vitamins from the orange and pineapple, and healthy sources of fat in the almond milk and chia seeds.

This recipe is also a great source of calcium, iron, protein, and fiber.

INGREDIENTS

1 orange, peeled and seeded

1 cup cubed pineapple

2 small stalks celery

1 teaspoon chia seeds, soaked for
5 minutes

1 cup fresh baby spinach

1/4 cup fresh parsley

4 ounces homemade almond milk
(page 64)

NUTRITION INFO

*Calories: 191 • Fat: 1g • Protein: 5g
Carbs: 43g • Calcium: 13%
Iron: 2.5mg • Vitamin A: 33%
Vitamin C: 255%*

APPLE-MANGO GREEN SMOOTHIE

Apples are loaded with fiber that helps support colon function. Just one apple contains 17 percent of your recommended daily value of fiber. The water-rich lemon and cucumber help make this the perfect cleansing smoothie.

INGREDIENTS

1/2 mango, peeled
1 green apple, cored
1/4 lemon, peeled
1/2 cucumber, chopped
1 cup fresh baby spinach
4 ounces filtered water

NUTRITION INFO

*Calories: 203 • Fat: 1g • Protein: 4g
Carbs: 52g • Calcium: 7%
Iron: 1.7mg • Vitamin A: 32%
Vitamin C: 99%*

SWEET GRAPEFRUIT SMOOTHIE

Oranges and grapefruits are rich in the antioxidants known as flavonoids, which expel damaging free radicals from your body and protect against cell damage and disease.

INGREDIENTS

1 orange, peeled and seeded
1/2 grapefruit, peeled and seeded
1/2 cup cubed frozen pineapple
Seeds scraped from 1 vanilla bean
   or 1/2 teaspoon pure vanilla
   extract (alcohol-free)
1/4 cup butterhead lettuce, torn
8 ounces filtered water

NUTRITION INFO

*Calories: 168 • Fat: 1g • Protein: 3g
Carbs: 42g • Calcium: 8%
Iron: 0.5mg • Vitamin A: 13%
Vitamin C: 214%*

If you are on medication, please check with your doctor before consuming grapefruit, as it can have a negative reaction that can be fatal.

GREEN GOODNESS DETOX SMOOTHIE

The cucumber and grapes in this green smoothie recipe are especially hydrating, while the apple gives this smoothie 17 percent of your recommended daily value of fiber.

Flaxseeds are so small that most blenders cannot pulverize them. Therefore, I recommend grinding them in a coffee grinder prior to use.

INGREDIENTS

1 green apple, cored
1/2 cup green grapes
Juice of 1/2 lime
1 cup fresh baby spinach
1/2 cucumber, chopped
1/4 cup fresh flat-leaf parsley
1 tablespoon ground flaxseeds
4 ounces filtered water

NUTRITION INFO

Calories: 219 • Fat: 4g • Protein: 5g
Carbs: 48g • Calcium: 9%
Iron: 3.1mg • Vitamin A: 31%
Vitamin C: 58%

CRANBERRY CLEANSE SMOOTHIE

Cranberries are loaded with free radical–purging antioxidants. Combine that with the powerful cleansing properties of water and fiber-rich oranges and you have a tasty detox smoothie.

The pear and orange help to sweeten the cranberries without having to use additional sweeteners.

INGREDIENTS

1/2 cup cranberries
1 pear, cored
1 orange, peeled
2 cups fresh baby spinach
4 ounces filtered water

NUTRITION INFO

Calories: 207 • Fat: 1g • Protein: 4g
Carbs: 53g • Calcium: 12%
Iron: 2.3mg • Vitamin A: 43%
Vitamin C: 152%

ORANGE-PEAR SMOOTHIE

Pears are a great source of fiber. Just one pear provides 22 percent of your recommended daily value of fiber. That's even more than an apple! They are also a great source of copper, magnesium, potassium, and vitamins K and C.

There is no need to add liquid to this recipe since the oranges are water-rich already.

INGREDIENTS

2 oranges, peeled
1 pear, cored
1 teaspoon grated ginger
2 cups fresh baby spinach

NUTRITION INFO

*Calories: 252 • Fat: 1g • Protein: 5g
Carbs: 65g • Calcium: 16%
Iron: 2.3mg • Vitamin A: 45%
Vitamin C: 253%*

STRAWBERRY-LEMONADE SMOOTHIE

Swiss chard contains high amounts of vitamin K, which helps to reduce inflammation. It's also a great source of protein, calcium, and fiber.

INGREDIENTS

10 strawberries
1/2 lemon, peeled
1 frozen banana, peeled and sliced
2 chard leaves, stems removed
6 ounces filtered water

NUTRITION INFO

*Calories: 170 • Fat: 1g • Protein: 4g
Carbs: 15g • Calcium: 7%
Iron: 2.7mg • Vitamin A: 43%
Vitamin C: 167%*

CHAPTER FIVE

WEIGHT LOSS GREEN SMOOTHIES

Pineapple-Mango Green Smoothie • 101

Strawberry-Orange Smoothie • 101

Banana-Pineapple Green Smoothie • 102

Cherry-Pineapple Green Smoothie • 102

Mango-Kiwifruit Smoothie • 103

Peach-Cherry Smoothie • 103

Spiced Blueberry and Pear Smoothie • 104

Healthy Chocolate Smoothie • 104

Carrot-Papaya Smoothie • 105

Apple-Broccoli Smoothie • 105

Watermelon-Mint Smoothie • 106

Chocolate-Grape-Strawberry Smoothie • 106

Peach-Strawberry Green Smoothie • 107

Coconut-Mango Green Smoothie with Lime • 107

Kiwifruit-Broccoli Smoothie • 108

Apple-Cherimoya Smoothie • 108

Chocolate-Kiwifruit Smoothie • 109

Banana-Pineapple Smoothie with Aloe and Kale • 109

Green smoothies are an excellent weight-loss tool. I used green smoothies as an integral part of a whole foods diet to lose forty pounds, and now I use them to maintain my weight.

Over the years, I've collected firsthand accounts from people who have lost anywhere from twenty-five pounds to more than a hundred pounds by embracing a green smoothie and whole foods lifestyle. Their transformations have been impressive, especially those who have lost a hundred pounds and now run marathons!

Over and over again, I've heard firsthand accounts from people who tried every type of diet imaginable. I've even heard from people who went through gastric bypass and ended up putting weight back on!

Their lives changed when they finally discovered green smoothies. These delicious beverages kick-started a cascade of *sustainable* changes in their diet and lifestyle that they could stick to for life.

The result? Easy weight loss and long-term maintenance of a healthier weight.

How Green Smoothies Help You Lose Weight

Forget about those canned weight-loss shakes you find in drugstores. Green smoothies are nothing like those! Instead of cutting calories from your diet through a liquid weight-loss shake, green smoothies feed your body with whole foods and facilitate healthy, natural weight loss in several ways.

First of all, they can replace unhealthy meals. What better way to start your day than with a green smoothie meal containing up to three servings of fresh fruit and two servings of leafy greens (the taste of which is hidden by the sweet fruit)? Add some protein powder and some omega-3 fatty acid–rich flax or chia seeds and you'll have a satisfying breakfast that will keep you energized and focused until lunch.

Contrast that with a heavy, greasy breakfast of pancakes, eggs, and bacon. Not only does this sit heavily in your stomach, but the great amount of fat (most of it saturated fat) and sugar (from the pancakes and syrup) often leads to a mid-morning energy crash. Not to mention the greasy breakfast can have *triple* the calories of the green smoothie breakfast. And there's not one fruit or vegetable in sight (no, blueberries in your pancakes or ketchup on your eggs don't count!).

A less dramatic example of an unhealthy breakfast is a large muffin or even a bagel with cream cheese. A large muffin has more than 500 calories. A bagel with cream cheese has up to 450 calories—if you only put two tablespoons of cream cheese on it. Neither of these two breakfast items will keep you satisfied until lunch, since the sugar content will give you a surge of energy shortly after eating them, followed by a crash mid-morning.

In contrast, a large, 32-ounce green smoothie contains around 350 calories. It's hard to make a green smoothie that exceeds 400 calories. That would be a rather huge smoothie!

A green smoothie can also replace lunch or even dinner. The contrast between the amount of calories in a green smoothie versus the typical fast-food lunch (burger, fries, and a soft drink) is astounding. Just check the nutrition labels at your usual fast-food lunch spot, and remind yourself that a green smoothie is much more nourishing, will satisfy your hunger, and provides less than 400 calories on average.

Plus, one of the biggest benefits of green smoothies is that they are grab-and-go, so they can be as convenient as a muffin for breakfast or a fast-food lunch—with fewer calories and a whole lot more nutrition!

Secondly, a green smoothie made with sweet fruits not only hides the bitter flavors of leafy greens or other vegetables, it satisfies your sweet tooth without added sugars. I have often craved a donut or something sugary, only to have the Banana-Pineapple Green Smoothie (page 102) make me forget why I even wanted to put a calorie-dense, sugar-drenched glazed donut in my body to begin with.

Thirdly, green smoothies give you energy to exercise. They are a potent source of vitamins, minerals, antioxidants, healthy carbohydrates, healthy fats, and protein. Because they are blended, green smoothies support efficient digestion and absorption of nutrients, which means that your cells get the nourishment they need. And that translates into more energy! If you use that energy to exercise, you'll kick off a snowball effect of accelerating weight loss, building muscle, and improving your metabolism.

And finally, they "reset" your taste buds so that you learn to enjoy healthy foods. Over time, you will be drawn to healthy fruits and vegetables and away from old indulgences. I find that a lot of my old junk-food favorites are too sweet or too greasy or just don't taste as good as I remember. Instead, I savor the flavors of fruits, vegetables, and healthy, whole foods meals that I can cook at home. And I feel so much better for it!

Should I Do a Green Smoothie-Only Diet?

No! I do not promote a green smoothie–only diet or a green smoothie "fast." Temporary crash diets provide temporary weight loss. However, once you stop dieting, the weight comes right back.

Instead, I encourage people to incorporate green smoothies into their current diet and slowly work toward a whole food, plant-based diet.

Not only is a whole foods diet that includes green smoothies healthy and promotes weight loss, it is sustainable long term. You can eat a whole foods diet every day for the rest of your life and never go hungry or feel deprived. You can enjoy a green smoothie every single day.

By implementing a long-term diet overhaul, you have a much greater chance of not only losing the weight, but keeping it off for good. Think about it: What's the point of losing sixty pounds if you're just going to put it back on after you stop dieting?

But I'm on a Low-Carb Diet. Will These Green Smoothies Sabotage My Weight Loss?

As you read in Chapter One, green smoothies are not in the same league as donuts and pasta. Green smoothies will not make you fat. Yes, they contain carbohydrates and fructose. But because you are consuming these substances in a whole food form, the vitamins, minerals, antioxidants, fiber, and other nutrients cancel out the potential negative effects and promote overall health and a healthy weight.

When it comes to fruits and vegetables, I don't really count them as carbohydrates, nor do I count the sugar content unless there is a medical reason to do so (e.g., diabetes).

About These Recipes

You'll notice that all of the green smoothie recipes in this section contain fruits, vegetables, greens, and superfoods, but they do not contain dairy milk or processed ingredients like yogurts. You can get enough calcium from fruits and vegetables that you don't need to add milk or yogurt. These foods contain excess fat, hormones, and other additives that may sabotage your efforts to lose weight.

You can, however, add high-protein foods like goji berries, hemp seeds, and dark leafy greens. Dark greens like kale and dandelion greens are also going to be a great source of calcium.

PINEAPPLE-MANGO GREEN SMOOTHIE

Goji berries are great for weight loss. Protein, fiber, and vitamins are all packed in this little berry. I often carry a small bag of goji berries around with me when I know I'm going to be out for a while. They make a wonderful, portable snack when I'm on the go.

This delicious smoothie satisfies my sweet tooth, while the fiber and protein help fight off hunger.

INGREDIENTS

1 mango, peeled and pitted

1/2 cup cubed pineapple

2 tablespoons goji berries

2 cups fresh baby spinach

4 ounces homemade almond milk
   (page 64)

NUTRITION INFO

Calories: 272 • Fat: 1g • Protein: 7g
Carbs: 61g • Calcium: 10%
Iron: 3.2mg • Vitamin A: 210%
Vitamin C: 204%

STRAWBERRY-ORANGE SMOOTHIE

Strawberries are an excellent low-calorie berry. Just six large strawberries contain 9 percent of your recommended daily value of fiber, as well as 6 percent of your recommended daily value of omega-3 fatty acids. Of course, they are also a great source of vitamin C with 85 percent of your recommended daily value.

The strawberries and orange help to mask the flavor of the celery, while the banana helps to make this smoothie creamy.

INGREDIENTS

1 banana, peeled

6 large strawberries

1 orange, peeled and seeded

1 stalk celery, chopped

8 ounces filtered water

NUTRITION INFO

Calories: 203 • Fat: 1g • Protein: 3g
Carbs: 51g • Calcium: 8%
Iron: 1mg • Vitamin A: 4%
Vitamin C: 182%

BANANA-PINEAPPLE GREEN SMOOTHIE

This smoothie reminds me of a tropical drink you'd get on the beach. Unlike those high-calorie, sugar-laden drinks, however, this smoothie is low calorie and loaded with fiber to help you lose weight.

The addition of spinach gives this smoothie a little extra calcium and iron as well as various vitamins and minerals.

INGREDIENTS

1 banana, peeled
1/2 cup cubed frozen pineapple
2 cups fresh baby spinach
Seeds scraped from 1/2 vanilla bean
    or 1/4 teaspoon pure vanilla
    extract (alcohol-free)
4 ounces coconut water

NUTRITION INFO

Calories: 187 • Fat: 2g • Protein: 3g
Carbs: 40g • Calcium: 6%
Iron: 2.2mg • Vitamin A: 41%
Vitamin C: 89%

CHERRY-PINEAPPLE GREEN SMOOTHIE

Cherries might be a pain to pit, but they are well worth it. One cup of cherries contains only 97 calories, but they are a great source of B vitamins, antioxidants, and fiber.

Pears are also loaded with fiber to help fill you up.

INGREDIENTS

1 cup cherries, pitted
1/2 cup cubed pineapple
1 pear, cored
1 large collard leaf
4 to 6 ounces filtered water

NUTRITION INFO

Calories: 251 • Fat: 1g • Protein: 4g
Carbs: 65g • Calcium: 11%
Iron: 1.3mg • Vitamin A: 14%
Vitamin C: 94%

MANGO-KIWIFRUIT SMOOTHIE

When it comes to losing weight, mangoes are your friends. Just one medium mango has around 150 calories and is loaded with nutrients!

One mango contains 16 percent of your recommended daily value of fiber, 2 grams of protein, and 121 percent of your recommended daily value of vitamin C.

INGREDIENTS

1 mango, peeled and pitted

2 kiwifruit, ends removed

4 ounces coconut water

NUTRITION INFO

*Calories: 258 • Fat: 2g • Protein: 4g
Carbs: 64g • Calcium: 8%
Iron: 0.8mg • Vitamin A: 20%
Vitamin C: 366%*

PEACH-CHERRY SMOOTHIE

This smoothie combines low-calorie cherries with high-fiber fruits like mango and peach to create a perfect smoothie that is not only delicious but nutritious!

Coconut water is nature's sports drink. It's loaded with electrolytes to give you energy.

INGREDIENTS

1/2 mango, peeled and pitted

1 large peach, pitted

1/2 cup cherries, pitted
    (fresh or frozen)

2 collard leaves, stems removed

8 ounces coconut water

NUTRITION INFO

*Calories: 248 • Fat: 1g • Protein: 5g
Carbs: 61g • Calcium: 13%
Iron: 1.1mg • Vitamin A: 27%
Vitamin C: 234%*

SPICED BLUEBERRY AND PEAR SMOOTHIE

Adding spices to smoothies is a great way to add a lot of flavor without adding additional calories.

Frozen wild blueberries are a great low-calorie fruit that is loaded with 25 percent of your recommended daily value of fiber and 12 percent of your recommended daily value of zinc—with only 80 calories!

INGREDIENTS

1 medium pear, cored

1 cup frozen wild blueberries

1/4 teaspoon ground cinnamon

1/4 teaspoon ground nutmeg

4 ounces homemade almond milk
   (page 64)

NUTRITION INFO

Calories: 208 • Fat: 1g • Protein: 2g
Carbs: 49g • Calcium: 3%
Iron: 0.8mg • Vitamin A: 1%
Vitamin C: 29%

HEALTHY CHOCOLATE SMOOTHIE

This smoothie is a chocolate lover's dream come true. It's a healthy way to enjoy chocolate without the guilt. Cacao is raw chocolate and it is very bitter on its own. I added banana and pear to sweeten this recipe. It's better than a chocolate bar!

INGREDIENTS

1 banana, peeled

1 large pear, cored

1 tablespoon cacao powder

1 cup fresh baby spinach

6 ounces homemade almond milk
   (page 64)

NUTRITION INFO

Calories: 268 • Fat: 1g • Protein: 5g
Carbs: 60g • Calcium: 5%
Iron: 2mg • Vitamin A: 21%
Vitamin C: 35%

CARROT-PAPAYA SMOOTHIE

Carrot juice is a great source of vitamins A and K. I added carrot juice instead of a whole carrot to this smoothie to make it a little creamier—carrots can be very pulpy.

Papayas are high in vitamin C and are a good source of folate, potassium, fiber, and vitamins A, E, and K. Papayas are also rich in antioxidants and the enzyme papain, which helps promote digestive health.

INGREDIENTS

1 banana, peeled

1 cup cubed papaya

1/2 teaspoon ground cinnamon

1 cup fresh baby spinach

4 ounces carrot juice

NUTRITION INFO

Calories: 222 • Fat: 1g • Protein: 4g
Carbs: 55g • Calcium: 8%
Iron: 2mg • Vitamin A: 191%
Vitamin C: 156%

APPLE-BROCCOLI SMOOTHIE

Don't be afraid to blend broccoli in a green smoothie. Not only does it provide minerals such as calcium, iron, and antioxidants, it's easily masked by sweet fruit. Frozen broccoli has a milder flavor and adds a nice chill to your smoothie.

Apples are a great source of fiber to help fill you up and keep you feeling fuller longer. This is a great low-calorie smoothie for a mid-afternoon snack.

INGREDIENTS

1 green apple, cored

1/2 cup frozen broccoli

1/2 banana, peeled

1 stalk celery

1 cup fresh baby spinach

8 ounces homemade almond milk
   (page 64)

NUTRITION INFO

Calories: 223 • Fat: 1g • Protein: 5g
Carbs: 47g • Calcium: 8%
Iron: 1.8mg • Vitamin A: 31%
Vitamin C: 98%

WATERMELON-MINT SMOOTHIE

Watermelon is almost 90 percent water, so it's great for weight loss. Two cups of watermelon chunks contain 33 percent of your recommended daily value of vitamin C, 7 percent of your recommended daily value of potassium, and 5 percent of your recommended daily value of fiber.

Strawberries are also loaded with nutrients with very few calories. Just twelve strawberries contain 113 percent of your recommended daily value of vitamin C and 12 percent of your recommended daily value of fiber with only 46 calories.

INGREDIENTS

2 cups seedless watermelon chunks

12 strawberries

1 banana, peeled

5 mint leaves

8 ounces filtered water

NUTRITION INFO

Calories: 243 • Fat: 1g • Protein: 4g
Carbs: 61g • Calcium: 4%
Iron: 1.7mg • Vitamin A: 13%
Vitamin C: 160%

CHOCOLATE-GRAPE-STRAWBERRY SMOOTHIE

This smoothie is great for weight loss because it's loaded with protein and 42 percent of your recommended daily value of fiber with only 256 calories.

I used water-rich grapes so you can use less almond milk. The almond milk helps to add a little healthy fat to your smoothie and to give it a slightly creamier texture.

INGREDIENTS

1 cup red grapes

10 large strawberries

1/2 pear, cored

1 teaspoon cacao powder

1 cup fresh baby spinach

2 ounces homemade almond milk
(page 64)

NUTRITION INFO

Calories: 256 • Fat: 1g • Protein: 5g
Carbs: 60g • Calcium: 8%
Iron: 3mg • Vitamin A: 21%
Vitamin C: 164%

PEACH-STRAWBERRY GREEN SMOOTHIE

Dandelion greens are amazing for many reasons. They are loaded with protein, fiber, calcium, and iron. They are also very cleansing and great for detox.

One cup of dandelion greens contains only 24 calories, but it has 40 percent of your recommended daily value of vitamin A, 1.7 mg of iron, and 2 grams of protein.

INGREDIENTS

2 medium peaches, pitted

10 medium strawberries

Seeds scraped from 1 vanilla bean
   or 1/2 teaspoon pure vanilla
   extract (alcohol-free)

1 small carrot, sliced

1 cup dandelion greens, chopped

8 ounces homemade almond milk
   (page 64)

NUTRITION INFO

*Calories: 235 • Fat: 2g • Protein: 7g
Carbs: 48g • Calcium: 13%
Iron: 3.1mg • Vitamin A: 106%
Vitamin C: 150%*

COCONUT-MANGO GREEN SMOOTHIE WITH LIME

This smoothie will remind you of a tropical beach drink. Unlike those drinks, however, this smoothie is loaded with nutrients.

Two cups of kale provide this smoothie with enough protein and fiber to drink it as a meal—and it's filling enough to keep you going until your next meal.

INGREDIENTS

1 mango, peeled and pitted

1/2 lime, peeled and seeded

1/2 frozen banana, peeled and sliced

2 cups fresh curly kale

4 ounces unsweetened coconut milk

NUTRITION INFO

*Calories: 293 • Fat: 5g • Protein: 9g
Carbs: 63g • Calcium: 23%
Iron: 2.9mg • Vitamin A: 126%
Vitamin C: 343%*

KIWIFRUIT-BROCCOLI SMOOTHIE

Cucumbers and kiwifruit are water rich and offer a lot of fiber. Adding water-rich ingredients to your smoothie is a great way to fill you up without a lot of calories.

Since frozen broccoli has a much less pungent flavor than fresh, I recommend using frozen in a green smoothie.

INGREDIENTS

1 medium frozen banana, peeled and sliced

1/2 cup frozen broccoli

2 organic kiwifruit with peel

1/2 cucumber, chopped

4 ounces filtered water

NUTRITION INFO

Calories: 239 • Fat: 2g • Protein: 6g
Carbs: 58g • Calcium: 9%
Iron: 1.7mg • Vitamin A: 11%
Vitamin C: 257%

APPLE-CHERIMOYA SMOOTHIE

Cherimoyas and apples are a delicious combination. Cherimoyas have an apple- and pear-like flavor, so adding an apple complements the flavor nicely.

I only added half a teaspoon of cinnamon, but you can add a whole teaspoon if you'd like. Cinnamon is great for adding a lot of flavor without additional calories.

INGREDIENTS

1/2 cup cherimoya, peeled and seeded (about 1 medium cherimoya)

1/2 medium apple, cored

1/2 medium frozen banana, peeled and sliced

1/2 teaspoon ground cinnamon

1 small carrot, sliced

1/2 head butterhead lettuce, chopped

4 ounces filtered water

NUTRITION INFO

Calories: 191 • Fat: 1g • Protein: 4g
Carbs: 47g • Calcium: 5%
Iron: 1.6mg • Vitamin A: 80%
Vitamin C: 34%

CHOCOLATE-KIWIFRUIT SMOOTHIE

I added mint tea instead of water to this smoothie. Adding tea that you have brewed and cooled is another great weight-loss trick. Like spices, it adds a lot of flavor without adding additional calories.

The peel of a kiwifruit is loaded with antioxidants. I recommend buying organic kiwifruit and leaving the peel on for the extra nutrients. Simply cut the ends off and add it to your blender. The little black seeds are a great source of omega-3 fatty acids.

INGREDIENTS

2 kiwifruit, ends removed

1 tablespoon cacao powder

1 medium banana, peeled

2 cups fresh baby spinach

4 ounces chilled mint tea

NUTRITION INFO

Calories: 243 • Fat: 3g • Protein: 6g
Carbs: 55g • Calcium: 9%
Iron: 2.8mg • Vitamin A: 25%
Vitamin C: 198%

BANANA-PINEAPPLE SMOOTHIE WITH ALOE AND KALE

Adding aloe to your green smoothie is great for your digestive tract and it adds almost no calories to your smoothie.

You can find aloe as a leaf at most grocery stores. If you are going to use aloe from a tub, make sure it is meant to be consumed.

INGREDIENTS

1/4 cup aloe vera gel scraped from
   a leaf

1 banana, peeled

1 cup cubed pineapple

3 fresh kale leaves, stems removed

2 small celery stalks

6 ounces filtered water

NUTRITION INFO

Calories: 258 • Fat: 2g • Protein: 8g
Carbs: 61g • Calcium: 20%
Iron: 2.8mg • Vitamin A: 98%
Vitamin C: 335%

CHAPTER SIX

ANTIOXIDANT GREEN SMOOTHIES

Very Berry Green Smoothie • 115

Cherry-Plum Green Smoothie • 115

Blueberry-Persimmon Green Smoothie • 116

Frozen Raspberry-Lemonade Smoothie • 116

Blueberry-Cherry-Pomegranate Smoothie • 117

Raspberry-Orange-Pomegranate Smoothie • 117

Plum-Açaí Smoothie • 118

Mango-Papaya Green Smoothie with
Blueberries • 118

Pineapple-Plum Smoothie with Almond Milk • 119

Cherry-Pomegranate Smoothie • 119

Blackberry-Peach Smoothie • 120

Raspberry-Carrot Green Smoothie • 120

Black and Blue Smoothie • 121

Blackberry-Açaí Green Smoothie • 121

Super Antioxidant Blast Green Smoothie • 122

Cherry-Vanilla-Peach Green Smoothie • 122

Pineapple-Carrot Smoothie • 123

The green smoothie recipes in this chapter focus on antioxidant-rich fruits and berries.

Antioxidants include vitamins such as C and E, as well as naturally occurring chemical compounds in plants such as carotenoids (carotene, lycopene, lutein) and polyphenols (resveratrol, flavonoids).

Antioxidants play an important role in your health. They inhibit oxidation of other molecules, preventing free radicals from producing the negative chain reactions in the body that may ultimately lead to potentially cancer-causing cellular and DNA damage.

Scientific research has found that oxidative stress may be implicated in the development or increased risk of some chronic diseases, including neurodegenerative diseases such as Alzheimer's disease,[39] as well as schizophrenia,[40] cancer, and cardiovascular disease.[41] Oxidative stress may also exacerbate many medical conditions. For example, persons with diabetes may be susceptible to more oxidative stress in their bodies resulting from hyperglycemia.[42]

Despite the widespread idea that antioxidants provide anti-aging as well as disease-protective benefits, scientific studies have had limited success in establishing conclusive connections between antioxidant intake and disease prevention. However, most of these studies have used antioxidant supplements rather than dietary antioxidants from antioxidant-rich foods.

This does not necessarily mean that dietary antioxidants have no beneficial effect in the human body simply because antioxidant supplements have been shown to be minimally effective. Rather, it underscores the importance of obtaining as much nutrition as possible through diet instead of relying on synthetic "quick-fix" pills.

Despite the current debate in the scientific community about the overall role of antioxidants in human health and their ability to prevent disease, there is no debate that people who follow diets that are highest in antioxidant-rich fruits and vegetables tend to have a lower risk of developing many of the chronic illnesses that plague modern society.[43]

Whether antioxidants themselves provide the greatest protection against disease or work synergistically with other phytochemical compounds, vitamins, minerals, fiber, and other macronutrients (all of which are lacking in manufactured antioxidant pills), I have no reason to doubt the overall health benefits of antioxidant-rich fruits and vegetables in the diet.

The Top Antioxidant-Rich Fruits

All fruits and vegetables are rich in antioxidants, but fresh berries tend to have the highest levels. This includes blueberries, blackberries, raspberries, and strawberries, as well as grapes and exotic fruits like açaí berries.

About These Recipes

The recipes in this chapter focus on green smoothies that provide large amounts of vitamins C and E, as well as specific fruits and/or vegetables that have a particularly high concentration of a certain antioxidant (e.g., resveratrol in red grapes).

VERY BERRY GREEN SMOOTHIE

Goji berries, raspberries, blackberries, and blueberries are all extremely high in antioxidants. Blackberries and blueberries actually rank the highest in antioxidants of all the berries.

INGREDIENTS

1 cup blueberries

1/2 cup raspberries

1/2 cup blackberries

2 tablespoons goji berries, soaked
  for 5 minutes

1 tablespoon ground flaxseeds

2 cups butterhead lettuce, torn

8 ounces unsweetened coconut milk

NUTRITION INFO

*Calories: 299 • Fat: 10g • Protein: 9g
Carbs: 51.7g • Calcium: 10%
Iron: 4mg • Vitamin A: 178%
Vitamin C: 74%*

CHERRY-PLUM GREEN SMOOTHIE

Cherries, plums, and spinach are loaded with antioxidants. The antioxidants in plums are actually in their skin, so you don't want to peel them.

INGREDIENTS

1 cup Bing cherries, pitted

1 plum, pitted

1 tablespoon chia seeds, soaked
  for 5 minutes

Seeds scraped from 1/2 vanilla bean
  or 1/4 teaspoon pure vanilla
  extract (alcohol-free)

1/2 small zucchini

2 cups fresh baby spinach

4 ounces homemade almond milk
  (page 64)

NUTRITION INFO

*Calories: 190 • Fat: 2g • Protein: 6g
Carbs: 39g • Calcium: 10%
Iron: 2.9mg • Vitamin A: 44%
Vitamin C: 69%*

BLUEBERRY-PERSIMMON GREEN SMOOTHIE

Persimmons and cinnamon make a delicious combination. Use the flat, tomato-looking fuyu persimmons for a sweeter smoothie.

I added chard since it is a great source of protein. Each chard leaf contains 1 gram of protein.

INGREDIENTS

1 cup blueberries

2 fuyu persimmons, seeded

1 small banana, peeled

1/2 teaspoon ground cinnamon

2 chard leaves, stems removed

4 ounces filtered water

NUTRITION INFO

*Calories: 256 • Fat: 1g • Protein: 4g
Carbs: 65g • Calcium: 6%
Iron: 3.7mg • Vitamin A: 43%
Vitamin C: 113%*

FROZEN RASPBERRY-LEMONADE SMOOTHIE

You might be wondering why this recipe is with the antioxidant smoothies. Raspberries are a great source of antioxidants, of course, but did you know that spinach is also a great source of antioxidants?

If this smoothie is too bitter for you, you can use less lemon (one-quarter) or add a date to sweeten it. I recommend adding natural sweeteners instead of sugar or agave nectar to your smoothies.

INGREDIENTS

1 cup raspberries

1/2 small lemon, peeled and seeded

1 small frozen banana, peeled and
    sliced

Seeds scraped from 1 vanilla bean
    or 1/2 teaspoon pure vanilla
    extract (alcohol-free)

2 cups fresh baby spinach

4 ounces homemade almond milk
    (page 64)

NUTRITION INFO

*Calories: 190 • Fat: 2g • Protein: 5g
Carbs: 43g • Calcium: 9%
Iron: 2.9mg • Vitamin A: 41%
Vitamin C: 98%*

BLUEBERRY-CHERRY-POMEGRANATE SMOOTHIE

Pomegranates can stain when you try to remove the arils. To remove the arils without making a mess, cut the pomegranate in half, submerse each half in water, and pull apart the arils from the white pith.

Butterhead lettuce has a delicate flavor that will easily be masked by the fruit. If you can't find butterhead lettuce, you can always replace it with spinach or a large collard leaf.

INGREDIENTS

1/2 cup blueberries
1/2 cup pomegranate arils
1 cup Bing cherries, pitted
1/2 head butterhead lettuce, chopped
1/2 teaspoon ground cinnamon
4 ounces filtered water

NUTRITION INFO

Calories: 173 • Fat: 2g • Protein: 4g
Carbs: 41g • Calcium: 4%
Iron: 1.8mg • Vitamin A: 20%
Vitamin C: 33%

RASPBERRY-ORANGE-POMEGRANATE SMOOTHIE

I added a pear to give this green smoothie a creamy texture. Depending on the season, you can replace the pear with a banana or mango.

The orange and collard leaves give this smoothie a boost in calcium. The collard leaves are also a great source of protein.

INGREDIENTS

1 cup raspberries
1 orange, peeled and seeded
1/4 cup pomegranate arils
1 small pear, cored
2 medium collard leaves, stems
  removed
4 ounces filtered water

NUTRITION INFO

Calories: 276 • Fat: 2g • Protein: 6g
Carbs: 67g • Calcium: 23%
Iron: 1.8mg • Vitamin A: 29%
Vitamin C: 202%

ANTIOXIDANT GREEN SMOOTHIES

PLUM-AÇAÍ SMOOTHIE

I recommend adding açaí purée instead of powder or juice. The purée contains heart-healthy omega-3 fatty acids as well as fiber.

The chia seeds add a little extra omega-3 fatty acids and some extra protein.

INGREDIENTS

2 black plums, pitted
1 pouch (100 grams) frozen açaí
  purée
1 teaspoon chia seeds, soaked for
  5 minutes
1 fuyu persimmon, seeded
6 ounces homemade almond milk
  (page 64)

NUTRITION INFO

*Calories: 203 • Fat: 7g • Protein: 4g
Carbs: 28g • Calcium: 5%
Iron: 0.9mg • Vitamin A: 35%
Vitamin C: 45%*

MANGO-PAPAYA GREEN SMOOTHIE WITH BLUEBERRIES

The frozen mango in this recipe creates a chilled, refreshing smoothie.

Escarole lettuce is just as nutritious as romaine lettuce, but it has an even milder flavor. It's a great source of iron, protein, and calcium. If you can't find escarole lettuce, you can use butterhead lettuce, green leaf lettuce, or collard leaves.

INGREDIENTS

1 cup cubed papaya
1 cup blueberries
1/2 cup cubed frozen mango
1/2 orange, peeled and seeded
1/4 teaspoon grated ginger
2 cups escarole lettuce, torn
4 ounces filtered water

NUTRITION INFO

*Calories: 248 • Fat: 2g • Protein: 4g
Carbs: 62g • Calcium: 11%
Iron: 1.9mg • Vitamin A: 113%
Vitamin C: 241%*

PINEAPPLE-PLUM SMOOTHIE WITH ALMOND MILK

Adding almond milk to your smoothies helps to add a little extra protein. It also adds a little extra healthy fat.

INGREDIENTS

2 plums, pitted

1/2 cup cubed pineapple

6 medium strawberries

2 medium collard leaves, stems
   removed

4 ounces homemade almond milk
   (page 64)

NUTRITION INFO

Calories: 162 • Fat: 1g • Protein: 5g
Carbs: 35g • Calcium: 16%
Iron: 1.1mg • Vitamin A: 29%
Vitamin C: 160%

CHERRY-POMEGRANATE SMOOTHIE

Pomegranate arils and cherries are loaded with antioxidants, but did you know carrots are also loaded with antioxidants? Red and purple carrots are rich in anthocyanin, while orange carrots are a great source of beta-carotene.

INGREDIENTS

1/2 cup pomegranate arils

1/2 orange, peeled and seeded

1 small banana, peeled

1 cup Bing cherries, pitted

1 small carrot, sliced

6 ounces filtered water

NUTRITION INFO

Calories: 314 • Fat: 2g • Protein: 5g
Carbs: 78g • Calcium: 7%
Iron: 1.3mg • Vitamin A: 62%
Vitamin C: 97%

BLACKBERRY-PEACH SMOOTHIE

Not only are chia seeds a great source of omega-3 fatty acids, they are also a great source of antioxidants, protein, and fiber.

Soaking the chia seeds helps to soften them so they will blend up in your smoothie. You can also grind the seeds with a coffee grinder instead of soaking them. If you grind the seeds, be sure to add an extra ounce of almond milk before blending since chia seeds will absorb water and gel, potentially making your smoothie thicker than you expected.

INGREDIENTS

1 cup blackberries

1 large peach, pitted

1/2 orange, peeled and seeded

1 teaspoon chia seeds, soaked for
    5 minutes

2 cups fresh baby spinach

4 ounces homemade almond milk
    (page 64)

NUTRITION INFO

Calories: 200 • Fat: 2g • Protein: 7g
Carbs: 42g • Calcium: 12%
Iron: 3.1mg • Vitamin A: 48%
Vitamin C: 133%

RASPBERRY-CARROT GREEN SMOOTHIE

This smoothie has so many antioxidant-rich ingredients. Orange carrots are a great source of beta-carotene, while raspberries and kale are also loaded with antioxidants.

In fact, the health benefits of kale are numerous. Kale contains beta-carotene, vitamins C and K, lutein, zeaxanthin (a carotenoid similar to lutein), calcium, and fiber.

INGREDIENTS

1 cup raspberries

1 large carrot, sliced

1/2 orange, peeled and seeded

1/4 teaspoon grated ginger

1/2 pear, cored

1 teaspoon ground cinnamon

2 cups fresh baby kale leaves

4 ounces filtered water

NUTRITION INFO

Calories: 214 • Fat: 1g • Protein: 5g
Carbs: 49g • Calcium: 20%
Iron: 2.4mg • Vitamin A: 130%
Vitamin C: 197%

BLACK AND BLUE SMOOTHIE

Yes, this recipe contains zucchini, and, yes, it is still delicious! Why zucchini? It is low in calories but will help fill you up, making it a great weight-loss food. Leave the peel on since it is loaded with fiber and beta-carotene.

INGREDIENTS

1 cup blackberries

1 cup blueberries

1/2 small zucchini, chopped

1/2 medium banana, peeled

4 ounces filtered water

NUTRITION INFO

*Calories: 209 • Fat: 2g • Protein: 5g
Carbs: 51g • Calcium: 5%
Iron: 1.7mg • Vitamin A: 4%
Vitamin C: 80%*

BLACKBERRY-AÇAÍ GREEN SMOOTHIE

Açaí is a berry that grows in Central and South America. It contains a large seed that cannot be eaten. The best way to eat the fruit is as a frozen purée. While you can find it in juice and powder forms, the frozen purée keeps most of the nutrients, including the fiber, intact. You can find frozen açaí purée in the freezer aisle at health food stores or order it online.

INGREDIENTS

2 cups blackberries

1 pouch (100 grams) frozen açaí
    purée

1 banana, peeled

2 cups butterhead lettuce, torn

8 ounces filtered water

NUTRITION INFO

*Calories: 323 • Fat: 8g • Protein: 9g
Carbs: 61g • Calcium: 14%
Iron: 3.5mg • Vitamin A: 63%
Vitamin C: 106%*

SUPER ANTIOXIDANT BLAST GREEN SMOOTHIE

This smoothie is called the Super Antioxidant Blast Green Smoothie because all of the ingredients contain antioxidants. While pomegranates, açaí, and spinach contain the most antioxidants, even bananas contain some of the potent, disease-protecting phytonutrients.

INGREDIENTS

1/4 cup fresh pomegranate arils

1 pouch (100 grams) frozen açaí purée

1 banana, peeled

3 cups fresh baby spinach

8 ounces filtered water

NUTRITION INFO

*Calories: 224 • Fat: 7g • Protein: 6g
Carbs: 38g • Calcium: 11%
Iron: 2.8mg • Vitamin A: 93%
Vitamin C: 57%*

CHERRY-VANILLA-PEACH GREEN SMOOTHIE

Not only are peaches a great source of antioxidant phenols, they are a great source of vitamin C, fiber, and potassium.

Cherries contain beta-carotene, vitamin C, potassium, magnesium, iron, folate, and fiber. Tart or sour cherries contain more beta-carotene and slightly more vitamin C.

Anthocyanins are antioxidants that give the cherry its red color.

INGREDIENTS

1 large peach, pitted

1 cup cherries, pitted

Seeds scraped from 1 vanilla bean or 1/2 teaspoon pure vanilla extract (alcohol-free)

2 cups romaine lettuce, chopped

1 medium carrot, sliced

4 ounces filtered water

NUTRITION INFO

*Calories: 203 • Fat: 1g • Protein: 5g
Carbs: 48g • Calcium: 7%
Iron: 2mg • Vitamin A: 135%
Vitamin C: 37%*

PINEAPPLE-CARROT SMOOTHIE

Carrots are a great source of dietary fiber and beta-carotene. They are also a great source of vitamins B3, B6, C, E, and K, as well as minerals such as iron, magnesium, phosphorus, calcium, molybdenum, and potassium.

INGREDIENTS

1 cup cubed pineapple

1 large carrot, sliced

1 orange, peeled and seeded

1/2 banana, peeled

4 ounces filtered water

NUTRITION INFO

Calories: 233 • Fat: 1g • Protein: 4g
Carbs: 60g • Calcium: 9%
Iron: 1mg • Vitamin A: 89%
Vitamin C: 228%

CHAPTER SEVEN

FITNESS AND ENERGY GREEN SMOOTHIES

Apple-Lime Green Smoothie • 130

Goji Berry–Maca Smoothie • 130

Berry–Chia Seed Smoothie • 131

Chocolate–Peanut Butter Smoothie • 131

Blueberry-Oat Smoothie • 132

Berry-Kale Smoothie • 132

Mango-Avocado Smoothie • 133

Blueberry-Maca Smoothie • 133

Peach-Oat Smoothie • 134

Ginger-Berry-Oat Smoothie • 134

Chocolate-Cherry Smoothie • 135

Cherry-Banana Smoothie • 135

Vanilla-Avocado Smoothie • 136

Apple-Avocado Smoothie • 136

Cucumber-Kale Smoothie • 137

Peanut Butter–Raspberry Smoothie • 137

Ginger-Citrus Green Smoothie with Kale • 138

Green smoothies are my go-to post-workout recovery drink. They replace lost electrolytes and give my body a much-needed dose of protein. Green smoothies are my sports drink!

While I recommend green smoothies as a post-workout recovery drink, some people like to have a small smoothie before exercising to fuel their workout. This is fine for short-duration exercises (for example, a thirty-minute treadmill workout).

I have included a few recipes in this chapter that provide some options for pre-workout smoothies. These recipes are smaller and less likely to cause bloating, which may interfere with your performance. Any of the recipes that have 200 calories or less are fine to drink before a workout.

I don't recommend drinking a green smoothie before *and* after your workouts because you could potentially consume more calories than you burn. The only exception to this would be if you are doing hardcore, extremely demanding exercise regimens (e.g., an hour or more in the gym or a ten-mile run).

The Importance of Electrolytes

Electrolytes are naturally occurring salt ions that have the ability to carry electrical impulses. Maintaining a proper balance of electrolytes in your body is critical because they help regulate voltage within cells and carry electrical impulses that drive nerve and muscle function.

During strenuous exercise, your body loses electrolytes through sweat, leading to an imbalance of electrolytes that may cause fatigue and improper muscle function. Extreme imbalances of electrolytes exacerbated by dehydration or over-hydration can be fatal.

Fortunately, electrolytes are easy to replenish—even when you are doing strenuous exercise. The most important electrolytes in your body include sodium, potassium, chloride, calcium, magnesium, bicarbonate, phosphate, and sulfate.

In addition to coconut water, some of the top electrolyte-rich foods that you can use in a green smoothie include: sea vegetables (kelp, dulse, wakame, and hijiki), kale, spinach, celery, Swiss chard, collard greens, beets, oranges, bananas, avocados, tomatoes, apricots, beet greens, papaya, romaine lettuce, turnip greens, cantaloupe, carrots, strawberries, kiwifruit, prunes, grapes, broccoli, sesame seeds, figs, dandelion greens, young Thai coconuts, parsley, almonds and almond milk, cacao (raw chocolate), and cucumber.

Protein for Your Green Smoothies

Protein is another critical component of a fitness-supporting green smoothie. The recipes in this chapter all have at least 10 grams of protein per recipe.

You can double the protein content of these recipes by using a quality protein powder. I recommend plant-based brown rice, hemp, or sprouted protein powders. Brands that I have used and enjoy include Epic Protein by Sprout Living and NutriBiotic.

If you are avoiding genetically modified foods (GMOs), then skip soy protein powders. And while whey protein is extremely popular, I do not believe that it has any more benefit than any plant-based protein powders, which also offer a complete spectrum of essential amino acids.

Building Muscle with Plant-Based Green Smoothie Proteins

You need to do more than just consume protein in order to build muscle. While your body tends to "automatically" get fat when you consume excess calories, it does not automatically get buff from eating excess protein.

To build muscle, you have to do more than just increase protein intake. You also have to work your muscles through consistent resistance training. One of the best ways to "direct" your dietary protein intake into your muscles is through weight training. However, you don't have to adopt a bodybuilder's exercise regimen. Lifting heavy weights (15-pound dumbbells, for example) in a routine that works out all of your major muscle groups three times per week can be enough to increase muscle definition and overall strength.

About These Recipes

Aside from a few pre-workout smoothies, most of the recipes in this chapter are designed to help you recover from your workouts. They use fruit and vegetable ingredients that provide an excellent source of electrolytes as well as protein.

After you work out, your body is going to burn the calories it consumed very quickly. You are going to want a smoothie with lots of calories to refuel yourself and replenish nutrients used to strengthen your body.

A few of the recipes in this chapter can be used to fuel your body before a workout.

APPLE-LIME GREEN SMOOTHIE

Most of the protein in this smoothie comes from the kale. Two cups of kale contains almost 6 grams of protein. The almond milk will also help to give this smoothie an additional protein boost, making it an excellent post- or pre-workout smoothie.

INGREDIENTS

1 banana, peeled

1 green apple, cored

1 stalk celery, chopped

1/4 lime, peeled

2 cups fresh kale, chopped

8 ounces homemade almond milk
(page 64)

NUTRITION INFO

*Calories: 312 • Fat: 2g • Protein: 9g
Carbs: 67g • Calcium: 20%
Iron: 2.7mg • Vitamin A: 98%
Vitamin C: 247%*

GOJI BERRY-MACA SMOOTHIE

This smoothie might be small, but it's loaded with nutrients. The chia seeds, spinach, and goji berries give this smoothie a protein boost to fuel your workout.

Two tablespoons of goji berries contain 2 grams of protein and are loaded with antioxidants. And not only are chia seeds loaded with protein, but they are also a great source of omega-3 fatty acids. Just one teaspoon contains 16 percent of your recommended daily value of omega-3 fatty acids.

INGREDIENTS

1 frozen banana, peeled and sliced

2 tablespoons goji berries, soaked
for 5 minutes

10 medium strawberries

1 teaspoon maca powder

1 teaspoon chia seeds, soaked for
5 minutes

2 cups fresh baby spinach

8 ounces homemade almond milk
(page 64)

NUTRITION INFO

*Calories: 247 • Fat: 1g • Protein: 7g
Carbs: 49g • Calcium: 9%
Iron: 3.4mg • Vitamin A: 191%
Vitamin C: 138%*

BERRY-CHIA SEED SMOOTHIE

This is a great pre-workout smoothie. It's not a very large smoothie, so it won't leave you feeling bloated before your workout, but it gives you just enough protein to fuel your fitness routine.

Just two large collard leaves provide 14 percent of your recommended daily value of calcium, so they are great for healthy bones.

INGREDIENTS

12 medium strawberries

1/2 cup raspberries

1/2 cup blueberries

2 tablespoons goji berries, soaked for 5 minutes

1 tablespoon chia seeds, soaked for 5 minutes

2 collard leaves, stems removed

4 ounces filtered water

NUTRITION INFO

Calories: 196 • Fat: 2g • Protein: 6g
Carbs: 43g • Calcium: 14%
Iron: 2.5mg • Vitamin A: 164%
Vitamin C: 169%

CHOCOLATE-PEANUT BUTTER SMOOTHIE

This smoothie is a chocolate lover's dream. This recipe has healthy chocolate without the added sugar.

This green smoothie tastes like a peanut butter cup, and you'll never notice the mineral boost from the lettuce hidden beneath the chocolate–peanut butter goodness.

INGREDIENTS

1 banana, peeled

1 tablespoon all-natural peanut butter

1 tablespoon cacao powder

Seeds scraped from 1 vanilla bean or 1/2 teaspoon pure vanilla extract (alcohol-free)

1/2 head butterhead lettuce, torn

4 ounces filtered water

NUTRITION INFO

Calories: 250 • Fat: 10g • Protein: 7g
Carbs: 37g • Calcium: 4%
Iron: 2mg • Vitamin A: 20%
Vitamin C: 18%

BLUEBERRY-OAT SMOOTHIE

A lot of people eat oatmeal for breakfast since it is loaded with fiber and protein. It's a great way to start your breakfast, so why not add it to your green smoothie?

Just one-quarter cup of oats contains 7 grams of protein and 17 percent of your recommended daily value of fiber.

INGREDIENTS

1/4 cup dry old-fashioned rolled oats

1/2 banana, peeled

1/4 teaspoon ground cinnamon

1/2 cup blueberries

2 collard leaves, stems removed

6 ounces filtered water

NUTRITION INFO

*Calories: 257 • Fat: 3g • Protein: 9g
Carbs: 52g • Calcium: 9%
Iron: 2.4mg • Vitamin A: 13%
Vitamin C: 33%*

BERRY-KALE SMOOTHIE

Both the goji berries and the kale in this green smoothie recipe are great sources of protein. Goji berries are particularly good for boosting the protein content of a smoothie without dramatically increasing the size of the smoothie.

Blueberries and cinnamon is one of my favorite flavor combinations.

INGREDIENTS

1/2 cup blueberries

2 tablespoons goji berries, soaked
   for 5 minutes

1/2 teaspoon ground cinnamon

1 cup fresh curly kale, stems
   removed

1/2 orange, peeled

4 ounces homemade almond milk
   (page 64)

NUTRITION INFO

*Calories: 211 • Fat: 1g • Protein: 7g
Carbs: 45g • Calcium: 15%
Iron: 2.3mg • Vitamin A: 201%
Vitamin C: 235%*

MANGO-AVOCADO SMOOTHIE

This green smoothie works best as a post-workout snack, since it is high in protein and contains slower-digesting fat from the avocado.

INGREDIENTS

1/2 cup cubed mango

1/4 avocado, peeled and pitted

1 kiwifruit, peeled

1 stalk celery

2 cups fresh kale, stems removed

6 ounces filtered water

NUTRITION INFO

*Calories: 269 • Fat: 10g • Protein: 9g
Carbs: 46g • Calcium: 22%
Iron: 2.7mg • Vitamin A: 107%
Vitamin C: 369%*

BLUEBERRY-MACA SMOOTHIE

Not only is maca great for one's libido, it can also boost one's energy and stamina. It's loaded with fatty acids and amino acids. The flavor, however, might be an acquired taste for some. While maca powder smells like butterscotch, it doesn't quite taste like it. That's why I never add more than a tablespoon, and some people who are sensitive to the flavor may need to start with less maca and work their way up.

INGREDIENTS

1 cup blueberries

1 banana, peeled

Seeds scraped from 1 vanilla bean
    or 1/2 teaspoon pure vanilla
    extract (alcohol-free)

1/2 teaspoon ground cinnamon

1 tablespoon maca powder

2 collard leaves, stems removed

4 ounces unsweetened coconut
    milk

NUTRITION INFO

*Calories: 153 • Fat: 3g • Protein: 4g
Carbs: 32g • Calcium: 19%
Iron: 1mg • Vitamin A: 37%
Vitamin C: 48%*

PEACH-OAT SMOOTHIE

The oats and chia seeds in this smoothie help pack a one-two protein punch. Adding dry, old-fashioned rolled oats is a great high-calorie, high-protein option with very little extra bulk.

INGREDIENTS

1 large peach, pitted

1 tablespoon chia seeds, soaked
    for 5 minutes

1/4 cup dry old-fashioned rolled oats

1/2 orange, peeled and seeded

2 cups fresh baby spinach

4 ounces filtered water

NUTRITION INFO

*Calories: 252 • Fat: 4g • Protein: 10g
Carbs: 50g • Calcium: 11%
Iron: 3.9mg • Vitamin A: 45%
Vitamin C: 93%*

GINGER-BERRY-OAT SMOOTHIE

Just one-quarter cup of oats contains 7 grams of protein and 17 percent of your recommended daily value of fiber. The rest of the protein in this smoothie comes from the spinach.

Spinach, strawberries, and blackberries are all excellent sources of antioxidants and vitamins. They are all great low-sugar ingredients to fuel your workout and give you energy throughout the day without a sugar crash.

INGREDIENTS

1 cup blackberries

10 medium strawberries

1/4 teaspoon grated ginger

1/4 cup dry old-fashioned rolled oats

1 cup fresh baby spinach

4 ounces homemade almond milk
    (page 64)

NUTRITION INFO

*Calories: 246 • Fat: 3g • Protein: 9g
Carbs: 45g • Calcium: 9%
Iron: 3.7mg • Vitamin A: 23%
Vitamin C: 146%*

CHOCOLATE-CHERRY SMOOTHIE

This smoothie is a great morning or afternoon pick-me-up. Both maca and cacao are known for their energy-boosting properties.

This chocolate-cherry smoothie is not only tasty, it's loaded with nutrients to fill you up and help you start your day. Pears actually have more fiber than apples. Just half a pear contains 11 percent of your recommended daily value of fiber.

INGREDIENTS

1 cup frozen cherries

1/2 pear, cored

1 tablespoon cacao powder

1 teaspoon maca powder

Seeds scraped from 1 vanilla bean
or 1/2 teaspoon pure vanilla
extract (alcohol-free)

2 cups fresh baby spinach

8 ounces homemade almond milk
(page 64)

NUTRITION INFO

Calories: 216 • Fat: 1g • Protein: 6g
Carbs: 43g • Calcium: 8%
Iron: 3mg • Vitamin A: 41%
Vitamin C: 40%

CHERRY-BANANA SMOOTHIE

This is a great pre-workout smoothie. It's low in calories but has enough protein to fuel a workout.

Dandelion greens are a powerhouse green that is loaded with calcium, iron, protein, essential vitamins, and minerals.

INGREDIENTS

1/2 cup frozen cherries

1/2 orange, peeled

1 small banana, peeled

1 cup dandelion greens

4 ounces unsweetened coconut milk

NUTRITION INFO

Calories: 210 • Fat: 1g • Protein: 5g
Carbs: 48g • Calcium: 12%
Iron: 2.3mg • Vitamin A: 42%
Vitamin C: 99%

VANILLA-AVOCADO SMOOTHIE

Your body sweats out potassium when you exercise, so it is essential for you to replenish it. Avocados are a great source of potassium, as well as slow-digesting fats to help regulate energy levels and keep you satisfied until your next meal.

INGREDIENTS

1 banana, peeled

Seeds scraped from 1 vanilla bean
    or 1/2 teaspoon pure vanilla
    extract (alcohol-free)

1/4 avocado, peeled and pitted

3 large Swiss chard leaves, stems
    removed

8 ounces homemade almond milk
    (page 64)

NUTRITION INFO

Calories: 247 • Fat: 8g • Protein: 6g
Carbs: 37g • Calcium: 7%
Iron: 3.2mg • Vitamin A: 64%
Vitamin C: 78%

APPLE-AVOCADO SMOOTHIE

This smoothie is great for a little energy kick. The apple is loaded with fiber and natural sugars to give you a pick-me-up that will keep you going.

Not only is kale loaded with calcium, protein, and iron, but it is also loaded with vitamins and minerals. Just two cups of kale provides 14 percent of your recommended daily value of potassium.

INGREDIENTS

1 apple, cored

1/4 avocado, peeled and pitted

1/2 cucumber with peel

1 tablespoon chia seeds, soaked for
    5 minutes

2 cups fresh kale, stems removed

8 ounces filtered water

NUTRITION INFO

Calories: 261 • Fat: 9g • Protein: 9g
Carbs: 47g • Calcium: 22%
Iron: 3.1mg • Vitamin A: 98%
Vitamin C: 237%

CUCUMBER-KALE SMOOTHIE

Pineapples are a great source of vitamin C. Just half a cup contains 53 percent of your recommended daily value. They are also a great source of fiber. Pineapple also has a very strong flavor, so it easily helps to mask the bitterness of kale.

While cucumbers are relatively low in calories, they are loaded with vitamins and minerals. Just one cucumber contains 9 percent of your recommended daily value of potassium.

INGREDIENTS

1/2 cup cubed pineapple

1/2 cup raspberries

1 cucumber with peel

2 cups fresh kale, stems removed

4 ounces filtered water

NUTRITION INFO

*Calories: 184 • Fat: 2g • Protein: 9g
Carbs: 41g • Calcium: 23%
Iron: 3.5mg • Vitamin A: 98%
Vitamin C: 300%*

PEANUT BUTTER-RASPBERRY SMOOTHIE

Peanut butter is loaded with protein and calories to fuel your workout. Make sure you are using an all-natural peanut butter and not one that contains sugar and extra additives.

Not only are bananas a great source of potassium, but they are a great source of healthy carbohydrates to give you energy throughout the day.

INGREDIENTS

1 small banana, peeled

1 tablespoon all-natural peanut
    butter

1/2 cup raspberries

Seeds scraped from 1 vanilla bean
    or 1/2 teaspoon pure vanilla
    extract (alcohol-free)

1 cup fresh baby spinach

8 ounces homemade almond milk
    (page 64)

NUTRITION INFO

*Calories: 268 • Fat: 10g • Protein: 7g
Carbs: 35g • Calcium: 4%
Iron: 1.5mg • Vitamin A: 21%
Vitamin C: 44%*

GINGER-CITRUS GREEN SMOOTHIE WITH KALE

Oranges are high in vitamin C as well as vitamins A and B1, potassium, folate, calcium, and dietary fiber.

Almond milk, while it doesn't contain a lot of protein, does give this smoothie a little extra boost of protein and heart-healthy fats. It also helps to naturally sweeten the kale while enhancing the creaminess of this smoothie.

INGREDIENTS

1 cup cubed pineapple

1/2 orange, peeled and seeded

1 teaspoon grated ginger

2 cups fresh curly kale, stems
  removed

8 ounces homemade almond milk
  (page 64)

NUTRITION INFO

*Calories: 220 • Fat: 2g • Protein: 8g
Carbs: 43g • Calcium: 21%
Iron: 2.6mg • Vitamin A: 98%
Vitamin C: 375%*

CHAPTER EIGHT

IMMUNE-BOOSTING GREEN SMOOTHIES

Orange-Ginger Smoothie • 143

Papaya-Mint Smoothie • 143

Lemon-Kiwifruit Smoothie • 144

Pear-Broccoli Smoothie • 144

Zucchini-Vanilla Smoothie • 145

Cinnamon-Strawberry Smoothie • 145

Vanilla-Cantaloupe Smoothie • 146

Happy Berry Muffin Smoothie • 146

Sweet Potato Smoothie • 147

Cherry–Sweet Potato Smoothie • 147

Kiwifruit-Grape Smoothie with Broccoli • 148

Cantaloupe-Papaya Smoothie • 148

Pear-Kiwifruit Smoothie • 149

Mango-Lime Smoothie • 149

Ginger-Carrot Smoothie • 150

Refreshing Lemon-Cucumber Smoothie • 150

Pineapple-Ginger Smoothie • 151

You've heard that an apple a day keeps the doctor away. Well, this same saying can be applied to green smoothies.

There is an overwhelming number of published scientific studies that show a correlation between higher intakes of fruits and vegetables and a lower incidence of disease—both acute and chronic.[44]

There are some specific fruits and vegetables that appear to have a direct, therapeutic effect on certain health conditions or that dramatically reduce the risk of getting certain diseases. I even have a whole e-book on this subject titled *Green Smoothie Remedies & Prevention* (available on my website at www.incrediblesmoothies.com).

How Green Smoothies Protect Your Body

Green smoothies are the easiest way to get five or more servings of fruits and vegetables every single day. This alone gives you a much greater chance of skipping whatever illness is going around. It may even reduce your risk of getting the same chronic conditions as your parents.

Since 2008, I have been drinking a green smoothie daily and I rarely get sick. I can't even remember the last time I had a cold. And I'm not a special case. I've heard thousands of others sing the praises of their super-resilient immune system thanks (at least in part!) to delicious green smoothies.

Green smoothies are full of nutrition. All of those vitamins, minerals, and antioxidants work far more effectively when they come from whole foods than from pills and powders. Green smoothies are also an excellent source of dietary fiber. Fiber supports colon health and keeps your bowels doing what they are supposed to do. This alone is a significant boost to your health and may help reduce the risk of colon cancer.

Another potential health-promoting effect of green smoothies is that they may help maintain critical microflora in your intestines that support nutrient extraction and keep harmful bacteria from colonizing your digestive tract.[45] Scientists are just starting to explore the complex relationships between our gut microflora and our overall health, and it's too early to make broad claims about gut bacteria and disease prevention. But what we do know is that diet can directly alter the populations and diversity of beneficial bacteria in our intestines and colon.[46] Some studies have found a potential link between the diversity of gut microflora and overall levels of health.[47] While we can't yet draw conclusions about the implications of this finding (more research is needed), my guess is that a healthier diet rich in fruits and vegetables not only provides nutrients that our body needs to maintain health but also supports our microbiome and the many critical functions it performs within our bodies.

About These Recipes

The green smoothie recipes in this chapter focus on water-rich fruits and vegetables that are full of vitamin C and other antioxidants, which generally help boost your immune system. Other recipes include ingredients that may help alleviate acute symptoms of illness. For example, bananas are said to have an "antacid effect" on the stomach, and many people who have nausea or heartburn benefit from a creamy banana smoothie. Ginger is also well known for its nausea-fighting properties, as well as its digestive stimulation—perfect for when you need to keep things moving along in your body.

ORANGE-GINGER SMOOTHIE

Ginger is widely known for its immune-boosting and stomach-settling properties. It also adds a warming, spicy flavor to smoothies.

Pineapples have anti-inflammatory properties and they help with digestion. They contain an enzyme, bromelain, that helps break down proteins.

INGREDIENTS

1/2 cup cubed pineapple

1/4 teaspoon grated ginger

1 orange, peeled and seeded

1 cup fresh baby spinach

1 large collard leaf, stem removed

4 ounces filtered water

NUTRITION INFO

*Calories: 129 • Fat: 1g • Protein: 4g
Carbs: 32g • Calcium: 15%
Iron: 1.4mg • Vitamin A: 36%
Vitamin C: 191%*

PAPAYA-MINT SMOOTHIE

Papayas are high in vitamin C and are a good source of folate, potassium, fiber, and vitamins A, E, and K. They're also rich in antioxidants and the enzyme papain, which helps promote digestive health.

INGREDIENTS

2 cups cubed papaya

1 small pear, cored

10 fresh mint leaves

2 cups fresh baby spinach

4 ounces filtered water

NUTRITION INFO

*Calories: 223 • Fat: 1g • Protein: 4g
Carbs: 56g • Calcium: 11%
Iron: 2.6mg • Vitamin A: 60%
Vitamin C: 266%*

LEMON-KIWIFRUIT SMOOTHIE

Kiwifruit are rich in fiber, which helps improve digestion. The edible seeds contain omega-3 fatty acids.

Bananas are high in vitamins B6 and C, potassium, magnesium, and dietary fiber. They are the perfect fruit for giving smoothies a creamy texture and to sweeten bitter greens.

INGREDIENTS

2 kiwifruit, ends removed

Juice of 1/2 lemon

1 small banana, peeled

2 fresh kale leaves, stems removed

1/2 teaspoon maca powder

4 ounces filtered water

NUTRITION INFO

Calories: 245 • Fat: 2g • Protein: 9g
Carbs: 57g • Calcium: 21%
Iron: 2.7mg • Vitamin A: 97%
Vitamin C: 409%

PEAR-BROCCOLI SMOOTHIE

Broccoli might not be on the top of your smoothie ingredient list, but it is extremely nutritious. Broccoli is a great source of vitamins A (as beta-carotene) and C, as well as folate. You can mask the bitterness with sweet fruits like pears and oranges.

INGREDIENTS

1 large pear, cored

1/2 cup frozen broccoli

1/2 orange, peeled

4 ounces filtered water, if needed

NUTRITION INFO

Calories: 213 • Fat: 1g • Protein: 3g
Carbs: 55g • Calcium: 8%
Iron: 0.9mg • Vitamin A: 7%
Vitamin C: 157%

ZUCCHINI-VANILLA SMOOTHIE

Zucchini is a great source of B vitamins and minerals. It's great for bulking up a low-calorie smoothie, and the flavor is mild and easily masked with sweeter fruit, like bananas.

Bananas are an excellent source of potassium and fiber. They are also a great source of vitamins B6 and C, as well as antioxidants.

INGREDIENTS

1 large zucchini, chopped

1 small banana, peeled

Seeds scraped from 1 vanilla bean
  or 1/2 teaspoon pure vanilla
  extract (alcohol-free)

4 ounces homemade almond milk
  (page 64)

NUTRITION INFO

*Calories: 162 • Fat: 1g • Protein: 6g
Carbs: 33g • Calcium: 5%
Iron: 1.5mg • Vitamin A: 5%
Vitamin C: 89%*

CINNAMON-STRAWBERRY SMOOTHIE

I love adding spices like cinnamon and vanilla to smoothies. They contain almost no calories but offer a unique spin on familiar fruity flavors.

Dandelion greens can be very bitter. By using spices and sweet fruits like oranges and strawberries, you will mask some of the bitterness, making these greens much more palatable.

Dandelion greens are loaded with iron, calcium, protein, and vitamins A (as beta-carotene) and C (which helps facilitate iron absorption).

INGREDIENTS

2 oranges, peeled and seeded

10 large strawberries

Seeds scraped from 1 vanilla bean
  or 1/2 teaspoon pure vanilla
  extract (alcohol-free)

1/2 teaspoon ground cinnamon

1 cup fresh baby spinach

1 cup dandelion greens

NUTRITION INFO

*Calories: 227 • Fat: 2g • Protein: 6g
Carbs: 55g • Calcium: 23%
Iron: 3.6mg • Vitamin A: 65%
Vitamin C: 399%*

VANILLA-CANTALOUPE SMOOTHIE

Cantaloupes contain enzymes that help with digestion. They are also a great source of copper, potassium, magnesium, iron, phosphorus, zinc, and manganese.

I love blending cantaloupe with vanilla. I think they accent each other nicely. The simple way to use vanilla in a green smoothie is to either use an alcohol-free pure vanilla extract or use a vanilla bean. If using a vanilla bean, simply cut it open lengthwise and scrape out the seeds.

INGREDIENTS

2 cups cubed cantaloupe

1 small banana, peeled

2 tablespoons goji berries, soaked
   for 5 minutes

Seeds scraped from 1 vanilla bean
   or 1/2 teaspoon pure vanilla
   extract (alcohol-free)

2 collard leaves, stems removed

8 ounces homemade almond milk
   (page 64)

NUTRITION INFO

*Calories: 272 • Fat: 1g • Protein: 8g
Carbs: 64g • Calcium: 18%
Iron: 2.2mg • Vitamin A: 253%
Vitamin C: 210%*

HAPPY BERRY MUFFIN SMOOTHIE

This smoothie reminds me of a berry muffin, thanks to the way that oats suggest a "baked goods" flavor. Hidden in this muffin-flavored goodness is butterhead lettuce, which adds calcium and iron, as well as vitamins A and K.

To help keep the calories down, I only added 1/8 cup of oats. Even though you are only adding a little bit of oats, they still offer a significant amount of fiber and protein.

INGREDIENTS

10 large strawberries

1/2 cup blueberries

1/8 cup dry old-fashioned rolled
   oats

1 small frozen banana

1 cup butterhead lettuce, torn

2 to 4 ounces filtered water

NUTRITION INFO

*Calories: 270 • Fat: 3g • Protein: 7g
Carbs: 61g • Calcium: 6%
Iron: 2.8mg • Vitamin A: 14%
Vitamin C: 165%*

SWEET POTATO SMOOTHIE

Sweet potato is an often overlooked hidden gem when it comes to green smoothie ingredients. Just half a cup of sweet potato contains 2 grams of protein, 13 percent of your recommended daily value of fiber, and 137 percent of your recommended daily value of vitamin A (as beta-carotene). Sweet potato is also loaded with antioxidants.

You can use it raw or cooked. I prefer to use cooked and cooled sweet potato since cooking it brings out more of the flavor.

INGREDIENTS

1/2 cup cubed sweet potato, cooked
   and cooled

1 medium banana, peeled

1 medium carrot, sliced

1/4 teaspoon ground cinnamon

1/4 teaspoon ground nutmeg

1 cup butterhead lettuce, torn

8 ounces homemade almond milk
   (page 64)

NUTRITION INFO

*Calories: 262 • Fat: 1g • Protein: 6g
Carbs: 54g • Calcium: 7%
Iron: 1.9mg • Vitamin A: 223%
Vitamin C: 47%*

CHERRY-SWEET POTATO SMOOTHIE

Sweet potato and cherries are an excellent flavor combination and complement each other nicely. They are both a great source of antioxidants.

Cherries contain beta-carotene, vitamin C, potassium, magnesium, iron, folate, and fiber. Tart or sour cherries contain more beta-carotene and slightly more vitamin C than regular cherries.

INGREDIENTS

1/2 cup cubed sweet potato, cooked
   and cooled

1 cup Bing cherries, pitted

1 tablespoon chia seeds, soaked for
   5 minutes

1/4 teaspoon ground cinnamon

4 ounces homemade almond milk
   (page 64)

NUTRITION INFO

*Calories: 219 • Fat: 1g • Protein: 5g
Carbs: 47g • Calcium: 6%
Iron: 1.5mg • Vitamin A: 138%
Vitamin C: 41%*

KIWIFRUIT-GRAPE SMOOTHIE WITH BROCCOLI

A lot of people are reluctant to use broccoli in a green smoothie. If you've ever blended raw broccoli, you have probably vowed to never do it again.

However, frozen broccoli is much less pungent, and it doesn't overpower sweet fruits in a green smoothie. The added bonus is that frozen broccoli is almost as nutritious as fresh and keeps for much longer in the freezer.

INGREDIENTS

1/2 cup frozen broccoli

2 kiwifruit, ends removed

1 cup green grapes

1 cup fresh baby spinach

4 ounces filtered water

NUTRITION INFO

Calories: 223 • Fat: 1g • Protein: 5g
Carbs: 54g • Calcium: 10%
Iron: 2.3mg • Vitamin A: 30%
Vitamin C: 256%

CANTALOUPE-PAPAYA SMOOTHIE

This is a delicious green smoothie with a tropical flair. I recommend using young Thai coconuts (the cone-shaped, white ones often found in Asian or Mexican markets).

Coconuts are a great source of calcium, iron, zinc, potassium, phosphorus, magnesium, and vitamins B1, B2, B3, B5, B6, folate, and C.

INGREDIENTS

1 cup cubed cantaloupe

1 cup cubed papaya

Juice of 1/2 lime

1 cup fresh baby spinach

1/4 cup coconut meat

NUTRITION INFO

Calories: 161 • Fat: 4g • Protein: 3g
Carbs: 33g • Calcium: 6%
Iron: 1.7mg • Vitamin A: 68%
Vitamin C: 216%

PEAR-KIWIFRUIT SMOOTHIE

Kiwifruit are a rich source of vitamin C. They are also a good source of vitamins A, B6, E, and K, as well as folate, magnesium, phosphorus, copper, and dietary fiber. The edible seeds contain omega-3 fatty acids.

The pear and kiwifruit really help to sweeten the kale and the cilantro, while the ginger gives this smoothie a little extra bite—in a good way!

INGREDIENTS

1 large pear, cored

2 kiwifruit, ends removed

2 fresh curly kale leaves, stems removed

1/4 cup cilantro

1/4 teaspoon grated ginger

4 ounces filtered water

NUTRITION INFO

Calories: 282 • Fat: 2g • Protein: 8g
Carbs: 67g • Calcium: 23%
Iron: 2.9mg • Vitamin A: 99%
Vitamin C: 400%

MANGO-LIME SMOOTHIE

I love the sweet and sour flavors of mango and lime together. Personally, I prefer ice-cold mangoes in my smoothies. I use frozen mango or mango from the refrigerator in order to get this refreshing chill. You can buy mango that is already frozen or you can buy fresh mango, peel it, cut it into chunks, and freeze it yourself.

Mangoes are a super fruit high in dietary fiber as well as vitamins A, B6, C, E, and K.

INGREDIENTS

1 cup frozen mango

1/2 lime, peeled and seeded

2 fresh kale leaves, stems removed

1 tablespoon chia seeds, soaked for 5 minutes

1 kiwifruit, ends removed

4 ounces unsweetened coconut milk

NUTRITION INFO

Calories: 257 • Fat: 6g • Protein: 9g
Carbs: 52g • Calcium: 27%
Iron: 3.2mg • Vitamin A: 120%
Vitamin C: 393%

GINGER-CARROT SMOOTHIE

Carrots can be hard on some department-store blenders. Unless you are using a high-speed blender, I recommend chopping the carrots into half-inch pieces to make sure they blend up completely. You can also use carrot juice instead of the almond milk for this recipe.

This is one of my favorite smoothies. I've made it for a few people and they all loved it.

Ginger is great for boosting your immune system and settling upset stomachs.

INGREDIENTS

1/2 teaspoon grated ginger
2 medium carrots, sliced
1/2 cup cubed pineapple
1/2 cup cubed mango
4 ounces homemade almond milk
    (page 64)

NUTRITION INFO

*Calories: 159 • Fat: 1g • Protein: 3g
Carbs: 35g • Calcium: 5%
Iron: 0.7mg • Vitamin A: 152%
Vitamin C: 102%*

REFRESHING LEMON-CUCUMBER SMOOTHIE

This is a very low-calorie smoothie, but adding the cucumber peel and the collard leaves helps to boost the nutrients.

Just two large collard leaves contain 26 percent of your recommended daily value of vitamin A (as beta-carotene), 34 percent of your recommended daily value of vitamin C, 350 percent of your recommended daily value of vitamin K, and 2.2 grams of protein.

Cucumbers are a good source of vitamin C and also contain vitamin A, molybdenum, folate, manganese, silica, potassium, and magnesium. They are also an excellent source of dietary fiber.

INGREDIENTS

1 large pear, cored
1/2 cucumber with peel, sliced
Juice of 1/2 lemon
2 collard leaves, stems removed
4 ounces filtered water

NUTRITION INFO

*Calories: 182 • Fat: 1g • Protein: 4g
Carbs: 46g • Calcium: 18%
Iron: 1.2mg • Vitamin A: 27%
Vitamin C: 65%*

PINEAPPLE-GINGER SMOOTHIE

Pineapples have anti-inflammatory properties and they help with digestion. They contain an enzyme, bromelain, that helps break down protein.

While kale is highly nutritious, it also has a very strong flavor. The pineapple and orange in this smoothie help to sweeten the bitterness of the kale.

INGREDIENTS

1 cup cubed pineapple

1/2 teaspoon grated ginger

1/2 orange, peeled and seeded

2 fresh curly kale leaves, stems
    removed

4 ounces homemade almond milk
    (page 64)

NUTRITION INFO

*Calories: 201 • Fat: 2g • Protein: 8g
Carbs: 42g • Calcium: 21%
Iron: 2.5mg • Vitamin A: 98%
Vitamin C: 375%*

CHAPTER NINE

CALCIUM-RICH GREEN SMOOTHIES

Coconut–Goji Berry Smoothie • 158
Sweet Potato–Orange Smoothie • 158
Nectarine-Cherry Smoothie • 159
Pear-Tangerine Smoothie • 159
Red Grape–Fig Smoothie • 160
Banana-Orange Smoothie • 160
Pistachio-Banana Smoothie • 161
Coconut-Grapefruit Smoothie • 161
Peach-Strawberry-Coconut Smoothie • 162

Super Green and Peach Smoothie • 162
Pineapple-Citrus Smoothie • 163
Banana-Cranberry Smoothie • 163
Ginger-Peach Smoothie • 164
Pear-Aloe Smoothie • 164
Coconut-Peach Smoothie • 165
Pineapple-Orange Tropical Smoothie • 165
Strawberry-Raspberry Smoothie with Avocado • 166
Orange–Sesame Seed Smoothie • 166

Calcium is an important mineral for healthy, strong bones. However, you do not need to use dairy milk or yogurt in your smoothies to get calcium. In fact, you can make a green smoothie with more calcium than a glass of milk!

For example, two cups of kale or dandelion greens contain 17 percent of your recommended daily value of calcium. Just five figs contain 9 percent and one orange contains 6 percent of your recommended daily value. All of these ingredients can be blended into one green smoothie that will provide 32 percent of your recommended daily value of calcium (and a whole bunch of other nutrients and antioxidants that dairy milk lacks).

As you can see, the calcium content of a green smoothie recipe can add up quickly if you use the right ingredients.

How Much Calcium Do You Need?

Table 1: Recommended Dietary Allowances (RDAs) for Calcium				
AGE	MALE	FEMALE	PREGNANT	LACTATING
0–6 months*	200 mg	200 mg		
7–12 months*	260 mg	260 mg		
1–3 years	700 mg	700 mg		
4–8 years	1,000 mg	1,000 mg		
9–13 years	1,300 mg	1,300 mg		
14–18 years	1,300 mg	1,300 mg	1,300 mg	1,300 mg
19–50 years	1,000 mg	1,000 mg	1,000 mg	1,000 mg
51–70 years	1,000 mg	1,200 mg		
71+ years	1,200 mg	1,200 mg		
* Adequate Intake (AI)				

Calcium-Rich Green Smoothie Ingredients

While most fruits and vegetables that you can add to a green smoothie contain trace amounts of calcium, there are some calcium superstars of the plant world, which I've profiled below.

You can mix and match these ingredients to blend a green smoothie that has more calcium than a glass of dairy milk!

Parsley (1 cup, chopped)—83 mg

Dandelion greens (2 cups, chopped)—205 mg

Kale (2 cups, chopped)—181 mg

Spinach (2 cups, chopped)—59 mg

Papaya (1/2 Caribbean Red/Mexican)—78 mg

Orange (1 fruit, without peel)—60 mg

Cactus pear (1 fruit)—60 mg

Fig (5 medium fruits)—87 mg

Kiwifruit (1 fruit)—23.5 mg

Celery (2 stalks, medium length)—32 mg

Young Thai coconut (meat and water)—Up to 200 mg per coconut

Sesame seeds (1 tablespoon)—88 mg

Flaxseeds (2 tablespoons, whole)—52 mg

Chia seeds (2 tablespoons)—38 mg

Calcium Intake Alone Doesn't Build Strong Bones

Don't just consume calcium-rich foods and expect that your bones will automatically become stronger. Resistance training is one of the most important bone-building exercises that you can do, and it signals your body to use the calcium that you ingest to strengthen your bones.

You don't have to be a champion weightlifter or bench-press three times your weight to get the bone-strengthening benefits of dietary calcium. A simple free-weight workout a few times per week can signal your body to strengthen your bones, with the added bonus of losing weight and toning muscle!

About These Recipes

The recipes in this chapter focus on calcium-rich green smoothie ingredients. Every recipe in this section contains at least 10 percent of your recommended daily value of calcium. Several of the recipes have well over 300 mg of calcium—more than a glass of cow's milk.

COCONUT-GOJI BERRY SMOOTHIE

This green smoothie is loaded with calcium! Both the kale and the oranges, and even the coconut milk, are great sources of calcium. Some store-bought coconut milks are fortified with calcium, making this smoothie one of the best for strong bones and teeth.

INGREDIENTS

2 tablespoons goji berries, soaked
    for 5 minutes

1 small banana, peeled

1/2 orange, peeled and seeded

2 cups fresh curly kale, stems removed

8 ounces unsweetened coconut milk

NUTRITION INFO

*Calories: 290 • Fat: 7g • Protein: 11g
Carbs: 55g • Calcium: 21%
Iron: 3.2mg • Vitamin A: 247%
Vitamin C: 289%*

SWEET POTATO-ORANGE SMOOTHIE

Kale is a great source of calcium. Just two cups of kale contains 17 percent of your recommended daily value of calcium. It also contains 2 mg of iron and almost 6 grams of protein. Kale is definitely a smoothie superfood!

Sweet potato also contains calcium. Sweet potato contains 4 percent of your recommended daily value of calcium in just half a cup. It's also loaded with antioxidants.

INGREDIENTS

1 orange, peeled and seeded

1/2 cup cubed sweet potato,
    cooked and cooled

1/2 cup cubed papaya

2 cups fresh baby kale

4 ounces filtered water

NUTRITION INFO

*Calories: 259 • Fat: 1g • Protein: 6g
Carbs: 60g • Calcium: 22%
Iron: 2.6mg • Vitamin A: 234%
Vitamin C: 285%*

NECTARINE-CHERRY SMOOTHIE

While most of the calcium in this smoothie comes from the collard leaves, cherries, nectarines, and carrots actually contain a small amount of calcium.

A large collard leaf contains 7 percent of your recommended daily value of calcium. If you are looking to boost the calcium content of this smoothie further, you could always add three collard leaves.

INGREDIENTS

1 nectarine, pitted

1 cup cherries, pitted

2 large collard leaves, stems removed

1 small carrot, sliced

1 teaspoon ground sesame seeds

1/4 teaspoon ground cinnamon

4 ounces homemade almond milk
   (page 64)

NUTRITION INFO

Calories: 237 • Fat: 1g • Protein: 7g
Carbs: 49g • Calcium: 20%
Iron: 1.9mg • Vitamin A: 90%
Vitamin C: 62%

PEAR-TANGERINE SMOOTHIE

Not only are tangerines a great source of calcium, containing 5 percent of your recommended daily value in just two tangerines, but they are also a great source of vitamin C and fiber. Two tangerines also contain 63 percent of your recommended daily value of vitamin C and 13 percent of your recommended daily value of fiber.

Citrus fruits are also great for detox and cleansing since the pulp supports colon function.

INGREDIENTS

1 large pear, cored

1/2 teaspoon ground cinnamon

2 tangerines, peeled and seeded

2 large heads baby bok choy
   (about 2 cups)

4 ounces filtered water

NUTRITION INFO

Calories: 242 • Fat: 1g • Protein: 5g
Carbs: 62g • Calcium: 19%
Iron: 1.8mg • Vitamin A: 277%
Vitamin C: 160%

RED GRAPE–FIG SMOOTHIE

Figs can be hard to find in some areas and available only for a short period of time in others. However, if you can find this amazing little fruit, I recommend giving it a try. Just five medium figs contain 7 percent of your recommended daily value of calcium. They are also loaded with B vitamins, copper, fiber, and almost 2 grams of protein.

I used butterhead lettuce in this smoothie because it's relatively easy to find in most supermarkets and it has a very mild flavor. Since figs also have a mild flavor, I didn't want to add a bitter green like kale or dandelion that would overpower the delicate balance of flavors.

INGREDIENTS

5 medium figs

1/2 cup organic red grapes

1/2 head butterhead lettuce, torn

1/2 small banana, peeled

4 ounces filtered water

NUTRITION INFO

Calories: 293 • Fat: 1g • Protein: 4g
Carbs: 75g • Calcium: 11%
Iron: 2.3mg • Vitamin A: 22%
Vitamin C: 20%

BANANA–ORANGE SMOOTHIE

Kale really is a king of greens. Not only does two cups of kale contain 17 percent of your recommended daily value of calcium, it is also a great source of folate, vitamins A and C, copper, protein, potassium, iron, and fiber.

INGREDIENTS

1 medium banana, peeled

1 orange, peeled

1/4 teaspoon grated ginger

2 cups fresh kale, chopped

8 ounces filtered water

NUTRITION INFO

Calories: 241 • Fat: 2g • Protein: 7g
Carbs: 58g • Calcium: 21%
Iron: 2.8mg • Vitamin A: 701%
Vitamin C: 282%

PISTACHIO-BANANA SMOOTHIE

This smoothie is loaded with calcium from the kale and protein from both the kale and the pistachios. Pistachios are also a great source of vitamin B6.

If you really love pistachios and want to boost the pistachio flavor without adding a lot more calories, you can use 6 ounces of pistachio milk instead of the 6 ounces of water.

To make the pistachio milk, simply blend one cup of shelled pistachios that have been soaked for a least four hours with four cups of water. Strain it with a nut bag or fine sieve to remove the pulp. Add 6 ounces to this smoothie and you can use the rest for another recipe. Use it in anything you would use almond milk for.

INGREDIENTS

2 small bananas, peeled

Seeds scraped from 1 vanilla bean
    or 1/2 teaspoon pure vanilla
    extract (alcohol-free)

1/8 cup raw pistachios, shelled and
    soaked for 4 hours

2 cups fresh baby kale

6 ounces filtered water

NUTRITION INFO

*Calories: 283 • Fat: 6g • Protein: 7g
Carbs: 55g • Calcium: 14%
Iron: 2.1mg • Vitamin A: 44%
Vitamin C: 112%*

COCONUT-GRAPEFRUIT SMOOTHIE

This is one of my favorite grapefruit recipes. The coconut milk in this recipe helps to sweeten the grapefruit; however, it is still a little bitter.

The dulse flakes in this recipe are optional. Dulse does not add anything to the flavor of the recipe, but this sea vegetable is a great source of iodine.

INGREDIENTS

1/2 red grapefruit, peeled and
    seeded

1 banana, peeled

1/4 teaspoon dulse flakes
    (optional)

1 cup fresh kale, chopped

4 ounces unsweetened coconut
    milk

NUTRITION INFO

*Calories: 215 • Fat: 4g • Protein: 6g
Carbs: 46g • Calcium: 11%
Iron: 1.4mg • Vitamin A: 59%
Vitamin C: 172%*

Please note, if you are taking any medications, please check with your doctor before consuming grapefruit, since it can have a negative reaction that can be fatal.

PEACH-STRAWBERRY-COCONUT SMOOTHIE

Dandelion greens can be hard to find in some areas. I would not recommend picking them from your yard unless you live in a rural area and you are sure the soil is not contaminated.

Since they are a weed and grow very easily in most areas, you can grow your own in some organic potting soil. Make sure you harvest them before the flower starts to bud since the greens are less bitter when they are young.

Dandelion greens are just as nutritious as kale when it comes to protein, iron, and calcium. Two cups of dandelion greens contain 17 percent of your recommended daily value of calcium, 3.4 mg of iron, and 3 grams of protein.

INGREDIENTS

2 medium peaches, pitted

8 medium strawberries

1/2 orange, peeled and seeds
  removed

2 cups dandelion greens, chopped

4 ounces unsweetened coconut
  milk

NUTRITION INFO

Calories: 256 • Fat: 5g • Protein: 8g
Carbs: 55g • Calcium: 27%
Iron: 5mg • Vitamin A: 99%
Vitamin C: 208%

SUPER GREEN AND PEACH SMOOTHIE

Both dandelion greens and broccoli are great sources of calcium. I only added one cup of dandelion greens and half a cup of frozen broccoli since they are both slightly bitter.

The banana and peaches help to sweeten this smoothie nicely. Just make sure you are using very ripe fruit to really help sweeten it.

If you find the smoothie is too bitter for you, you can always add a soaked date to sweeten it further.

INGREDIENTS

1 banana, peeled

2 small peaches, pitted

1/2 cup frozen broccoli

1 cup dandelion greens, chopped

8 ounces filtered water

NUTRITION INFO

Calories: 245 • Fat: 2g • Protein: 6g
Carbs: 60g • Calcium: 12%
Iron: 2.9mg • Vitamin A: 51%
Vitamin C: 96%

PINEAPPLE-CITRUS SMOOTHIE

Parsley is extremely high in iron and calcium. It is, however, a very bitter green. I added a quarter cup to this smoothie so it would not overpower the rest of the ingredients. Pineapple and parsley are an amazing combination. If you are just starting to use parsley in your smoothies, I recommend adding pineapple until you have adjusted to the distinctive flavor of fresh parsley.

INGREDIENTS

1 small frozen banana, peeled and
   sliced
1 cup cubed pineapple
1/2 orange, peeled and seeded
1/2 cucumber with peel
1/4 cup fresh Italian parsley
1 cup dandelion greens, chopped
4 ounces filtered water

NUTRITION INFO

*Calories: 259 • Fat: 1g • Protein: 6g
Carbs: 65g • Calcium: 17%
Iron: 3.9mg • Vitamin A: 52%
Vitamin C: 230%*

BANANA-CRANBERRY SMOOTHIE

Cranberries can be very bitter, but they are extremely good for you. Cranberries are a good source of fiber and vitamin C. They also contain small amounts of vitamin K, magnesium, manganese, calcium, iron, potassium, and phosphorus. They are great for low-calorie smoothies.

The banana and orange really help to sweeten the cranberries and dandelion greens. The orange also helps to add a little extra fiber and calcium to this smoothie.

INGREDIENTS

1/2 cup fresh or frozen cranberries
Juice of 1/2 lime
2 small frozen bananas, peeled and
   sliced
1/2 orange, peeled and seeded
1 teaspoon ground cinnamon
2 cups dandelion greens, chopped
4 ounces filtered water

NUTRITION INFO

*Calories: 286 • Fat: 2g • Protein: 6g
Carbs: 71g • Calcium: 21%
Iron: 4.2mg • Vitamin A: 82%
Vitamin C: 139%*

GINGER-PEACH SMOOTHIE

If you can't find dandelion greens, you can always replace them with kale. They are equally nutritious. I love the flavor of dandelion greens with celery, though. They pair well in a green smoothie.

The pineapple helps to sweeten this smoothie without overpowering it. Make sure to use very ripe peaches since unripe peaches will not be as flavorful.

INGREDIENTS

1 teaspoon grated ginger
2 peaches, pitted
1/2 cup cubed pineapple
1 cup dandelion greens, chopped
2 stalks celery
6 ounces filtered water

NUTRITION INFO

Calories: 196 • Fat: 2g • Protein: 5g
Carbs: 47g • Calcium: 14%
Iron: 2.9mg • Vitamin A: 50%
Vitamin C: 108%

PEAR-ALOE SMOOTHIE

While aloe doesn't have much of a flavor, it is very good for your digestive health. I prefer to get my aloe gel right from the aloe leaf, but you can also find food-grade aloe gel in the store. Most aloe gel products sold in stores are topical, so double-check that any packaged aloe is safe to eat.

Pear and cinnamon is an amazing combination that even kids will like. You can add more or less cinnamon depending on your taste.

INGREDIENTS

2 small pears, cored
1 orange, peeled and seeded
1/2 teaspoon ground cinnamon
3 chard leaves, stems removed
1/4 cup aloe vera gel
4 ounces filtered water

NUTRITION INFO

Calories: 265 • Fat: 1g • Protein: 5g
Carbs: 68g • Calcium: 13%
Iron: 3.3mg • Vitamin A: 66%
Vitamin C: 185%

COCONUT-PEACH SMOOTHIE

Chard leaves are loaded with calcium. The larger the leaf, the better. One large leaf is the equivalent of about a cup, in case you can't find large leaves and need to use a few smaller leaves.

While peaches are not as high in calcium as chard leaves, they contain about 1 percent of your recommended daily value of calcium per peach. They are, however, a great source of fiber and vitamin C.

You can boost the calcium content of this smoothie further by using calcium-fortified coconut milk.

INGREDIENTS

2 peaches, pitted

1/2 mango, peeled and pitted

3 large chard leaves, stems removed

4 ounces unsweetened coconut milk

NUTRITION INFO

Calories: 245 • Fat: 4g • Protein: 7g
Carbs: 53g • Calcium: 13%
Iron: 3.9mg • Vitamin A: 90%
Vitamin C: 145%

PINEAPPLE-ORANGE TROPICAL SMOOTHIE

I added both chard and spinach to this smoothie to really boost the calcium. Dark leafy greens are loaded with nutrients. The chard and spinach also help to boost the protein in this smoothie.

While this smoothie is only about 20 ounces, it is loaded with 7 grams of protein.

The banana not only helps to sweeten the smoothie, but it also makes it creamy.

INGREDIENTS

1 orange, peeled and seeded

1/2 cup cubed pineapple

1 small banana, peeled

2 chard leaves, stems removed

1 cup fresh baby spinach

4 ounces unsweetened coconut milk

NUTRITION INFO

Calories: 257 • Fat: 4g • Protein: 7g
Carbs: 58g • Calcium: 20%
Iron: 4.4mg • Vitamin A: 96%
Vitamin C: 235%

STRAWBERRY-RASPBERRY SMOOTHIE WITH AVOCADO

Avocados are a great source of heart-healthy fats. They can also be high in calories, and that is why I only used a quarter of an avocado in this recipe. A quarter of an avocado is only about 80 calories and is just enough to give this smoothie a creamy, thick consistency.

It also blends nicely with the strawberries and raspberries. You can always add frozen raspberries and/or strawberries for a cold smoothie.

INGREDIENTS

10 large strawberries

1 cup raspberries

1/4 avocado, peeled and pitted

3 chard leaves, stems removed

6 ounces filtered water

NUTRITION INFO

Calories: 210 • Fat: 9g • Protein: 6g
Carbs: 34g • Calcium: 11%
Iron: 4.2mg • Vitamin A: 64%
Vitamin C: 201%

ORANGE-SESAME SEED SMOOTHIE

While sesame seeds have a very strong flavor, they are loaded with calcium. Just one tablespoon of sesame seeds contains 7 percent of your recommended daily value of calcium.

Since sesame seeds are so small, they might not blend up in all types of blenders. I recommend grinding the seeds before adding them to your smoothie. I used the orange to boost the calcium and to help mask the sesame seed flavor.

INGREDIENTS

1 tablespoon sesame seeds, ground
    into powder

1 orange, peeled and seeded

1/4 teaspoon ground cinnamon

1/2 cup raspberries

1 cup fresh baby spinach

4 ounces homemade almond milk
    (page 64)

NUTRITION INFO

Calories: 176 • Fat: 6g • Protein: 5g
Carbs: 28g • Calcium: 16%
Iron: 2.7mg • Vitamin A: 23%
Vitamin C: 143%

CHAPTER TEN

HEART-HEALTHY GREEN SMOOTHIES

Watermelon-Blueberry Green Smoothie • 171

Goji Berry Superfood Green Smoothie • 171

Creamy Chocolate and Vanilla Smoothie • 172

Kiwifruit-Orange Green Smoothie • 172

Tropical Green Smoothie • 173

Strawberry Goodness Smoothie • 173

Avocado-Peach Green Smoothie • 174

Cantaloupe-Raspberry Green Smoothie • 174

Strawberry-Avocado Smoothie • 175

Coconut-Apple-Ginger Smoothie • 175

Blackberry-Almond Smoothie • 176

Chia Seed–Red Grape Smoothie • 176

Raspberry-Avocado Smoothie • 177

Avocado-Berry Smoothie • 177

Blueberry-Flaxseed Smoothie • 178

Peach-Vanilla Smoothie • 178

Coconut-Persimmon Smoothie • 179

• •

As with most diseases, a large body of evidence suggests that a diet low in saturated fat and dietary cholesterol and rich in fresh fruits and vegetables reduces the risk of heart disease, high blood pressure, stroke, type-2 diabetes, and other risk factors for cardiovascular disease.

A study published in the *American Journal of Clinical Nutrition* in March 2007 showed a reduction of mortality from heart disease among those who consumed more fruits and vegetables in the diet. Of course, some fruits are going to stand out among the rest. Apples and pears were associated with a lower risk of mortality from coronary heart disease (CHD) and cardiovascular disease (CVD), grapefruit was associated with a lower risk of CHD, and strawberries and chocolate were associated with a lower mortality rate from CVD among postmenopausal women.[48] Resveratrol, an antioxidant compound found in fruits, especially in red grapes, has been studied extensively for its potential to reduce the risk of a variety of human diseases including cancer, stroke, and heart disease.[49]

Researchers at the University of Oslo in Norway also found that human volunteers in a random, crossover study who consumed two or three kiwifruit per day for twenty-eight days had an 18 percent lower platelet aggregation response to collagen and adenosine diphosphate (ADP). They also had lower blood triglyceride levels by 15 percent compared to the control group volunteers who did not eat kiwifruit.[50]

To the delight of most people, chocolate is also a heart-healthy food. Dark chocolate, for example, is loaded with antioxidants, which help rid your body of free radicals that cause oxidative damage to cells.

Of course, this doesn't mean that you should eat chocolate bars for lunch. However, healthier forms of chocolate include raw, minimally processed chocolate (also known as cacao). This form of chocolate is straight from the cacao fruit and contains high levels of minerals and antioxidants, without the added sugar and other unhealthy components in chocolate candy bars. Other kinds of chocolate, such as milk chocolate and white chocolate, simply do not provide the health benefits that raw, minimally processed cacao may provide.

Cacao is commonly sold in health food stores as powder (perfect for green smoothies), nibs (pieces), or whole beans.

About These Recipes

The green smoothies featured in this chapter will focus on ingredients such as raw cacao, apples, pears, and strawberries, all of which may help support a healthy heart.

WATERMELON-BLUEBERRY GREEN SMOOTHIE

Chia seeds are an excellent heart-healthy addition to your green smoothies. Just one tablespoon of chia seeds contains 49 percent of your recommended daily value of omega-3 fatty acids.

Blueberries contain anthocyanins, the antioxidants that give them their dark blue color. They are also loaded with fiber and vitamin C.

INGREDIENTS

1/2 cucumber, chopped

1 cup cubed watermelon

1 small banana, peeled

1 cup blueberries

2 cups fresh baby kale

1 tablespoon chia seeds, soaked for 5 minutes

4 ounces filtered water

NUTRITION INFO

Calories: 292 • Fat: 2g • Protein: 7g
Carbs: 70g • Calcium: 18%
Iron: 2.8mg • Vitamin A: 51%
Vitamin C: 141%

GOJI BERRY SUPERFOOD GREEN SMOOTHIE

I can't say enough good things about goji berries! They are an amazing nutrient-packed superfood in a tiny little berry. Not only are they loaded with protein and fiber, they are also a great source of antioxidants.

Both blueberries and strawberries contain anthocyanins, which are good for your heart. They are also a great source of fiber and vitamin C.

INGREDIENTS

5 large strawberries

1/2 cup blueberries

1/2 small pear, cored

1/2 small banana, peeled

1 teaspoon chia seeds, soaked for
    5 minutes

3 tablespoons goji berries, soaked
    for 5 minutes

2 cups fresh baby spinach

4 ounces filtered water

NUTRITION INFO

Calories: 251 • Fat: 1g • Protein: 7g
Carbs: 59g • Calcium: 10%
Iron: 3.9mg • Vitamin A: 266%
Vitamin C: 125%

CREAMY CHOCOLATE AND VANILLA SMOOTHIE

Avocados are a great source of heart-healthy omega-3 fatty acids. Just a quarter of an avocado contains 4 percent of your recommended daily value of omega-3 fatty acids, 6 percent of your recommended daily value of omega-6 fatty acids, and 11 percent of your recommended daily value of fiber.

Bananas are also a great source of fiber. One small banana contains 11 percent of your recommended daily value of fiber. A diet rich in dietary fiber may lower the risk of heart disease by reducing levels of total and LDL "bad" cholesterol.

INGREDIENTS

1/4 avocado, peeled and pitted

1 small frozen banana, peeled

1 tablespoon cacao powder

Seeds scraped from 1 vanilla bean
    or 1/2 teaspoon pure vanilla
    extract (alcohol-free)

6 ounces homemade almond milk
    (page 64)

NUTRITION INFO

Calories: 242 • Fat: 9g • Protein: 5g
Carbs: 35g • Calcium: 2%
Iron: 1.6mg • Vitamin A: 1%
Vitamin C: 18%

KIWIFRUIT-ORANGE GREEN SMOOTHIE

This green smoothie has so many health benefits. Not only are pears loaded with heart-healthy fiber, but just one teaspoon of ground flaxseeds is loaded with 44 percent of your recommended daily value of omega-3 fatty acids. A diet high in omega-3 fatty acids may decrease triglyceride levels.

INGREDIENTS

2 kiwifruit, ends removed

1 orange, peeled and seeded

1 pear, cored

1 teaspoon ground flaxseeds

3 cups escarole lettuce, torn

4 ounces filtered water

NUTRITION INFO

Calories: 300 • Fat: 3g • Protein: 6g
Carbs: 72g • Calcium: 19%
Iron: 2.7mg • Vitamin A: 180%
Vitamin C: 308%

TROPICAL GREEN SMOOTHIE

This is a delicious tropical smoothie with a green twist. It's loaded with hydrating and fiber-rich fruits and vegetables, which may provide both cleansing and heart-healthy benefits.

While kale doesn't contain as much heart-healthy omega-3 fatty acids as flaxseeds, just one cup of kale contains 11 percent of your recommended daily value. Kale is also a great source of protein, iron, and calcium.

INGREDIENTS

1/2 cup cubed papaya

1/2 cup cubed mango, peeled and pitted

1/2 cup cubed pineapple

1 teaspoon ground flaxseeds

1 stalk celery

1 large leaf fresh curly kale, stem removed

1/2 cucumber, chopped

1 cup fresh baby spinach

8 ounces unsweetened coconut milk

NUTRITION INFO

*Calories: 296 • Fat: 10g • Protein: 8g
Carbs: 51g • Calcium: 19%
Iron: 3.4mg • Vitamin A: 85%
Vitamin C: 312%*

STRAWBERRY GOODNESS SMOOTHIE

Papaya is a great source of fiber, which may help lower cholesterol. Just one cup of papaya contains 10 percent of your recommended daily value of fiber. Papaya is also a great source of vitamin C and folate.

Papaya has the best flavor when it is fully ripe. The peel should be yellow and spotting before you cut into it. After you cut into it, the fruit should be a deep pink color.

INGREDIENTS

15 large strawberries

1 tablespoon ground flaxseeds

1 large pear, cored

1/2 cup cubed papaya

8 ounces unsweetened coconut milk

NUTRITION INFO

*Calories: 354 • Fat: 9g • Protein: 6g
Carbs: 71g • Calcium: 9%
Iron: 2.9mg • Vitamin A: 30%
Vitamin C: 318%*

AVOCADO-PEACH GREEN SMOOTHIE

This smoothie is loaded with heart-hearty omega-3 fatty acids that may help decrease triglyceride levels. The avocado and flaxseeds contain 54 percent of your recommended daily value of omega-3 fatty acids. They also contain 29 percent of your recommended daily value of fiber.

Not only are peaches a great source of fiber, containing 9 percent of your recommended daily value, but they are also a great source of vitamin C.

INGREDIENTS

1 peach, pitted

1 cup fresh curly kale, chopped

1 cup fresh baby spinach

1/2 avocado, peeled and pitted

Seeds scraped from 1 vanilla bean
    or 1/2 teaspoon pure vanilla
    extract (alcohol-free)

1 teaspoon ground flaxseeds

6 ounces filtered water

NUTRITION INFO

Calories: 273 • Fat: 17g • Protein: 7g
Carbs: 31g • Calcium: 13%
Iron: 2.9mg • Vitamin A: 72%
Vitamin C: 145%

CANTALOUPE-RASPBERRY GREEN SMOOTHIE

Raspberries contain anthocyanins, which are good for your heart. They are also a great source of heart-healthy fiber and vitamin C.

Just one teaspoon of ground flaxseeds is loaded with 44 percent of your recommended daily value of omega-3 fatty acids.

Cantaloupes are a rich source of vitamins A (as beta-carotene) and C. They also contain good levels of B vitamins and vitamin K.

INGREDIENTS

1/2 cantaloupe, cubed

1 cup raspberries

1/2 banana, peeled

2 cups fresh baby spinach

1 teaspoon ground flaxseeds

4 ounces filtered water

NUTRITION INFO

Calories: 242 • Fat: 3g • Protein: 7g
Carbs: 53g • Calcium: 11%
Iron: 3.4mg • Vitamin A: 107%
Vitamin C: 207%

STRAWBERRY-AVOCADO SMOOTHIE

Using spices like cinnamon and nutmeg in your green smoothies makes for some delicious surprises. If you feel like you are getting into a rut with your green smoothies, look to your spice rack to . . . spice things up!

I usually use organic strawberries, and when I do, I leave the green tops on and blend them whole. Like any leafy green, strawberry tops help boost the mineral content of your green smoothie.

INGREDIENTS

10 large strawberries

1/2 avocado, pitted

1/2 teaspoon ground cinnamon

1/4 teaspoon ground nutmeg

4 ounces homemade almond milk
    (page 64)

NUTRITION INFO

*Calories: 226 • Fat: 16g • Protein: 3g
Carbs: 19g • Calcium: 4%
Iron: 1.2mg • Vitamin A: 1%
Vitamin C: 108%*

COCONUT-APPLE-GINGER SMOOTHIE

Eating an apple a day may reduce your cholesterol. Just one medium apple contains 17 percent of your recommended daily value of fiber. They are also a great source of vitamin C.

Nutrients in carrots have been shown to reduce the risk of heart attacks and may help regulate blood sugar levels. Two medium carrots contain just 50 calories, and they are a great source of vitamin A (as beta-carotene) and fiber.

INGREDIENTS

1 large red delicious apple, cored

2 medium carrots, sliced into
    1-inch pieces

1 teaspoon grated ginger

1 tablespoon chia seeds, soaked for
    5 minutes

4 ounces unsweetened coconut milk

NUTRITION INFO

*Calories: 206 • Fat: 4g • Protein: 3g
Carbs: 44g • Calcium: 10%
Iron: 1.2mg • Vitamin A: 157%
Vitamin C: 23%*

BLACKBERRY-ALMOND SMOOTHIE

Blackberries are among the top-ranked antioxidant-rich fruits and also contain high levels of fiber, manganese, copper, and vitamin C. They also contain only 61 calories per cup and boost the protein level per cup by 2 grams.

INGREDIENTS

1 cup blackberries (fresh or frozen)

1 banana, peeled

2 teaspoons chia seeds, soaked for
    5 minutes

1 cup fresh baby spinach

6 ounces homemade almond milk
    (page 64)

NUTRITION INFO

*Calories: 203 • Fat: 2g • Protein: 5g
Carbs: 42g • Calcium: 7%
Iron: 2mg • Vitamin A: 23%
Vitamin C: 65%*

CHIA SEED-RED GRAPE SMOOTHIE

Just one tablespoon of chia seeds contains 49 percent of your recommended daily value of omega-3 fatty acids.

Sesame seeds are a great source of calcium and may also help lower your LDL "bad" cholesterol. I recommend grinding your sesame seeds before adding them to your smoothie. The seeds are very small and might not grind up in all blenders.

INGREDIENTS

1 cup red grapes

1 teaspoon chia seeds, soaked for
    about 5 minutes

1 small banana, peeled

3 cups romaine lettuce

1/2 tablespoon ground sesame
    seeds

4 ounces filtered water

NUTRITION INFO

*Calories: 249 • Fat: 4g • Protein: 5g
Carbs: 57g • Calcium: 57%
Iron: 2.9mg • Vitamin A: 89%
Vitamin C: 26%*

RASPBERRY-AVOCADO SMOOTHIE

Avocados can make a great base for a high-energy green smoothie that will keep you satisfied until your next meal. They are also high in good fats and contain the fat-soluble vitamin E, as well as antioxidants that may help prevent heart disease.

While I prefer to use the seeds scraped from a vanilla bean, you can easily use alcohol-free pure vanilla extract in this recipe instead.

INGREDIENTS

1 cup raspberries

1 small frozen banana, peeled and sliced

Seeds scraped from 1 vanilla bean or 1/2 teaspoon pure vanilla extract (alcohol-free)

1/4 avocado, peeled and pitted

6 ounces filtered water

NUTRITION INFO

Calories: 234 • Fat: 9g • Protein: 4g
Carbs: 42g • Calcium: 3%
Iron: 1.4mg • Vitamin A: 1%
Vitamin C: 61%

AVOCADO-BERRY SMOOTHIE

Raspberries, strawberries, and cherries are loaded with antioxidants, such as anthocyanins, which give them their red color. Studies have shown that anthocyanins also have anti-inflammatory properties.

Oranges are high in vitamin C as well as vitamins A and B1, folate, potassium, calcium, and dietary fiber. Oranges have been shown to lower high blood pressure and cholesterol.

INGREDIENTS

1/2 cup raspberries

5 large strawberries

1/2 cup cherries, pitted

1 orange, peeled and seeded

1/4 avocado, peeled and pitted

4 ounces filtered water

NUTRITION INFO

Calories: 249 • Fat: 8g • Protein: 4g
Carbs: 46g • Calcium: 8%
Iron: 1.4mg • Vitamin A: 3%
Vitamin C: 193%

BLUEBERRY-FLAXSEED SMOOTHIE

Flaxseeds are a good source of omega-3 fatty acids and fiber, both of which may help protect against heart disease.

Bananas are one of the most popular fruits in the world. It's easy to see why people love them since they are creamy, making them the perfect smoothie base fruit. Bananas are an excellent source of potassium and fiber. They are good sources of vitamins B6 and C and antioxidants.

INGREDIENTS

1/2 orange, peeled

1 small frozen banana, peeled and sliced

1 cup blueberries

1 tablespoon ground flaxseeds

1/2 head butterhead lettuce, torn

6 ounces filtered water

NUTRITION INFO

*Calories: 257 • Fat: 4g • Protein: 5g
Carbs: 57g • Calcium: 8%
Iron: 2.2mg • Vitamin A: 22%
Vitamin C: 90%*

PEACH-VANILLA SMOOTHIE

Peaches are a good source of vitamin C, potassium, lycopene, and lutein. Research shows that lycopene and lutein may help prevent heart disease.

Spinach is the most popular smoothie green. It's a good thing that it is also loaded with nutrients, low in calories, and the flavor is easily hidden by almost any fruit.

INGREDIENTS

1 small frozen banana, peeled and sliced

2 medium peaches, pitted

2 cups fresh baby spinach

Seeds scraped from 1 vanilla bean or 1/2 teaspoon pure vanilla extract (alcohol-free)

1 teaspoon chia seeds, soaked for 5 minutes

4 ounces filtered water

NUTRITION INFO

*Calories: 226 • Fat: 2g • Protein: 6g
Carbs: 54g • Calcium: 7%
Iron: 2.7mg • Vitamin A: 47%
Vitamin C: 61%*

COCONUT-PERSIMMON SMOOTHIE

I love to use the non-astringent fuyu persimmons in green smoothies. Fuyu persimmons are the squat, pumpkin- or tomato-shaped ones—as opposed to the astringent acorn or elongated persimmons.

When fuyu persimmons are ripe, they are very sweet. Persimmons are a good source of fiber, vitamin C, and antioxidants.

INGREDIENTS

3 very ripe fuyu persimmons, seeded

1/4 cup coconut meat from young Thai coconut

Seeds scraped from 1/2 vanilla bean or 1/4 teaspoon pure vanilla extract (alcohol-free)

1/4 teaspoon ground cinnamon

2 cups fresh baby spinach

4 ounces unsweetened coconut milk

NUTRITION INFO

Calories: 205 • Fat: 10g • Protein: 4g
Carbs: 31g • Calcium: 11%
Iron: 4.3mg • Vitamin A: 51%
Vitamin C: 89%

CHAPTER ELEVEN

IRON-RICH GREEN SMOOTHIES

Cherry-Kiwifruit Green Smoothie • 186

The Veggie Green Smoothie • 186

Chocolate-Raspberry Green Smoothie • 187

Star Fruit–Peach Smoothie • 187

Peach-Mango Smoothie • 188

Refreshing Apple Smoothie • 188

Mango-Pear Smoothie • 189

Kale-Parsley Smoothie • 189

Chocolate-Mango Smoothie • 190

Chocolate-Açaí Smoothie • 190

Broccoli-Kale Smoothie • 191

Parsley-Pear Smoothie • 191

Cucumber-Parsley Smoothie • 192

Peach-Pear Smoothie • 192

Pear-Grape Smoothie • 193

Nectarine–Goji Berry Smoothie • 193

Cucumber-Aloe Smoothie • 194

Ginger-Spinach Smoothie • 194

Iron is an extremely important mineral. Your body needs iron to create hemoglobin, which is a protein in red blood cells that transports oxygen to all of your body's other cells. Without oxygen, these cells would die.

How Much Iron Do You Need?

Different groups of people have different iron intake requirements. Therefore, it is best to ignore the percent daily value listed in the nutrition facts on labels and instead focus on the total milligrams per serving.

Nutrition facts labels are based on a 2,000-calorie diet and typically follow guidelines for adult men. A vegetarian female could obtain 100 percent of her recommended daily value of iron *according to the nutrition facts label* but still fall short of her actual iron intake requirement.

The following dietary iron recommendations were established in 2000 by the Institute of Medicine at the National Academy of Sciences. These guidelines factor in age, gender, and diet to determine the proper amount of dietary iron necessary to avoid anemia.

Vegetarians, Vegans & Raw Food Vegans (Adults)

Since non-heme, plant-based iron is less absorbable than heme-iron from animal products, vegetarians, vegans, and raw food vegans should abide by the following adequate intake recommendations. Percent daily value (%DV) commonly listed on packaged foods should NOT be followed by vegans and vegetarians.

- Adult men: 14 mg
- Adult women (premenopausal): 33 mg
- Adult women (postmenopausal): 14 mg

Omnivore Diet (Adults)

- Men 19+ years: 8 mg
- Women 19–50 years (premenopausal): 18 mg
- Women 51+ years (postmenopausal): 8 mg

- Pregnant women 14–50 years: 27 mg
- Lactating women 14–18 years: 10 mg
- Lactating women 19–50 years: 9 mg

- Adult women taking oral contraceptives (premenopausal): 10.9 mg

How Much Iron Can You Get from Green Smoothies?

Based on the above recommendations, omnivores can get a significant amount of their iron from the dark leafy greens in green smoothies.

For vegetarians, vegans, raw food vegans, and women (who have higher iron requirements than adult men), green smoothies can contribute to their overall iron requirements.

Some of the most iron-rich green smoothie ingredients include:

Parsley (1 cup, chopped)—3.7 mg

Dandelion greens (2 cups, chopped)—3.4 mg

Kale (2 cups, chopped)—2.3 mg

Spinach (2 cups, chopped)—1.6 mg

Flaxseeds (2 tablespoons whole)—1.2 mg

Raw cacao (varies depending on brand)—Anywhere from 1 mg to more than 36 mg per serving

About These Recipes

Dark leafy greens such as kale, dandelion greens, and parsley are excellent sources of iron in a green smoothie. Of course, they are also very bitter. Fortunately, even the bitterest greens can be masked by sweet fruit. Trust me, you won't taste them at all in these delicious recipes!

In this chapter, I will show you how to use these three greens as well as other iron-rich foods like cacao to make tasty green smoothies.

CHERRY-KIWIFRUIT GREEN SMOOTHIE

Dark leafy greens are an excellent source of iron. Most of the iron in this smoothie comes from the lettuce, but pear, kiwifruit, and cherries all contain small amounts of iron.

INGREDIENTS

1 large pear, cored

2 kiwifruit, ends removed

1 cup cherries, pitted

1/2 head butterhead lettuce, torn

4 to 6 ounces filtered water

NUTRITION INFO

Calories: 323 • Fat: 2g • Protein: 5g
Carbs: 82g • Calcium: 10%
Iron: 2.4mg • Vitamin A: 21%
Vitamin C: 202%

THE VEGGIE GREEN SMOOTHIE

This smoothie isn't as sweet as some of my other smoothies. It's more of a veggie lovers smoothie. I added both a banana and an apple to sweeten the bitterness of the kale, and to add some fiber.

I love apples and tomatoes together. I think that is one of my favorite fruit and vegetable combinations.

Kale and spinach are great sources of iron, calcium, protein, and fiber.

INGREDIENTS

1 celery stalk

1 Campari tomato, cut in half

5 baby carrots, sliced

1 apple, cored

1 banana, peeled

2 cups fresh baby spinach

2 cups fresh kale, chopped

8 ounces filtered water

NUTRITION INFO

Calories: 329 • Fat: 3g • Protein: 11g
Carbs: 75g • Calcium: 27%
Iron: 4.9mg • Vitamin A: 193%
Vitamin C: 282%

CHOCOLATE-RASPBERRY GREEN SMOOTHIE

Cacao is another great source of iron. Cacao is raw chocolate. However, it is very bitter on its own. The banana, raspberries, and even the almond milk in this recipe mask the bitterly dark chocolate.

Cacao comes in whole beans, nibs, and powder. I find the powder to be the creamiest in smoothies. If you don't have a high-speed blender and want to use the whole bean or the nibs, I recommend grinding them in a coffee grinder before adding them to your smoothie.

Just two tablespoons of cacao will contain around 1.4 mg of iron, depending on where it is grown.

INGREDIENTS

1 frozen banana, chopped

1 cup fresh raspberries

2 tablespoons powdered cacao

2 cups fresh baby spinach, chopped

8 ounces homemade almond milk
  (page 64)

NUTRITION INFO

*Calories: 263 • Fat: 3g • Protein: 8g
Carbs: 51g • Calcium: 9%
Iron: 3.9mg • Vitamin A: 41%
Vitamin C: 79%*

STAR FRUIT-PEACH SMOOTHIE

Two cups of spinach contain about 1.6 mg of iron. Spinach is also a great source of vitamins A (as beta-carotene), B1, B2, B3, B6, C, E, K, folate, dietary fiber, calcium, selenium, zinc, phosphorus, potassium, copper, and omega-3 fatty acids.

It's a super green with a very mild flavor. I use spinach in a lot of my smoothies as it is relatively cheap and it is available in most places.

INGREDIENTS

1 medium peach, pitted

1/2 large banana, peeled

2 large star fruit (also called
  carambola), seeded

1/2 teaspoon ground cinnamon

2 cups fresh baby spinach

4 ounces filtered water

NUTRITION INFO

*Calories: 210 • Fat: 2g • Protein: 6g
Carbs: 48g • Calcium: 7%
Iron: 2.4mg • Vitamin A: 45%
Vitamin C: 157%*

PEACH-MANGO SMOOTHIE

Rainbow chard is such a great source of iron. Just three large leaves contain 2.6 mg of iron. They also contain 6 percent of your recommended daily value of calcium and almost 3 grams of protein!

I love how nicely the vanilla complements the peach in this smoothie. Peaches are one of my favorite stone fruits.

INGREDIENTS

1/2 mango, peeled and pitted

1 large peach, pitted

3 large rainbow chard leaves,
   stems removed

Seeds scraped from 1/2 vanilla
   bean or 1/4 teaspoon pure
   vanilla extract (alcohol-free)

4 ounces homemade almond milk
   (page 64)

NUTRITION INFO

Calories: 293 • Fat: 1g • Protein: 9g
Carbs: 37g • Calcium: 8%
Iron: 3.1mg • Vitamin A: 75%
Vitamin C: 126%

REFRESHING APPLE SMOOTHIE

Parsley has a distinctive flavor that is best used in small amounts and blended with the proper fruits, like apples, pears, and bananas.

INGREDIENTS

1 small apple, cored

1 small banana, peeled

1 cup fresh parsley, chopped

1/2 cucumber, peeled

8 ounces filtered water

NUTRITION INFO

Calories: 212 • Fat: 1g • Protein: 4g
Carbs: 53g • Calcium: 10%
Iron: 4.6mg • Vitamin A: 38%
Vitamin C: 133%

MANGO-PEAR SMOOTHIE

This is a great smoothie for people who are just starting to use kale in their smoothies. Mangoes are full of flavor to help offset the kale while the pear helps to sweeten the smoothie.

Kale is a powerhouse green and a great source of iron, calcium, magnesium, and potassium, as well as protein and vitamins A, C, and K.

INGREDIENTS

1/2 cup mango, peeled and pitted
1/2 pear, cored
1/2 orange, peeled and seeded
1 cup fresh kale, chopped
1 cup fresh baby spinach
4 ounces filtered water

NUTRITION INFO

Calories: 174 • Fat: 1g • Protein: 5g
Carbs: 42g • Calcium: 15%
Iron: 2.2mg • Vitamin A: 76%
Vitamin C: 219%

KALE-PARSLEY SMOOTHIE

This green smoothie might be a little advanced for some people. Kale and parsley have very strong flavors, but they both offer a lot of nutrients in return.

Two large kale leaves (about two cups of kale) and a quarter cup of parsley offer 18 percent of your recommended daily value of calcium, 2.7 mg of iron, 6 grams of protein, and over 100 percent of your recommended daily value of vitamins A, C, and K.

INGREDIENTS

1 pear, cored
1/2 cup cubed pineapple
2 large fresh curly kale leaves,
    stems removed
1/4 cup parsley, chopped
4 ounces homemade almond milk
    (page 64)

NUTRITION INFO

Calories: 198 • Fat: 1g • Protein: 5g
Carbs: 45g • Calcium: 12%
Iron: 2.4mg • Vitamin A: 57%
Vitamin C: 196%

CHOCOLATE-MANGO SMOOTHIE

Who doesn't love chocolate? The fact that this is a healthy chocolate smoothie makes it even better.

Mango sweetens the bitter chocolate while cinnamon deliciously accents the flavor.

INGREDIENTS

1 mango, peeled and pitted
1/4 teaspoon ground cinnamon
1 tablespoon cacao powder
1 cup fresh baby spinach
4 ounces homemade almond milk
    (page 64)

NUTRITION INFO

*Calories: 205 • Fat: 2g • Protein: 5g
Carbs: 43g • Calcium: 6%
Iron: 2mg • Vitamin A: 39%
Vitamin C: 133%*

CHOCOLATE-AÇAÍ SMOOTHIE

Açaí is loaded with antioxidants. It has a wine-and-chocolate flavor on its own, so adding cacao to this smoothie only enhances the chocolate flavor.

I recommend using açaí purée, as you will get more nutrients and fiber than you would from juice or powder supplements. You can find the frozen purée in the freezer aisle of health food stores and some grocery stores.

The butterhead lettuce helps to add a little more iron as well as vitamins A, C, and K. It also has a mild flavor so it doesn't overpower the açaí and cacao.

INGREDIENTS

1 pouch (100 grams) frozen açaí
    purée
Seeds scraped from 1/2 vanilla bean
    or 1/4 teaspoon pure vanilla
    extract (alcohol-free)
1 tablespoon cacao powder
1 pear, cored
1/2 head butterhead lettuce, torn
4 ounces filtered water

NUTRITION INFO

*Calories: 222 • Fat: 7g • Protein: 5g
Carbs: 37g • Calcium: 8%
Iron: 2.1mg • Vitamin A: 52%
Vitamin C: 21%*

BROCCOLI-KALE SMOOTHIE

I love adding broccoli to my smoothies. I often add frozen broccoli to give my smoothie an extra dose of vitamin C, calcium, iron, and fiber. Just half a cup of broccoli also contains 2 grams of protein.

The banana helps to sweeten the broccoli and kale in this recipe, and provides potassium and dietary fiber.

INGREDIENTS

1/2 cup frozen broccoli

1 cup fresh kale, chopped

1 medium apple, cored

1/2 small banana, peeled

4 ounces homemade almond milk
(page 64)

NUTRITION INFO

*Calories: 217 • Fat: 1g • Protein: 6g
Carbs: 48g • Calcium: 12%
Iron: 1.9mg • Vitamin A: 57%
Vitamin C: 192%*

PARSLEY-PEAR SMOOTHIE

While most of the iron in this smoothie comes from the parsley, the avocado also contributes a small amount of iron, as well as omega-3 fatty acids.

Pears are a great source of fiber, vitamin C, vitamin K, and copper. They also contain a small amount of calcium, iron, and zinc.

INGREDIENTS

1 Bartlett pear, cored

1/4 avocado, peeled

1/2 banana, peeled

1/2 cup parsley, chopped

4 ounces filtered water

NUTRITION INFO

*Calories: 255 • Fat: 8g • Protein: 3g
Carbs: 46g • Calcium: 6%
Iron: 2.6mg • Vitamin A: 19%
Vitamin C: 77%*

CUCUMBER-PARSLEY SMOOTHIE

I didn't peel the cucumber before I added it to this smoothie. The cucumber peel is a great source of antioxidants as well as vitamin K, magnesium, potassium, and zinc.

The pineapple and banana help to sweeten the parsley while the avocado helps to make the smoothie creamy without sweetening it too much.

INGREDIENTS

1/2 banana, peeled

1/4 avocado, peeled

1 cup sliced cucumber

1/2 cup parsley, chopped

1/4 cup cubed pineapple

4 ounces unsweetened coconut milk

NUTRITION INFO

*Calories: 193 • Fat: 8g • Protein: 4g
Carbs: 29g • Calcium: 6%
Iron: 2.7mg • Vitamin A: 20%
Vitamin C: 92%*

PEACH-PEAR SMOOTHIE

Dandelion greens are one of my favorite greens. They can be hard to find in some areas, but if you can find them, I recommend giving them a try. They are slightly bitter like kale and parsley, but you can easily sweeten them with fruits like peach, pear, pineapple, or orange.

Just one cup of dandelion greens contains 9 percent of your recommended daily value of calcium, 1.7 mg of iron, 2 grams of protein, 40 percent of your recommended daily value of vitamin A, and 26 percent of your recommended daily value of vitamin C.

INGREDIENTS

1 peach, pitted

1 pear, cored

Seeds scraped from 1/2 vanilla
bean or 1/4 teaspoon pure
vanilla extract (alcohol-free)

1 cup dandelion greens, chopped

4 ounces homemade almond milk
(page 64)

NUTRITION INFO

*Calories: 202 • Fat: 1g • Protein: 4g
Carbs: 46g • Calcium: 11%
Iron: 2.4mg • Vitamin A: 44%
Vitamin C: 49%*

PEAR-GRAPE SMOOTHIE

I didn't add a lot of water to this smoothie as the grapes are already water-rich. Adding water would have made this smoothie too thin and watery.

Grapes are a great source of antioxidants (resveratrol), vitamin K, and fiber. They help to mask the bitterness of kale.

INGREDIENTS

1 Bartlett pear, cored

1/2 cup red grapes

2 cups fresh curly kale, chopped

2 to 4 ounces filtered water

NUTRITION INFO

Calories: 229 • Fat: 2g • Protein: 7g
Carbs: 52g • Calcium: 19%
Iron: 2.6mg • Vitamin A: 96%
Vitamin C: 228%

NECTARINE-GOJI BERRY SMOOTHIE

Collards are a delicious and hardy green that you can grow in a garden pretty easily. One large leaf is about one cup. I remove the stem, as it helps to cut the bitterness a little. The stem can also be hard to blend for some blenders.

Nectarines and goji berries complement each other nicely in this smoothie. Nectarines are a great source of vitamins C and E, as well as potassium and fiber. Goji berries are also a great source of vitamin C and fiber, as well as protein.

INGREDIENTS

1/2 mango, peeled and pitted

1 nectarine, pitted

2 tablespoons goji berries, soaked
    for 5 minutes

1 cup collard leaves, chopped

1 cup fresh baby spinach

4 ounces filtered water

NUTRITION INFO

Calories: 205 • Fat: 1g • Protein: 7g
Carbs: 47g • Calcium: 13%
Iron: 2.5mg • Vitamin A: 196%
Vitamin C: 107%

CUCUMBER-ALOE SMOOTHIE

Aloe doesn't offer a lot of flavor to this smoothie. Its mild flavor is easily masked, but it offers a lot of health benefits. Aloe is great for your digestive tract.

If you buy organic kiwifruit, cut off the ends but leave the peel on. In the peel are extra antioxidants and fiber. Kiwifruit are an excellent source of vitamins C and K. The tiny black seeds contain omega-3 fatty acids.

INGREDIENTS

1 1/2 cups cucumber with peel, sliced

2 large kiwifruit, ends removed

2 cups fresh baby spinach

1/2 cup fresh aloe vera gel

1 banana, peeled

8 ounces filtered water

NUTRITION INFO

Calories: 226 • Fat: 2g • Protein: 6g Carbs: 55g • Calcium: 11% Iron: 2.8mg • Vitamin A: 43% Vitamin C: 213%

GINGER-SPINACH SMOOTHIE

Ginger is great for calming the stomach and giving smoothies a warming feeling. It complements the mango nicely and adds a lot of flavor to this smoothie without a lot of additional calories.

INGREDIENTS

1 teaspoon grated ginger

1/2 banana, peeled

1 cup mango, peeled and pitted

1/2 cucumber with peel, sliced

2 cups fresh baby spinach

8 ounces homemade almond milk (page 64)

NUTRITION INFO

Calories: 227 • Fat: 1g • Protein: 6g Carbs: 47g • Calcium: 9% Iron: 2.5mg • Vitamin A: 54% Vitamin C: 115%

CHAPTER TWELVE

MOOD-ENHANCING GREEN SMOOTHIES

Strawberry-Banana Smoothie • 200

Cherry-Apple Smoothie • 200

Berry-Banana Smoothie • 201

Spiced Pineapple Smoothie • 201

Coconut-Vanilla-Peach Smoothie • 202

Maca-Cacao Smoothie • 202

Maca-Almond Smoothie • 203

Mango-Maca Smoothie • 203

Mesquite Cacao Smoothie • 204

Chocolate-Kale Smoothie • 204

We know that green smoothies are effective for weight loss and can boost energy levels. Because of this, many of my readers who have changed their lives with green smoothies are now running 5Ks and marathons or, at the very least, working out more than they ever have in their lives.

What does this have to do with elevating mood? Plenty!

Exercise has known mental health benefits, and it can have a powerful effect on depression and anxiety. Exercise releases "feel-good" chemicals in your brain—endorphins and neurotransmitters. Regular exercise can also facilitate weight loss and increase fitness, both of which may boost your confidence and energy levels, having a direct effect on your mood and outlook on life.

But boosting energy to exercise is not the only mood-enhancing benefit of green smoothies. The ingredients you use may also play a role in lifting your mood!

Mood-Enhancing Green Smoothie Foods

Dark leafy greens such as spinach, turnip greens, and romaine lettuce are high in folic acid, a nutrient that the National Institutes of Health (NIH) report as alleviating depression and reducing fatigue.[51]

Symptoms of vitamin C deficiency include low energy, depressed mood, and irritability. An increase in citrus fruits such as oranges and grapefruit, as well as vitamin C–rich goji berries, may give you a little extra pep in your step if you are low in this nutrient.

Omega-3 fatty acids are widely promoted as a key component of alternative treatments for depression. Particular emphasis has been placed on increasing marine-sourced EPA and DHA omega-3 fatty acids, but plant-based ALA omega-3 fatty acids found in flaxseeds, chia seeds, and other plant foods may also provide a benefit to those suffering from mild to moderate depression. Your body also converts some ALA omega-3 fatty acids into EPA and DHA.[52]

Studies in mice have also shown that flaxseed oil provides anti-anxiety benefits in mice. While the anti-anxiety benefit of flaxseed oil has not been studied extensively in humans, it doesn't hurt to add nutritious flaxseeds to your green smoothies.[53]

Cacao is a mood enhancer. Both anandamide (a.k.a. "The Bliss Chemical") and phenylethylamine (a.k.a. "The Love Chemical") are found abundantly in raw chocolate. The theobromine in chocolate is a mild stimulant, similar to caffeine, and it can give a temporary boost of energy. While cacao may temporarily alleviate low mood or mild depressive symptoms, it can potentially exacerbate anxiety. If you are sensitive to caffeine, it is best to avoid or limit your use of cacao.

Maca root powder is another ingredient that I recommend for mood-boosting smoothies. Maca root can provide a boost of energy without the crash that other stimulants like caffeine and cacao may produce in some people. Maca also has the added benefit of boosting libido.

Magnesium deficiency has been implicated as a potential cause for mood disorders, including anxiety and depression.[54] A diet that includes a lot of processed foods can be lower in magnesium than a whole foods diet. For example, whole-grain bread has significantly more magnesium than white bread. Leafy greens are also abundant in magnesium, and just two cups of kale in a green smoothie provide 46 mg of magnesium.

Tryptophan is an essential amino acid found in many fruits and vegetables. It plays an important role in the synthesis of serotonin, which is a neurotransmitter that helps regulate mood and sleep patterns. Just two cups of spinach contain up to 312 mg of tryptophan.

About These Recipes

The green smoothie recipes in this section include the mood-enhancing foods discussed in the previous paragraphs. Special focus was given to foods highest in mood-supporting nutrients (vitamin C, folic acid, omega 3s, magnesium, tryptophan), as well as foods that may temporarily boost mood and energy levels, such as cacao and maca root powder.

STRAWBERRY-BANANA SMOOTHIE

This smoothie is a great source of protein for only 149 calories. Most of that protein comes from the chard. While chard has a fairly strong flavor, it is also loaded with nutrients such as protein, fiber, calcium, and iron.

To help sweeten the chard, I also added strawberry and banana to this smoothie. Make sure to use very ripe fruits or the smoothie might be too bitter.

The maca root powder in this smoothie helps boost energy levels, which may also boost mood.

INGREDIENTS

1 banana, peeled
8 medium strawberries
1/2 teaspoon maca powder
2 cups chard, chopped
4 to 6 ounces filtered water

NUTRITION INFO

Calories: 149 • Fat: 1g • Protein: 3g
Carbs: 37g • Calcium: 6%
Iron: 2mg • Vitamin A: 32%
Vitamin C: 118%

CHERRY-APPLE SMOOTHIE

Apples are a great source of fiber, vitamin C, and antioxidants. Most of the antioxidants are in the peel, so I would recommend using organic apples that you don't need to peel.

Cherries are also a great source of antioxidants, vitamin C, potassium, magnesium, iron, folate, and fiber. Frozen cherries will help make this smoothie cold; however, you can also use fresh cherries and add ice, if you prefer.

INGREDIENTS

1 cup pitted cherries (fresh or frozen)
1 apple, cored
Seeds scraped from 1 vanilla bean or 1/2 teaspoon pure vanilla extract (alcohol-free)
2 cups fresh baby spinach
4 to 6 ounces filtered water

NUTRITION INFO

Calories: 205 • Fat: 1g • Protein: 4g
Carbs: 52g • Calcium: 9%
Iron: 2.4mg • Vitamin A: 42%
Vitamin C: 48%

BERRY-BANANA SMOOTHIE

The flavor will change slightly depending on whether you use fresh or frozen blueberries (fresh has a stronger blueberry taste).

Frozen wild blueberries are higher in zinc than their cultivated counterparts, but both fresh and frozen blueberries are loaded with antioxidants, manganese, dietary fiber, and vitamins B6, C, and K.

INGREDIENTS

8 medium strawberries

1/2 cup blueberries (fresh or frozen)

1 banana, peeled

3 chard leaves

6 ounces homemade almond milk (page 64)

NUTRITION INFO

*Calories: 232 • Fat: 1g • Protein: 6g
Carbs: 50g • Calcium: 8%
Iron: 3.5mg • Vitamin A: 64%
Vitamin C: 156%*

SPICED PINEAPPLE SMOOTHIE

The spice in this smoothie comes from the cooled chai tea. I've made this smoothie several times for myself and my friends, and everyone loves it. I have often called it "heaven in a glass."

INGREDIENTS

1 cup cubed pineapple

1 frozen banana, peeled and sliced

1/2 teaspoon grated ginger

2 cups fresh baby spinach

6 ounces chai tea, brewed and cooled

NUTRITION INFO

*Calories: 201 • Fat: 1g • Protein: 4g
Carbs: 50g • Calcium: 7%
Iron: 2.4mg • Vitamin A: 41%
Vitamin C: 141%*

COCONUT-VANILLA-PEACH SMOOTHIE

Two cups of spinach contain 5 percent of your recommended daily value of calcium, 1.6 mg of iron, 40 percent of your recommended daily value of vitamin A, and 2 grams of protein.

Spinach also contains selenium, zinc, phosphorus, potassium, copper, omega-3 fatty acids, and vitamins B1, B2, B3, B6, and E.

INGREDIENTS

1 peach, pitted

1/2 frozen banana, thawed slightly
    and peeled

Seeds scraped from 1/2 vanilla
    bean or 1/4 teaspoon pure
    vanilla extract (alcohol-free)

2 cups fresh baby spinach

4 ounces unsweetened coconut milk

NUTRITION INFO

Calories: 149 • Fat: 3g • Protein: 4g
Carbs: 31g • Calcium: 10%
Iron: 2.5mg • Vitamin A: 55%
Vitamin C: 43%

MACA-CACAO SMOOTHIE

Both maca and cacao are natural mood enhancers. Cacao is a stimulant, so if you are sensitive to caffeine, I would omit it from this recipe and instead use carob powder, which has a chocolate-like flavor.

Goji berries, blueberries, and cacao powder are all loaded with antioxidants, so they're not only delicious but nutritious as well!

INGREDIENTS

2 tablespoons goji berries, soaked
    for 5 minutes

1 tablespoon cacao powder

1 tablespoon maca powder

1/2 cup frozen blueberries

1 banana, peeled

1/2 head butterhead lettuce, torn

6 ounces homemade almond milk
    (page 64)

NUTRITION INFO

Calories: 261 • Fat: 1g • Protein: 7g
Carbs: 54g • Calcium: 6%
Iron: 3.3mg • Vitamin A: 170%
Vitamin C: 27%

MACA-ALMOND SMOOTHIE

I added almond butter to this recipe to give it a creamier texture as well as extra protein and a little healthy fat. One tablespoon of almond butter contains almost 4 grams of protein.

Since the almond butter is higher in calories, I flavored this smoothie with maca, cinnamon, and vanilla rather than more sweet fruits since they add almost no additional calories.

INGREDIENTS

1 frozen banana, peeled
1 tablespoon almond butter
1/2 tablespoon maca powder
1 teaspoon ground cinnamon
Seeds scraped from 1 vanilla bean
    or 1/2 teaspoon pure vanilla
    extract (alcohol-free)
2 collard leaves, stems removed
8 ounces homemade almond milk
    (page 64)

NUTRITION INFO

*Calories: 241 • Fat: 9g • Protein: 7g
Carbs: 32g • Calcium: 11%
Iron: 1.2mg • Vitamin A: 13%
Vitamin C: 31%*

MANGO-MACA SMOOTHIE

I added a half of a banana and a half of a mango since they complement each other and neither flavor will dominate the smoothie. I wanted to make sure you could taste the strawberries.

Strawberries are high in vitamin C, antioxidants, and manganese. They are also good sources of potassium, folate, riboflavin, vitamin B5, vitamin B6, vitamin K, omega-3 fatty acids, magnesium, and copper.

INGREDIENTS

1/2 mango, peeled and pitted
1/2 banana, peeled
8 large strawberries
2 cups escarole lettuce, torn
1/2 tablespoon maca powder
8 ounces homemade almond milk
    (page 64)

NUTRITION INFO

*Calories: 210 • Fat: 1g • Protein: 5g
Carbs: 50g • Calcium: 11%
Iron: 2.4mg • Vitamin A: 129%
Vitamin C: 193%*

MESQUITE CACAO SMOOTHIE

Mesquite powder and cacao powder complement each other nicely in a smoothie. Mesquite powder has a molasses-like flavor with a hint of caramel, while cacao lends a bitter dark chocolate flavor.

Chia seeds are a great source of protein and omega-3 fatty acids. They have a slightly nutty flavor that pairs well with the mesquite and cacao.

INGREDIENTS

1 large pear, cored
1 tablespoon cacao powder
1 tablespoon mesquite powder
1 tablespoon chia seeds, soaked
    for 5 minutes
2 cups fresh baby spinach
6 ounces unsweetened coconut
    milk

NUTRITION INFO

*Calories: 224 • Fat: 6g • Protein: 5g
Carbs: 44g • Calcium: 15%
Iron: 3.5mg • Vitamin A: 56%
Vitamin C: 36%*

CHOCOLATE-KALE SMOOTHIE

Cacao powder and kale are both great sources of iron. However, they are both bitter on their own, so I added a banana to help offset some of the bitter flavor.

Bananas are an excellent source of potassium and fiber. They are a good source of vitamins B6, C, and antioxidants.

INGREDIENTS

1 frozen banana, peeled and sliced
1 tablespoon chia seeds, soaked
    for 5 minutes
1 cup fresh curly kale, chopped
1 tablespoon cacao powder
8 ounces homemade almond milk
    (page 64)

NUTRITION INFO

*Calories: 217 • Fat: 3g • Protein: 7g
Carbs: 38g • Calcium: 11%
Iron: 2.2mg • Vitamin A: 48%
Vitamin C: 121%*

Notes

[1] Bingham, S., Day, N., Luben, R., Ferrari, P., Silmani, N., Norat, T., et al. "Dietary Fibre in Food and Protection against Colorectal Cancer in the European Prospective Investigation into Cancer and Nutrition (EPIC): An Observational Study." *The Lancet*, 361 (May 2003): 1496–1501. http://igitur-archive.library.uu.nl/med/2006 -0803-200520/Peeters_03_Dietaryfibreinfoodandprotectionagainstcolorectalcancer .pdf.

[2] Ou, S., Kwok, K., Li, Y., and Fu, L. "In Vitro Study of Possible Role of Dietary Fiber in Lowering Postprandial Serum Glucose." *Journal of Agricultural and Food Chemistry*, 49, no. 2 (February 2001): 1026–1029, doi:10.1021/jf000574n.

[3] Gu, Y., Nieves, J. W., Stern, Y., Luchsinger, J. A., and Scarmeas, N. "Food Combination and Alzheimer Disease Risk." *Archives of Neurology*, 67, no. 6 (June 2010): 699–706, doi:10.1001/archneurol.2010.84.

[4] Hosseinpour-Niazi, S., Mirmiran, P., Sohrab, G., Hosseini-Esfahani, F., and Azizi, F. "Inverse Association between Fruit, Legume, and Cereal Fiber and the Risk of Metabolic Syndrome: Tehran Lipid and Glucose Study." *Diabetes Research and Clinical Practice* (August 2011), doi:10.1016/j.diabres.2011.07.020.

[5] Bazzano, L., Li, T., Joshipura, K., and Hu, F. "Intake of Fruit, Vegetables, and Fruit Juices and Risk of Diabetes in Women." *Diabetes Care*, 31, no. 7 (July 2008): 1311–1317, doi:10.2337/dc08-0080.

[6] Carter, P., Gray, L., Troughton, J., Khunti, K., and Davies, M. "Fruit and Vegetable Intake and Incidence of Type 2 Diabetes Mellitus: Systematic Review and Meta-Analysis." *British Medical Journal*, 341 (2010): c4229, doi:10.1136/bmj.c4229.

[7] Schulze, M., Schulz, M., Heidemann, C., Schienkiewitz, A., Hoffmann, K., and Boeing, H. "Fiber and Magnesium Intake and Incidence of Type 2 Diabetes." *Archives of Internal Medicine*, 167, no. 9 (May 2007): 956–965. http://www.ncbi.nlm.nih.gov/pubmed/17502538.

[8] Zunino, S. "Type 2 Diabetes and Glycemic Response to Grapes or Grape Products." *Journal of Nutrition*, 139, no. 9 (September 2009): 17945–18005, doi:10.3945/jn.109.107631.

[9] Harding, A., Wareham, N., Bringham, S., Khaw, K., Luben, R., Welch, A., et al. "Plasma Vitamin C Level, Fruit and Vegetable Consumption, and the Risk of New-Onset Type 2 Diabetes Mellitus." *Archives of Internal Medicine*, 168, no. 14 (July 2008): 1493–1499. http://www.ncbi.nlm.nih.gov/pubmed/18663161.

[10] Appel, L., Moore, T., Obarzanek, E., Vollmer, W., Svetkey, L., Sacks, F., et al. "A Clinical Trial of the Effects of Dietary Patterns on Blood Pressure." *New England Journal of Medicine*, 336 (April 1997): 1117–1124. http://www.nejm.org/doi/full/10.1056/NEJM199704173361601.

[11] John, J., Ziebland, S., Yudkin, P., Roe, L., and Neil, H. "Effects of Fruit and Vegetable Consumption on Plasma Antioxidant Concentrations and Blood Pressure: A Randomised Controlled Trial." *The Lancet*, 359, no. 9322 (June 2002): 1969–1974, doi:10.1016/S0140-6736(02)98858-6.

[12] Jenkins, D., Nguyen, T., Kendall, C., Faulkner, D., Bashyam, B., Kim, I., et al. "The Effect of Strawberries in a Cholesterol-Lowering Dietary Portfolio." *Metabolism*, 57, no. 12 (December 2008): 1636–1644. doi:10.1016/j.metabol.2008.07.018.

[13] Hansen, L., Vehof, H., Dragsted, O., Olsen, A., Christensen, J., Overvad, K., et al. "Fruit and Vegetable Intake and Serum Cholesterol Levels: A Cross-Sectional Study in the Diet, Cancer and Health Cohort." *Journal of Horticultural Science & Biotechnology*, Special Issue (2009), 42–46. http://www.jhortscib.com/isafruit/isa_pp042_046.pdf.

[14] Mink, P., Scrafford, C., Barraj, L., Harnack, L., Hong, C., Nettleton, J., and Jacobs, D. Jr. "Flavonoid Intake and Cardiovascular Disease Mortality: A Prospective Study in Postmenopausal Women." *American Journal of Clinical Nutrition*, 85, no. 3 (March 2007): 895–909. http://www.ajcn.org/content/85/3/895.short.

[15] Tabak, C., Smit, H. A., Heederik, D., Ocke, M. C., and Kromhout, D. "Diet and Chronic Obstructive Pulmonary Disease: Independent Beneficial Effects of Fruits, Whole Grains, and Alcohol (the MORGEN Study)." *Clinical & Experimental Allergy*, 31, no. 5 (2001): 747–755, doi:10.1046/j.1365-2222.2001.01064.x.

[16] Tabak, C., Smit, H. A., Heederik, D., Ocke, M. C., and Kromhout, D. "Chronic Obstructive Pulmonary Disease and Intake of Catechins, Flavonols, and Flavones."

American Journal of Respiratory and Critical Care Medicine, 164, no. 1 (2001): 61–64, doi:10.1136/thx.2006.069419.

[17] Hirayama, F., Lee, A. H., Binns, C. W., Zhao, Y., Hiramatsu, T., Tanikawa, Y., Nishimura, K., and Taniguchi, H. "Do Vegetables and Fruits Reduce the Risk of Chronic Obstructive Pulmonary Disease? A Case-Control Study in Japan." *Preventative Medicine*, 49, no. 2–3 (2009): 184–189, doi:10.1016/j.ypmed.2009.06.010.

[18] Jacka, F. N., Pasco, J. A., Mykletun, A., Williams, L. J., Hodge, A. M., O'Reilly, S. L., et al. "Association of Western and Traditional Diets with Depression and Anxiety in Women." *American Journal of Psychiatry*, 167 (January 2010): 305–311, doi:10.1176/appi.ajp.2009.09060881.

[19] Akbaraly, T., Brunner, E., Ferrie, J., Marmot, M., Kivimaki, M., and Singh-Manoux, A. "Dietary Pattern and Depressive Symptoms in Middle Age." *British Journal of Psychiatry*, 195, no. 5 (November 2009): 408–419. http://www.ncbi.nlm.nih.gov/pubmed/19880930?dopt=Abstract.

[20] Gao, X., Chen, H., Fung, T., Logroscino, G., Schwarzschild, M., Hu, F., and Ascherio, A. "Prospective Study of Dietary Pattern and Risk of Parkinson Disease." *American Journal of Clinical Nutrition*, 86, no. 5 (November 2007): 1486–1494. http://www.ajcn.org/content/86/5/1486.short.

[21] He, F., Nowson, C., and MacGregor, G. "Fruit and Vegetable Consumption and Stroke: Meta-Analysis of Cohort Studies." *The Lancet*, 367, no. 9507 (2006): 320–326, doi:10.1016/S0140-6736(06)68069-0.

[22] Griep, L., Verschuren, M., Kromhout, D., Ocke, M., and Geleijnse, J. "Colors of Fruit and Vegetables and 10-Year Incidence of Stroke." *Stroke AHA*, Published online before print (September 2011), doi:10.1161/STROKEAHA.110.611152.

[23] Shwu-Jiuan Sheu, Ni-Chun Liu, and Jiunn-Liang Chen. "Resveratrol Protects Human Retinal Pigment Epithelial Cells from Acrolein-Induced Damage." *Journal of Ocular Pharmacology and Therapeutics*, 26, no. 3 (June 2010): 231–236, doi:10.1089/jop.2009.0137.

[24] "Nutrition to Reduce Cancer Risk." Stanford Medicine Cancer Institute (2011). http://cancer.stanford.edu/information/nutritionAndCancer/reduceRisk/.

[25] Deneo-Pellegrini, H., De Stefani, E., and Ronco, A. "Vegetables, Fruits, and Risk of Colorectal Cancer: A Case-Control Study from Uruguay." *Nutrition and Cancer*, 25, no. 3 (1996): 297–304. http://www.ncbi.nlm.nih.gov/pubmed/8771572.

[26] Zhang, C., Ho, S., Chen, Y., Fu, J., Cheng, S., and Lin, F. "Greater Vegetable and Fruit Intake Is Associated with a Lower Risk of Breast Cancer among Chinese Women." *International Journal of Cancer*, 125, no. 1 (July 2009): 181–188. http://www.ncbi.nlm.nih.gov/pubmed/19358284.

[27] Rashidkhani, B., Lindblad, P., and Wolk, A. "Fruits, Vegetables and Risk of Renal Cell Carcinoma: A Prospective Study of Swedish Women." *International Journal of Cancer*, 113, no. 3 (January 2005): 451–455. http://www.ncbi.nlm.nih.gov/pubmed/15455348.

[28] Gerhauser, C. "Cancer Chemopreventive Potential of Apples, Apple Juice, and Apple Components." *Planta Medica*, 74, no. 13 (2008): 1608–1624, doi:10.1055/s-0028-1088300.

[29] Keck, A. and Finley, J. "Cruciferous Vegetables: Cancer Protective Mechanisms of Glucosinolate Hydrolysis Products and Selenium." *Integrative Cancer Therapies*, 3, no. 1 (March 2004): 5–12, doi:10.1177/1534735403261831.

[30] "Laboratory and Clinical Studies of Cancer Chemoprevention by Antioxidants in Berries." *Carcinogenesis*, 29, no. 9 (2008): 1665–1674, doi:10.1093/carcin/bgn142.

[31] Adhami, V., Khan, N., and Mukhtar, H. "Cancer Chemoprevention by Pomegranate: Laboratory and Clinical Evidence." *Nutrition and Cancer*, 61, no. 6 (November 2009): 811–815, doi:10.1080/01635580903285064.

[32] Lansky, E., and Newman, R. (2007, January). "Punica Granatum (Pomegranate) and Its Potential for Prevention and Treatment of Inflammation and Cancer." *Journal of Ethnopharmacology*, 109(2), 177–206. doi:10.1016/j.jep.2006.09.006. Retrieved from http://www.sciencedirect.com/science/article/pii/S0378874106004570.

[33] Malik, A., Afaq, F., Sarfaraz, S., Adhami, V., Syed, D., and Mukhtar, H. "Pomegranate Fruit Juice for Chemoprevention and Chemotherapy of Prostate Cancer." *PNAS*, 102, no. 41 (October 2005): 14813–14818, doi:10.1073/pnas.0505870102.

[34] Duke University Medical Center. "Flaxseed Stunts the Growth of Prostate Tumors." *ScienceDaily*, June 4, 2007. http://www.sciencedaily.com/releases/2007/06/070603215443.htm.

[35] Roberts, R., Green, J., and Lewis, B. "Lutein and Zeaxanthin in Eye and Skin Health." *Clinics in Dermatology*, 27, no. 2 (March–April 2009): 195–201, doi:10.1016/j.clindermatol.2008.01.011.

[36] Afaq, F. and Mukhtar, H. "Botanical Antioxidants for Skin Protection: An Overview." *Nutrition For Healthy Skin*, Part 2 (2011), 51–63, doi:10.1007/978-3-642-12264-4_5.

[37] "The Oxalate Content of Food." Oxalosis & Hyperoxaluria Foundation (OHF). http://www.ohf.org/docs/Oxalate2008.pdf.

[38] Pornsak Sriamornsak. "Chemistry of Pectin and Its Pharmaceutical Uses: A Review." *Silpakorn University International Journal*, 3, no. 1–2 (2003): 206.

[39] Engelhart, M., Geerlings, M., Ruitenberg, A., Swieten, J., et al. "Dietary Intake of Antioxidants and Risk of Alzheimer Disease Lipids in Healthy Human Volunteers." *Journal of the American Medical Association*, 287, no. 24 (2002), 3223–3229, doi:10.1001/jama.287.24.3223.

[40] Pae C.-U., Paik I.-H., Lee C., Lee S.-J., Kim J.-J., and Lee C.-U. "Decreased Plasma Antioxidants in Schizophrenia." *Korea Neuropsychobiology* 2004, no. 50: 54–56, doi:10.1159/000077942.

[41] Willcox, J., Ash, S., and Catignan, G. "Antioxidants and Prevention of Chronic Disease." *Critical Reviews in Food Science and Nutrition*, 44, no. 4 (2004): 275–295, doi:10.1080/10408690490468489.

[42] Johansen, J., Harris, A., Rychly, D., and Ergul, A. "Oxidative Stress and the Use of Antioxidants in Diabetes: Linking Basic Science to Clinical Practice." *Cardiovascular Diabetology*, 4, no. 5 (2005), doi:10.1186/1475-2840-4-5.

[43] Boeing, H., Bechthold, A., Bub, A., Ellinger, S., Haller, D., et al. "Critical Review: Vegetables and Fruit in the Prevention of Chronic Diseases." *European Journal of Nutrition*, 51, no. 6 (2012): 637–663, doi:10.1007/s00394-012-0380-y.

[44] Ibid.

[45] Guarner, F. "Gut Flora in Health and Disease." *The Lancet*, 361, no. 9356 (2003): 512–519. http://www.sciencedirect.com/science/article/pii/S0140673603124890.

[46] Li, F., Hullar, M., Schwarz, Y., and Lampe, J. "Human Gut Bacterial Communities Are Altered by Addition of Cruciferous Vegetables to a Controlled Fruit- and Vegetable-Free Diet." *The Journal of Nutrition*, 139, no. 9 (2009): 1685–1691, doi:10.3945/jn.109.108191.

[47] Claesson, M., Jeffery, I., Conde, S., Power, S., O'Connor, E., Cusack, S., et al. "Gut Microbiota Composition Correlates with Diet and Health in the Elderly." *Nature*, 488 (2012): 178–184. doi:10.1038/nature11319.

[48] Mink, P., Scrafford, C., Barraj, L., Harnack, L., Hong, C., Nettleton, J., and Jacobs, D. Jr. "Flavonoid Intake and Cardiovascular Disease Mortality: A Prospective Study in Postmenopausal Women." *American Journal of Clinical Nutrition*, 85, no. 3 (March 2007): 895–909. http://www.ajcn.org/content/85/3/895.short.

[49] Shankar, S., Singh, G., and Srivastava, R. "Chemoprevention by Resveratrol: Molecular Mechanisms and Therapeutic Potential." *Frontiers in Bioscience*, 12 (September 2007): 4839–4854. http://www.ncbi.nlm.nih.gov/pubmed/17569614.

[50] Duttaroy, A. and Jorgensen, A. "Effects of Kiwi Fruit Consumption on Platelet Aggregation and Plasma Lipids in Healthy Human Volunteers." *Platelets*, 15, no. 5 (August 2004): 287–292. http://www.ncbi.nlm.nih.gov/pubmed/15370099.

[51] "Folate: Dietary Supplement Fact Sheet." National Institutes of Health, Office of Dietary Supplements. http://ods.od.nih.gov/factsheets/Folate-HealthProfessional/.

[52] Blondeau, N., Nguemeni, C., Debruyne, D. N., Piens, M., Wu, X., Pan, H., Hu, X., Gandin, C., Lipsky, R. H., Plumier, J. C., Marini, A. M., and Heurteaux, C. "Subchronic Alpha-Linolenic Acid Treatment Enhances Brain Plasticity and Exerts an Antidepressive Effect: A Versatile Potential Therapy for Stroke." *Neuropsychopharmacology*, 34, no. 12 (November 2009): 2548–2559, doi:10.1038/npp.2009.84.

[53] Nain Parminder, et al. "Evaluation and Comparison of Anxiolytic Effect of Flaxseed Oil and Perilla Oil in Mice." *International Research Journal of Pharmacy*, 2, no. 4 (2011): 161–164. http://www.irjponline.com/admin/php/uploads/vol2/issue4/30.pdf.

[54] Eby, G., and Eby, K. "Rapid Recovery from Major Depression Using Magnesium Treatment." *Medical Hypotheses*, 67, no. 2 (2006): 362–370, doi:10.1016/j.mehy.2006.01.047.

Index

A

A Vitamins
  in Apricots, 42
  in Arugula, 51
  in Beet Greens, 51
  in Bell Peppers, 56
  in Broccoli, 56
  in Carrots, 57
  in Collard Greens, 52
  in Goji Berries, 59
  in Grapefruit, 48–49
  in Guavas, 45
  in Mangoes, 39
  in Melons, 49
  in Papaya, 40
  in Passion Fruits, 46
  in Peaches, 40
  in Plums, 47
  in Pumpkin, 40–41
  in Sapote, 41
  in Spinach, 55
  in Sweet Potatoes, 41
  in Swiss Chard, 55–56
  in Tangerines/Clementines, 50
  in Tomatoes, 58
  in Turnip Greens, 56
  in Watermelon, 50
  in Zucchini/Yellow Squash, 58
Açaí Berries, 41–42
Acerola, 42
Allergies, 19
Almond Milk, 63–64
Aloe Vera, 51
Alzheimers Disease, 7
American Diabetes Association, 15
Antioxidants, 6, 7, 10
  in Avocadoes, 38
  in Cherries, 43–44
  in Chocolate, 58
  in Goji Berries, 59
  in Passion Fruits, 46
Anxiety, 7
Apples, 24, 25, 32, 38
Apricots, 42

Arginine, 50
Art of Smoothie Making, 22–28
Arugula, 51
Asthma, 51
Avocadoes, 24, 30, 32, 38

B

B Vitamins
  in Avocadoes, 38
  in Bananas, 38–39
  in Cherimoyas, 43
  in Collard Greens, 52
  in Dandelion Greens, 52
  in Durian, 39
  in Figs, 39
  in Grapes, 49
  in Guavas, 45
  in Jackfruits, 45
  in Kale, 53
  in Lambsquarters, 53
  in Mangoes, 39
  in Melons, 49
  in Oranges, 50
  in Papaya, 40
  in Pineapple, 47
  in Pomegranates, 47–48
  in Pumpkin, 40–41
  in Sapote, 41
  in Spinach, 55
  in Spirulina, 61
  in Strawberries, 48
  in Sweet Potatoes, 41
  in Tomatoes, 58
  in Turnip Greens, 56
  in Zucchini/Yellow Squash, 58
Bananas, 24, 25, 32, 38–39
Base Fruits, 24, 27, 38–41, 69
Beet Greens, 51
Bell Peppers, 56
Beta-Carotene, 38
Bitter Flavors, 29
Blackberries, 42
Blenders, 20–21
Blendtec Blenders, 20–21

Blood Pressure, 7
Blood Thinners, 14–15
Blueberries, 25, 42–43
Bok Choy (Pak Choi/Chinese Spinach),
  51–52
Broccoli, 56
Bromelain, 47
Butterhead Lettuce, 53–54

C

C Vitamins
  in Acerolas, 42
  in Avocadoes, 38
  in Bell Peppers, 56
  in Blackberries, 42
  in Broccoli, 56
  in Cabbage, 52
  in Cactus Pears, 43
  in Collard Greens, 52
  in Durian, 39
  in Grapefruit, 48–49
  in Guavas, 45
  in Kiwifruit, 46
  in Lambsquarters, 53
  in Lemons/Limes, 49
  in Lychee, 46
  in Mangoes, 39
  in Melons, 49
  in Oranges, 50
  in Papaya, 40
  in Passion Fruits, 46
  in Peaches, 40
  in Pears, 40
  in Persimmons, 46–47
  in Pineapple, 47
  in Plums, 47
  in Raspberries, 48
  in Spirulina, 61
  in Strawberries, 48
  in Sweet Potatoes, 41
  in Tangerines/Clementines, 50
  in Watermelon, 50
  in Zucchini/Yellow Squash, 58
Cabbage, 52

Cactus (Nopal), 54
Cactus Pears, 43
Calcium
  in Bok Choy, 51
  in Cactus Pears, 43
  in Celery, 57
  in Coconut, 44
  in Dandelion Greens, 52
  in Figs, 39
  in Kale, 53
  in Lettuce, 54
  in Nopal (Cactus), 54
  in Oranges, 50
  in Radish Greens, 55
  in Sesame Seeds, 62
  in Sweet Potatoes, 41
  in Turnip Greens, 56
Calorie Counting, 22
Cancer, 7
Carbohydrates, 8, 10–11
Carotenoids, 57
Carrots, 57
Cauliflower, 56
Celery, 57
Chard, 33
Cherimoyas, 43
Cherries, 43–44
Chia Seeds, 61
Chocolate (Raw Cacao), 58–59
Chronic Health Conditions, 7
Cilantro (Coriander), 52
Cinnamon, 62
Cleansing Your Body, 7
Clove, 63
Coconut, 44
Coconut Butter, 66
Coconut Meat, 24
Coconut Milk, 64
Coconut Oil, 66
Coconut Water, 23, 64
Coffee, 64
Collard Greens, 33, 52
Colon Cancer, 7

Combining Foods, 11–12
Compost Bins, 22
COPD, 7
Copper
  in Bananas, 38–39
  in Blackberries, 42
  in Durian, 39
  in Flax Seeds, 62
  in Guavas, 45
  in Jackfruits, 45
  in Kiwifruit, 46
  in Lambsquarters, 53
  in Pears, 40
  in Pineapple, 47
  in Pumpkin, 40–41
  in Sweet Potatoes, 41
  in Turnip Greens, 56
Cranberries, 44
CRON-o-Meter, 22
Cruciferous Vegetables, 14, 26
Cucumbers, 57
Cupuacus, 44–45
Cutting Boards, 21

D
D Vitamins, in Spirulina, 61
Dandelion Greens, 33, 52–53
Depression, 7
Detoxification, 7, 52
Diabetes, 7, 15
Dieting, 8
Dill Weed, 53, 63
Disasters, Fixing, 28–30
Diseases, 7, 51
Durian, 24, 39

E
E Vitamins
  in Avocadoes, 38
  in Blackberries, 42
  in Dandelion Greens, 52
  in Kiwifruit, 46
  in Mangoes, 39

in Pomegranates, 47–48
in Pumpkin, 40–41
in Raspberries, 48
in Sapote, 41
in Spirulina, 61
in Sweet Potatoes, 41
in Turnip Greens, 56
Egg Protein Powder, 67
Elements of Natural Hygiene, 12
Energy, 8
Epic Protein, 68
Expenses, 70–72

F
Fats, 66
Fiber, 6, 7, 10, 13, 38
Figs, 39
Filtered Water, 23
Flavor Fruits, 48–50, 69
Flavor Mixing, 24–25, 27
Flaxseeds, 62
Food Allergies, 19
Food Servings, 6
Freezers, 31
Frozen Fruit, 28
Fructose, 11
Fruit Base, 24, 27
Fruit Juices, 23, 65
Fruit Markets, 72
Fruit Sugar, 15

G
Gardening, 71
Ginger, 63
Glass Straws, 21
Glucose, 8
GMOs, 73
Go-Anywhere Foods, 6
Goitrogenic Glucosinolates, 14, 26
Goji Berries, 59
Graham, Sylvester, 12
Grapefruit, 13, 23, 48–49
Grapes, 49

Green Leaf Lettuce, 54
Greens, 24, 25–27, 28, 32–33, 51–56
Guava, 45

H
Health Benefits, 7–8
Heart Disease, 7
Hemp Milk, 65
Hemp Protein Powder, 67
Hemp Seeds, 62
Hypothyroidism, 14

I
Ice, 28
Illness, 7
Incredible Smoothies (website), 7
Inflammatory Diseases, 51
Iron
   in Blackberries, 42
   in Bok Choy, 51
   in Cucumbers, 57
   in Dandelion Greens, 52
   in Figs, 39
   in Flax Seeds, 62
   in Kale, 53
   in Lambsquarters, 53
   in Lettuce, 54
   in Persimmons, 46–47
   in Pumpkin, 40–41
   in Spinach, 55
   in Strawberries, 48
   in Sweet Potatoes, 41

J
Jackfruit, 45
Jars, 21, 30
JTC OmniBlend V blender, 20–21
Juices, 23, 65

K
K Vitamins
   in Arugula, 51
   in Beet Greens, 51
   in Blackberries, 42

in Blueberries, 42–43
in Broccoli, 56
in Cabbage, 52
in Collard Greens, 52
in Cucumbers, 57
in Dandelion Greens, 52
in Grapes, 49
in Kale, 53
in Kiwifruit, 46
in Pomegranates, 47–48
in Raspberries, 48
in Spinach, 55
in Swiss Chard, 55–56
in Turnip Greens, 56
in Zucchini/Yellow Squash, 58
Kale, 33, 53
Kidney Stones, 14
Kiwifruit, 46
Knives, 21

L
Lambsquarters, 53
Leafy Greens, 14, 26–27
Lemons/Limes, 49
Lettuce, Butterhead, 53–54
Lettuce, Green and Red Leaf, 54
Lettuce, Romaine, 54
Liquid, 22–24
Liquids, 27, 63–65
Lutein, 38
Lychee, 46
Lycopene, 38

M
Maca, 60
Macular Degeneration, 7
Magnesium
in Bananas, 38–39
in Cactus Pears, 43
in Durian, 39
in Flax Seeds, 62
in Jackfruits, 45

in Nopal (Cactus), 54
in Sweet Potatoes, 41
Manganese
in Bananas, 38–39
in Blackberries, 42
in Durian, 39
in Flax Seeds, 62
in Nopal (Cactus), 54
in Pineapple, 47
in Sapote, 41
in Spinach, 55
in Strawberries, 48
in Sweet Potatoes, 41
in Turnip Greens, 56
Mangoes, 24, 25, 39
Mason Jars, 21, 30
Melons (Canteloupe/Honey Dew), 49
Milks, 23–24
Minerals, 6, 10. *See also* specific minerals
Minneola/Tangelos, 49
Mint, 63

N
Natural Hygiene philosophy, 12
Nectarines, 40
Ninja Blenders, 20
Nopal (Cactus), 54
Nut Butters, 66
Nut Milk Bags, 21
Nutmeg, 63
Nutrition, 8

O
Oat Milk, 65
Omega-3 Fatty Acids, 10
in Açaí Berries, 42
in Cherimoyas, 43
in Chia Seeds, 61
in Flax Seeds, 62
in in Hemp Protein Powder, 67
in Hemp Seeds, 62
in Jackfruits, 45

in Mangoes, 39
in Raspberries, 48
in Spirulina, 61
Omega-6 Fatty Acids, 58
in in Hemp Protein Powder, 67
Oranges, 23, 25, 32, 50
Oregano, 63
Organic Food, 71–72
Oro Blancos, 13, 48–49
Oxalates, 14, 26
Oxygen Radical Absorbance Capacity
(ORAC) Value, 42

P
Papain, 40
Papaya, 24, 40
Parkinson's Disease, 7
Parsley, 55, 63
Passion Fruit, 46
Peaches, 24, 40
Pears, 24, 25, 40
Pectin, 38
Persimmon, 46–47
Phosphorus
in Flax Seeds, 62
in Pumpkin, 40–41
in Sweet Potatoes, 41
Phytochemicals, 58
Pineapple, 25, 47
Plant Oils, 66
Plant-Based Diets, 8
Plums, 24, 47
Pluots, 47
Pomegranates, 47–48, 69
Pomelos, 13, 48–49
Potassium
in Bananas, 38–39
in Durian, 39
in Guavas, 45
in Jackfruits, 45
in Pumpkin, 40–41
in Sapote, 41
in Sweet Potatoes, 41

Prescription Medications, 8, 49
Produce, Storing, 31–32
Protein, 10
Protein Powders, 66–68
Pumpkin, 40–41

R
Radish Greens, 55
Raspberries, 48
Red Leaf Lettuce, 54
Rheumatoid Arthritis, 51
Rice Milk, 65
Rice Protein Powder, 67
Romaine Lettuce, 54

S
Sales, 70–71
Sapote (Mamey, Sapodilla), 41
Sea Vegetables, 60
Seeds, 61–62
Selenium, in Flax Seeds, 62
Sesame Seeds, 62
Shelton, Herbert M., 12
Snacks, 6
Sodium
in Celery, 57
in Sea Vegetables, 60
in Swiss Chard, 55–56
Soy Milk, 65
Soy Protein Powder, 67–68
Spices, 62–63
Spinach, 14, 33, 55
Spirulina, 61
Sprouted Living, 68
Sprouted Protein Powder, 68
Sprouts, 57–58
Stamina, 8
Storage Solutions, 30–31, 31–32, 32–33
Strawberries, 24, 25, 48
Straws, Glass, 21
Strokes, 7
Substitutions, 68–69
Sugar, 8, 9–10, 15

Superfoods, 39, 48, 58–61, 71
Sweet Potatoes, 41
Sweeteners, 29
Swiss Chard, 55–56

T
Tangerines, 23
Tangerines/Clementines, 50
Tea, 65
Texture, 24
Theacrines, 45
Thickeners, 29–30
Thyroid Diseases, 14
Tomatoes, 58
Turnip Greens, 56

U
Ugli Fruit, 50
Unhealthy Meals, 6
Urinary Tract Infections, 44

V
Vanilla, 63
Vegetable Markets, 72

Vegetables, 6, 14, 26–27, 28, 56–58
Vitamins, 6, 10, 14–15. *See also* specific
    vitamins
Vitamix Blenders, 20–21

W
Warehouse Clubs, 70
Water, 23, 65
Watermelon, 50
Weight, 7, 8, 11
Whey Protein Powder, 68–69
Whole Foods, 8
Workout Routines, 8

Y
Yellow Squash, 58

Z
Zinc
    in Flax Seeds, 62
    in Pomegranates, 47–48
    in Sapote, 41
Zucchini, 58

Recipe Index

A

Açaí Puree
  in Blackberry-Açaí Green Smoothies, 121
  in Chocolate-Açaí Smoothies, 190
  in Plum-Açaí Smoothies, 118
  in Super Antioxidant Blast Green Smooth
    ies, 122
**Almond Butter, in Maca-Almond Smooth-
  ies,** 203
Almond Milk
  in Apple-Broccoli Smoothies, 105
  in Apple-Lime Green Smoothies, 130
  in Berry-Banana Smoothies, 201
  in Berry-Kale Smoothies, 132
  in Blackberry-Almond Smoothies, 176
  in Blackberry-Peach Smoothies, 120
  in Blueberry-Lemonade Smoothies, 87
  in Broccoli-Kale Smoothies, 191
  in Cherry-Plum Green Smoothies, 115
  in Cherry–Sweet Potato Smoothies, 147
  in Chocolate-Cherry Smoothies, 135
  in Chocolate-Grape-Strawberry Smooth-
    ies, 106
  in Chocolate-Kale Smoothies, 204
  in Chocolate-Mango Smoothies, 190
  in Chocolate-Raspberry Green Smooth-
    ies, 187
  in Creamy Chocolate and Vanilla Smooth-
    ies, 172
  in Frozen Raspberry-Lemonade Smooth-
    ies, 116
  in Ginger-Berry-Oat Smoothies, 134
  in Ginger-Carrot Smoothies, 150
  in Ginger-Spinach Smoothies, 194
  in Goji Berry–Maca Smoothies, 130
  in Grapefruit-Orange Smoothies, 90
  in Healthy Chocolate Smoothies, 104
  in Kale-Parsley Smoothies, 189
  in Maca-Almond Smoothies, 203
  in Maca-Cacao Smoothies, 202
  in Mango-Maca Smoothies, 203
  in Nectarine-Cherry Smoothies, 159

in Orange–Sesame Seed Smoothies, 166
in Peach-Mango Smoothies, 188
in Peach-Pear Smoothies, 192
in Peach-Strawberry Green Smoothies, 107
in Peanut Butter–Raspberry Smoothies, 137, 138
in Pineapple-Celery Green Smoothies, 91
in Pineapple-Ginger Smoothies, 151
in Pineapple-Mango Green Smoothies, 101
in Pineapple-Plum Smoothies with Almond Milk, 119
in Plum-Açaí Smoothies, 118
in Spiced Blueberry and Pear Smoothies, 104
in Strawberry-Avocado Smoothies, 175
in Sweet Potato Smoothies, 147
in Vanilla-Avocado Smoothies, 136
in Vanilla-Cantaloupe Smoothies, 146
in Zucchini-Vanilla Smoothies, 145
Aloe Vera Gel
in Banana-Pineapple Smoothies with Aloe and Kale, 109
in Cucumber-Aloe Smoothies, 194
in Pear-Aloe Smoothies, 164
Apple-Avocado Smoothie, 136
Apple-Broccoli Smoothie, 105
Apple-Cherimoya Smoothie, 108
Apple-Lime Green Smoothie, 130
Apple-Mango Green Smoothie, 92
Apples
in Apple-Avocado Smoothies, 136
in Apple-Broccoli Smoothies, 105
in Apple-Cherimoya Smoothies, 108
in Apple-Lime Green Smoothies, 130
in Apple-Mango Green Smoothies, 92
in Broccoli-Kale Smoothies, 191
in Cherry-Apple Smoothies, 200
in Coconut-Apple-Ginger Smoothies, 175
in Green Apple Smoothies, 87
in Green Goddess Detox Smoothies, 93
in Refreshing Apple Smoothies, 188
in The Veggie Green Smoothie, 186
Avocado-Berry Smoothie, 177

Avocadoes
in Apple-Avocado Smoothies, 136
in Avocado-Berry Smoothies, 177
in Avocado-Peach Green Smoothies, 174
in Creamy Chocolate and Vanilla Smoothies, 172
in Cucumber-Parsley Smoothies, 192
in Dandelion-Orange Smoothies, 90
in Mango-Avocado Smoothies, 133
in Parsley-Pear Smoothies, 191
in Raspberry-Avocado Smoothies, 177
in Strawberry-Avocado Smoothies, 175
in Strawberry-Raspberry Smoothies with Avocado, 166
in Vanilla-Avocado Smoothies, 136
Avocado-Peach Green Smoothie, 174

B
Banana-Cranberry Smoothie, 163
Banana-Orange Smoothie, 160
Banana-Pineapple Green Smoothie, 102
Banana-Pineapple Smoothie with Aloe and Kale, 109
Bananas
in Apple-Broccoli Smoothies, 105
in Apple-Cherimoya Smoothies, 108
in Apple-Lime Green Smoothies, 130
in Banana-Cranberry Smoothies, 163
in Banana-Orange Smoothies, 160
in Banana-Pineapple Green Smoothies, 102
in Banana-Pineapple Smoothies with Aloe and Kale, 109
in Berry-Banana Smoothies, 201
in Black and Blue Smoothies, 121
in Blackberry-Açaí Green Smoothies, 121
in Blackberry-Almond Smoothies, 176
in Blueberry-Flaxseed Smoothies, 178
in Blueberry-Lemonade Smoothies, 87
in Blueberry-Maca Smoothies, 133
in Blueberry-Oat Smoothies, 132
in Blueberry-Persimmon Green Smoothies, 116

in Broccoli-Kale Smoothies, 191

in Cantaloupe-Raspberry Green Smoothies, 174

in Carrot-Papaya Smoothies, 105

in Cherry-Banana Smoothies, 135

in Cherry-Pomegranate Smoothies, 119

in Chia Seed–Red Grape Smoothies, 176

in Chocolate-Kale Smoothies, 204

in Chocolate-Kiwifruit Smoothies, 109

in Chocolate–Peanut Butter Smoothies, 131

in Chocolate-Raspberry Green Smoothies, 187

in Coconut–Goji Berry Smoothies, 158

in Coconut-Grapefruit Smoothies, 161

in Coconut-Mango Green Smoothie with Lime, 107

in Coconut-Vanilla-Peach Smoothies, 202

in Creamy Chocolate and Vanilla Smoothies, 172

in Cucumber-Aloe Smoothies, 194

in Cucumber-Parsley Smoothies, 192

in Frozen Raspberry-Lemonade Smoothies, 116

in Ginger-Spinach Smoothies, 194

in Goji Berry Superfood Green Smoothies, 171

in Goji Berry–Maca Smoothies, 130

in Grapefruit-Orange Smoothies, 90

in The Green Machine, 91

in Happy Berry Muffin Smoothies, 146

in Healthy Chocolate Smoothies, 104

in Kiwifruit-Broccoli Smoothies, 108

in Lemon-Kiwifruit Smoothies, 144

in Lemon-Lime Green Smoothies, 89

in Maca-Almond Smoothies, 203

in Maca-Cacao Smoothies, 202

in Mango-Maca Smoothies, 203

in Parsley-Pear Smoothies, 191

in Peach-Vanilla Smoothies, 178

in Peanut Butter–Raspberry Smoothies, 137

in Pineapple-Citrus Smoothies, 163

in Pineapple-Lime-Cilantro Smoothie, 88

in Pineapple-Orange Tropical Smoothies, 165

in Pistachio-Banana Smoothies, 161

in Raspberry-Avocado Smoothies, 177

in Refreshing Apple Smoothies, 188

in Spiced Pineapple Smoothies, 201

in Star Fruit–Peach Smoothies, 187

in Strawberry-Banana Smoothies, 200

in Strawberry-Grapefruit Green Smoothies, 88

in Strawberry-Lemonade Smoothies, 94

in Strawberry-Orange Smoothies, 101

in Super Antioxidant Blast Green Smoothies, 122

in Super Green and Peach Smoothie, 162

in Sweet Potato Smoothies, 147

in Vanilla-Avocado Smoothies, 136

in Vanilla-Cantaloupe Smoothies, 146

in The Veggie Green Smoothie, 186

in Watermelon-Blueberry Green Smoothies, 171

in Watermelon-Mint Smoothies, 106

in Zucchini-Vanilla Smoothies, 145

Bartlett Pears

in Parsley-Pear Smoothies, 191

in Pear-Grape Smoothies, 193

Berry Cleansing Smoothie, 89

Berry-Banana Smoothie, 201

Berry–Chia Seed Smoothie, 131

Berry-Kale Smoothie, 132

Bing Cherries

in Blueberry-Cherry-Pomegranate Smoothies, 117

in Cherry-Plum Green Smoothies, 115

in Cherry-Pomegranate Smoothies, 119

in Cherry–Sweet Potato Smoothies, 147

Black and Blue Smoothie, 121

Black Plums, in Plum-Açaí Smoothies, 118

Blackberries

in Black and Blue Smoothies, 121

in Blackberry-Açaí Green Smoothies, 121

in Blackberry-Almond Smoothies, 176

in Blackberry-Peach Smoothies, 120

in Ginger-Berry-Oat Smoothies, 134

in Very Berry Green Smoothies, 115

Blackberry-Açaí Green Smoothie, 121

Blackberry-Almond Smoothie, 176

Blackberry-Peach Smoothie, 120

Blueberries

in Berry Cleansing Smoothies, 89

in Berry-Banana Smoothies, 201

In Berry–Chia Seed Smoothies, 131

in Berry-Kale Smoothies, 132

in Black and Blue Smoothies, 121

in Blueberry-Cherry-Pomegranate Smoothies, 117

in Blueberry-Flaxseed Smoothies, 178

in Blueberry-Lemonade Smoothies, 87

in Blueberry-Maca Smoothies, 133

in Blueberry-Oat Smoothies, 132

in Blueberry-Persimmon Green Smoothies, 116

in Goji Berry Superfood Green Smoothies, 171

in Happy Berry Muffin Smoothies, 146

in Maca-Cacao Smoothies, 202

in Mango-Papaya Green Smoothies with Blueberries, 118

in Spiced Blueberry and Pear Smoothies, 104

in Very Berry Green Smoothies, 115

in Watermelon-Blueberry Green Smoothies, 171

Blueberry-Cherry-Pomegranate Smoothie, 117

Blueberry-Flaxseed Smoothie, 178

Blueberry-Lemonade Smoothie, 87

Blueberry-Maca Smoothie, 133

Blueberry-Oat Smoothie, 132

Blueberry-Persimmon Green Smoothie, 116

Bok Choy, in Pear-Tangerine Smoothies, 159

Broccoli

in Apple-Broccoli Smoothies, 105

in Broccoli-Kale Smoothies, 191

in Kiwifruit-Broccoli Smoothies, 108

in Kiwifruit-Grape Smoothies with Broccoli, 148

in Pear-Broccoli Smoothies, 144

in Super Green and Peach Smoothie, 162

Broccoli-Kale Smoothie, 191

Butterhead Lettuce

in Apple-Cherimoya Smoothies, 108

in Blackberry-Açaí Green Smoothies, 121

in Blueberry-Cherry-Pomegranate Smoothies, 117

in Blueberry-Flaxseed Smoothies, 178

in Cherry-Kiwifruit Green Smoothies, 186

in Chocolate-Açaí Smoothies, 190

in Chocolate–Peanut Butter Smoothies, 131

in Happy Berry Muffin Smoothies, 146

in Maca-Cacao Smoothies, 202

in Red Grape–Fig Smoothies, 160

in Sweet Grapefruit Smoothies, 92

in Sweet Potato Smoothies, 147

in Very Berry Green Smoothies, 115

C

Cacao Powder

in Chocolate-Açaí Smoothies, 190

in Chocolate-Cherry Smoothies, 135

in Chocolate-Grape-Strawberry Smoothies, 106

in Chocolate-Kale Smoothies, 204

in Chocolate-Kiwifruit Smoothies, 109

in Chocolate-Mango Smoothies, 190

in Chocolate–Peanut Butter Smoothies, 131

in Chocolate-Raspberry Green Smoothies, 187

in Creamy Chocolate and Vanilla Smoothies, 172

in Healthy Chocolate Smoothies, 104

in Maca-Cacao Smoothies, 202

in Mesquite Cacao Smoothies, 204

Campari Tomatoes, in The Veggie Green Smoothie, 186

Cantaloupe
  in Cantaloupe-Papaya Smoothies, 148
  in Cantaloupe-Raspberry Green Smoothies, 174
  in Vanilla-Cantaloupe Smoothies, 146
Cantaloupe-Papaya Smoothie, 149
Cantaloupe-Raspberry Green Smoothie, 174
Carambola, in Star Fruit–Peach Smoothies, 187
Carrot Juice, in Carrot-Papaya Smoothies, 105
Carrot-Papaya Smoothie, 105
Carrots
  in Apple-Cherimoya Smoothies, 108
  in Cherry-Pomegranate Smoothies, 119
  in Cherry-Vanilla-Peach Green Smoothies, 122
  in Coconut-Apple-Ginger Smoothies, 175
  in Ginger-Carrot Smoothies, 150
  in Nectarine-Cherry Smoothies, 159
  in Peach-Strawberry Green Smoothies, 107
  in Pineapple-Carrot Smoothies, 123
  in Raspberry-Carrot Green Smoothies, 120
  in Sweet Potato Smoothies, 147
  in The Veggie Green Smoothie, 186
Celery
  in Apple-Broccoli Smoothies, 105
  in Apple-Lime Green Smoothies, 130
  in Banana-Pineapple Smoothies with Aloe and Kale, 109
  in Ginger-Peach Smoothies, 164
  in Mango-Avocado Smoothies, 133
  in Pear-Dandelion Green Smoothies, 86
  in Pineapple-Celery Green Smoothies, 91
  in Strawberry-Orange Smoothies, 101
  in Tropical Green Smoothies, 173
  in The Veggie Green Smoothie, 186
Chai Tea, in Spiced Pineapple Smoothies, 201

Chard
  in Berry-Banana Smoothies, 201
  in Blueberry-Persimmon Green Smoothies, 116
  in Coconut-Peach Smoothies, 165
  in Peach-Mango Smoothies, 188
  in Pear-Aloe Smoothies, 164
  in Pineapple-Orange Tropical Smoothies, 165
  in Strawberry-Banana Smoothies, 200
  in Strawberry-Lemonade Smoothies, 94
  in Strawberry-Raspberry Smoothies with Avocado, 166
Cherimoyas, in Apple-Cherimoya Smoothies, 108
Cherries
  in Avocado-Berry Smoothies, 177
  in Cherry-Apple Smoothies, 200
  in Cherry-Banana Smoothies, 135
  in Cherry-Kiwifruit Green Smoothies, 186
  in Cherry-Pineapple Green Smoothies, 102
  in Cherry-Plum Green Smoothies, 115
  in Cherry-Vanilla-Peach Green Smoothies, 122
  in Chocolate-Cherry Smoothies, 135
  in Nectarine-Cherry Smoothies, 159
  in Peach-Cherry Smoothies, 103
Cherries, Bing
  in Blueberry-Cherry-Pomegranate Smoothies, 117
  in Cherry-Pomegranate Smoothies, 119
  in Cherry–Sweet Potato Smoothies, 147
Cherry-Apple Smoothie, 200
Cherry-Banana Smoothie, 135
Cherry-Kiwifruit Green Smoothie, 186
Cherry-Pineapple Green Smoothie, 102
Cherry-Plum Green Smoothie, 115
Cherry-Pomegranate Smoothie, 119
Cherry–Sweet Potato Smoothie, 147

Cherry-Vanilla-Peach Green Smoothie, 122

Chia Seed–Red Grape Smoothie, 176

Chia Seeds

in Apple-Avocado Smoothies, 136

in Berry Cleansing Smoothies, 89

In Berry–Chia Seed Smoothies, 131

in Blackberry-Almond Smoothies, 176

in Blackberry-Peach Smoothies, 120

in Blueberry-Lemonade Smoothies, 87

in Cherry-Plum Green Smoothies, 115

in Cherry–Sweet Potato Smoothies, 147

in Chia Seed–Red Grape Smoothies, 176

in Chocolate-Kale Smoothies, 204

in Coconut-Apple-Ginger Smoothies, 175

in Goji Berry Superfood Green Smoothies, 171

in Goji Berry–Maca Smoothies, 130

in Mango-Lime Smoothies, 149

in Mesquite Cacao Smoothies, 204

In Peach-Oat Smoothies, 134

in Peach-Vanilla Smoothies, 178

in Pineapple-Celery Green Smoothies, 91

in Plum-Açaí Smoothies, 118

in Watermelon-Blueberry Green Smoothies, 171

Chocolate-Açaí Smoothie, 190

Chocolate-Cherry Smoothie, 135

Chocolate-Grape-Strawberry Smoothie, 106

Chocolate-Kale Smoothie, 204

Chocolate-Kiwifruit Smoothie, 109

Chocolate-Mango Smoothie, 190

Chocolate–Peanut Butter Smoothie, 131

Chocolate-Raspberry Green Smoothie, 187

Cilantro

in Pear-Kiwifruit Smoothies, 149

in Pineapple-Lime-Cilantro Smoothie, 88

Cinnamon

in Apple-Cherimoya Smoothies, 108

in Banana-Cranberry Smoothies, 163

in Berry-Kale Smoothies, 132

in Blueberry-Cherry-Pomegranate Smoothies, 117

in Blueberry-Maca Smoothies, 133

in Blueberry-Oat Smoothies, 132

in Blueberry-Persimmon Green Smoothies, 116

in Carrot-Papaya Smoothies, 105

in Cherry–Sweet Potato Smoothies, 147

in Chocolate-Mango Smoothies, 190

in Cinnamon-Strawberry Smoothies, 145

in Coconut-Persimmon Smoothies, 179

in Maca-Almond Smoothies, 203

in Nectarine-Cherry Smoothies, 159

in Orange–Sesame Seed Smoothies, 166

in Pear-Aloe Smoothies, 164

in Pear-Tangerine Smoothies, 159

in Raspberry-Carrot Green Smoothies, 120

in Spiced Blueberry and Pear Smoothies, 104

in Star Fruit–Peach Smoothies, 187

in Strawberry-Avocado Smoothies, 175

in Sweet Potato Smoothies, 147

Cinnamon-Strawberry Smoothie, 145

Coconut

in Cantaloupe-Papaya Smoothies, 148

in Coconut-Persimmon Smoothies, 179

Coconut Milk

in Berry Cleansing Smoothies, 89

in Blueberry-Maca Smoothies, 133

in Cherry-Banana Smoothies, 135

in Coconut-Apple-Ginger Smoothies, 175

in Coconut–Goji Berry Smoothies, 158

in Coconut-Grapefruit Smoothies, 161

in Coconut-Mango Green Smoothie with Lime, 107

in Coconut-Peach Smoothies, 165

in Coconut-Persimmon Smoothies, 179

in Coconut-Vanilla-Peach Smoothies, 202

in Cucumber-Parsley Smoothies, 192

in Mango-Lime Smoothies, 149

in Mesquite Cacao Smoothies, 204

in Peach-Strawberry-Coconut Smoothies, 162

in Pineapple-Orange Tropical Smoothies, 165

in Strawberry Goodness Smoothies, 173

in Tropical Green Smoothies, 173

in Very Berry Green Smoothies, 115

Coconut Water

in Banana-Pineapple Green Smoothies, 102

in Mango-Kiwifruit Smoothies, 103

in Peach-Cherry Smoothies, 103

Coconut-Apple-Ginger Smoothie, 175

Coconut–Goji Berry Smoothie, 158

Coconut-Grapefruit Smoothie, 161

Coconut-Mango Green Smoothie with Lime, 107

Coconut-Peach Smoothie, 165

Coconut-Persimmon Smoothie, 179

Coconut-Vanilla-Peach Smoothie, 202

Collard Leaves

In Berry–Chia Seed Smoothies, 131

in Blueberry-Maca Smoothies, 133

in Blueberry-Oat Smoothies, 132

in Cherry-Pineapple Green Smoothies, 102

in Maca-Almond Smoothies, 203

in Nectarine-Cherry Smoothies, 159

in Nectarine–Goji Berry Smoothies, 193

in Orange-Ginger Smoothies, 143

in Peach-Cherry Smoothies, 103

in Pineapple-Plum Smoothies with Almond Milk, 119

in Raspberry-Orange-Pomegranate Smoothies, 117

in Refreshing Lemon-Cucumber Smoothies, 150

in Vanilla-Cantaloupe Smoothies, 146

Cranberries

in Banana-Cranberry Smoothies, 163

in Cranberry Cleanse Smoothies, 93

Cranberry Cleanse Smoothie, 93

Creamy Chocolate and Vanilla Smoothie, 172

Cucumber-Aloe Smoothie, 194

Cucumber-Kale Smoothie, 137

Cucumber-Parsley Smoothie, 192

Cucumbers

in Apple-Avocado Smoothies, 136

in Apple-Mango Green Smoothies, 92

in Cucumber-Aloe Smoothies, 194

in Cucumber-Kale Smoothies, 137

in Cucumber-Parsley Smoothies, 192

in Ginger-Spinach Smoothies, 194

in Green Goddess Detox Smoothies, 93

in Kiwifruit-Broccoli Smoothies, 108

in Pineapple-Citrus Smoothies, 163

in Pineapple-Lime-Cilantro Smoothie, 88

in Refreshing Apple Smoothies, 188

in Refreshing Lemon-Cucumber Smoothies, 150

in Tropical Green Smoothies, 173

in Watermelon-Blueberry Green Smoothies, 171

D

Dandelion Greens

in Banana-Cranberry Smoothies, 163

in Berry Cleansing Smoothies, 89

in Cherry-Banana Smoothies, 135

in Cinnamon-Strawberry Smoothies, 145

in Dandelion-Orange Smoothies, 90

in Ginger-Peach Smoothies, 164

in Peach-Pear Smoothies, 192

in Peach-Strawberry Green Smoothies, 107

in Peach-Strawberry-Coconut Smoothies, 162

in Pineapple-Citrus Smoothies, 163

in Super Green and Peach Smoothie, 162

Dandelion-Orange Smoothie, 90

Dulse Flakes, in Coconut-Grapefruit Smoothies, 161

E

Escarole Lettuce

in Kiwifruit-Orange Green Smoothies, 172

in Mango-Maca Smoothies, 203

in Mango-Papaya Green Smoothies with Blueberries, 118

F

Figs, in Red Grape–Fig Smoothies, 160

Flaxseeds

in Avocado-Peach Green Smoothies, 174

in Blueberry-Flaxseed Smoothies, 178

in Cantaloupe-Raspberry Green Smoothies, 174

in Green Goddess Detox Smoothies, 93

in The Green Machine, 91

in Kiwifruit-Orange Green Smoothies,- 172

in Strawberry Goodness Smoothies, 173

in Tropical Green Smoothies, 173

in Very Berry Green Smoothies, 115

Frozen Raspberry-Lemonade Smoothie, 116

G

Ginger

in Banana-Orange Smoothies, 160

in Blueberry-Lemonade Smoothies, 87

in Coconut-Apple-Ginger Smoothies, 175

in Ginger-Berry-Oat Smoothies, 134

in Ginger-Carrot Smoothies, 150

in Ginger-Peach Smoothies, 164

in Ginger-Spinach Smoothies, 194

in Mango-Papaya Green Smoothies with Blueberries, 118

in Orange-Ginger Smoothies, 143

in Orange-Pear Smoothies, 94

in Pear-Kiwifruit Smoothies, 149

in Pineapple-Ginger Smoothies, 151

in Pineapple-Lime-Cilantro Smoothie, 88

in Raspberry-Carrot Green Smoothies, 120

in Spiced Pineapple Smoothies, 201

Ginger-Berry-Oat Smoothie, 134

Ginger-Carrot Smoothie, 150

Ginger-Citrus Green Smoothie with Kale, 138

Ginger-Peach Smoothie, 164

Ginger-Spinach Smoothie, 194

Goji Berries

In Berry–Chia Seed Smoothies, 131

in Berry-Kale Smoothies, 132

in Coconut–Goji Berry Smoothies, 158

in Goji Berry Superfood Green Smoothies, 171

in Goji Berry–Maca Smoothies, 130

in Maca-Cacao Smoothies, 202

in Nectarine–Goji Berry Smoothies, 193

in Pineapple-Mango Green Smoothies, 101

in Vanilla-Cantaloupe Smoothies, 146

in Very Berry Green Smoothies, 115

Goji Berry Superfood Green Smoothie, 171

Goji Berry–Maca Smoothie, 130

Grapefruit

in Coconut-Grapefruit Smoothies, 161

in Grapefruit-Orange Smoothies, 90

in Strawberry-Grapefruit Green Smoothies, 88

in Sweet Grapefruit Smoothies, 92

Grapefruit-Orange Smoothie, 90

Grapes

in Chocolate-Grape-Strawberry Smoothies, 106

in Green Apple Smoothies, 87

in Green Goddess Detox Smoothies, 93

in The Green Machine, 91

in Lemon-Lime Green Smoothies, 89

Grapes, Green

in Kiwifruit-Grape Smoothies with Broccoli, 148

Grapes, Red

in Chia Seed–Red Grape Smoothies, 176

in Pear-Grape Smoothies, 193

in Red Grape–Fig Smoothies, 160

Green Apple Smoothie, 87

Green Apples

in Apple-Broccoli Smoothies, 105

in Apple-Lime Green Smoothies, 130

in Apple-Mango Green Smoothies, 92

in Green Apple Smoothies, 87

in Green Goddess Detox Smoothies, 93

Green Goodness Detox Smoothie, 93

Green Grapes

in Green Apple Smoothies, 87

in Green Goddess Detox Smoothies, 93

in The Green Machine, 91

in Kiwifruit-Grape Smoothies with Broc
coli, 148
in Lemon-Lime Green Smoothies, 89
**Green Leaf Lettuce, in Green Apple
Smoothies,** 87
The Green Machine, 91

H

Happy Berry Muffin Smoothie, 146
Healthy Chocolate Smoothie, 104
Hemp Seeds, in Green Apple Smoothies, 87

K

Kale
in Apple-Avocado Smoothies, 136
in Apple-Lime Green Smoothies, 130
in Avocado-Peach Green Smoothies, 174
in Banana-Orange Smoothies, 160
in Banana-Pineapple Smoothies with Aloe
and Kale, 109
in Berry-Kale Smoothies, 132
in Broccoli-Kale Smoothies, 191
in Chocolate-Kale Smoothies, 204
in Coconut–Goji Berry Smoothies, 158
in Coconut-Grapefruit Smoothies, 161
in Coconut-Mango Green Smoothie with
Lime, 107
in Cucumber-Kale Smoothies, 137
in The Green Machine, 91
in Kale-Parsley Smoothies, 189
in Lemon-Kiwifruit Smoothies, 144
in Lemon-Lime Green Smoothies, 89
in Mango-Avocado Smoothies, 133
in Mango-Lime Smoothies, 149
in Mango-Pear Smoothies, 189
in Pear-Dandelion Green Smoothies, 86
in Pear-Grape Smoothies, 193
in Pear-Kiwifruit Smoothies, 149
in Pineapple-Ginger Smoothies, 151
in Pistachio-Banana Smoothies, 161
in Raspberry-Carrot Green Smoothies,
120

in Sweet Potato-Orange Smoothies, 158
in Tropical Green Smoothies, 173
in The Veggie Green Smoothie, 186
in Watermelon-Blueberry Green Smooth
ies, 171
Kale-Parsley Smoothie, 189
Kiwifruit
in Cherry-Kiwifruit Green Smoothies, 186
in Chocolate-Kiwifruit Smoothies, 109
in Cucumber-Aloe Smoothies, 194
in Kiwifruit-Broccoli Smoothies, 108
in Kiwifruit-Grape Smoothies with Broc
coli, 148
in Kiwifruit-Orange Green Smoothies, 172
in Lemon-Kiwifruit Smoothies, 144
in Mango-Avocado Smoothies, 133
in Mango-Kiwifruit Smoothies, 103
in Mango-Lime Smoothies, 149
in Pear-Kiwifruit Smoothies, 149
Kiwifruit-Broccoli Smoothie, 108
Kiwifruit-Grape Smoothie with Broccoli,
148
Kiwifruit-Orange Green Smoothie, 172

L

Lemon-Kiwifruit Smoothie, 144
Lemon-Lime Green Smoothie, 89
Lemons
in Apple-Mango Green Smoothies, 92
in Blueberry-Lemonade Smoothies, 87
in Frozen Raspberry-Lemonade Smoothies, 116
in Lemon-Kiwifruit Smoothies, 144
in Lemon-Lime Green Smoothies, 89
in Refreshing Lemon-Cucumber Smoothies, 150
in Strawberry-Lemonade Smoothies, 94
Lettuce, Butterhead
in Apple-Cherimoya Smoothies, 108
in Blackberry-Açaí Green Smoothies, 121
in Blueberry-Cherry-Pomegranate Smoothies, 117

in Blueberry-Flaxseed Smoothies, 178

in Cherry-Kiwifruit Green Smoothies, 186

in Chocolate-Açaí Smoothies, 190

in Chocolate–Peanut Butter Smoothies, 131

in Happy Berry Muffin Smoothies, 146

in Maca-Cacao Smoothies, 202

in Red Grape–Fig Smoothies, 160

in Sweet Grapefruit Smoothies, 92

in Sweet Potato Smoothies, 147

in Very Berry Green Smoothies, 115

Lettuce, Escarole

in Kiwifruit-Orange Green Smoothies, 172

in Mango-Maca Smoothies, 203

in Mango-Papaya Green Smoothies with Blueberries, 118

Lettuce, Romaine

in Cherry-Vanilla-Peach Green Smoothies, 122

in Chia Seed–Red Grape Smoothies, 176

Limes

in Apple-Lime Green Smoothies, 130

in Banana-Cranberry Smoothies, 163

in Cantaloupe-Papaya Smoothies, 148

in Coconut-Mango Green Smoothie with Lime, 107

in Green Goddess Detox Smoothies, 93

in Lemon-Lime Green Smoothies, 89

in Mango-Lime Smoothies, 149

in Pineapple-Lime-Cilantro Smoothie, 88

M

Maca Powder

in Blueberry-Maca Smoothies, 133

in Chocolate-Cherry Smoothies, 135

in Goji Berry–Maca Smoothies, 130

in Lemon-Kiwifruit Smoothies, 144

in Maca-Almond Smoothies, 203

in Maca-Cacao Smoothies, 202

in Mango-Maca Smoothies, 203

in Strawberry-Banana Smoothies, 200

Maca-Almond Smoothie, 203

Maca-Cacao Smoothie, 202

Mango-Avocado Smoothie, 133

Mangoes

in Apple-Mango Green Smoothies, 92

in Chocolate-Mango Smoothies, 190

in Coconut-Mango Green Smoothie with Lime, 107

in Coconut-Peach Smoothies, 165

in Ginger-Carrot Smoothies, 150

in Ginger-Spinach Smoothies, 194

in Mango-Avocado Smoothies, 133

in Mango-Kiwifruit Smoothies, 103

in Mango-Lime Smoothies, 149

in Mango-Maca Smoothies, 203

in Mango-Papaya Green Smoothies with Blueberries, 118

in Mango-Pear Smoothies, 189

in Nectarine–Goji Berry Smoothies, 193

in Peach-Cherry Smoothies, 103

in Peach-Mango Smoothies, 188

in Pineapple-Mango Green Smoothies, 101

in Tropical Green Smoothies, 173

Mango-Kiwifruit Smoothie, 103

Mango-Lime Smoothie, 149

Mango-Maca Smoothie, 203

Mango-Papaya Green Smoothie with Blueberries, 118

Mango-Pear Smoothie, 189

Mean Green Cleansing Smoothie, 86

Mesquite Cacao Smoothie, 204

Mesquite Powder, in Mesquite Cacao Smoothies, 204

Mint

in Green Apple Smoothies, 87

in Papaya-Mint Smoothies, 143

in Pear-Dandelion Green Smoothies, 86

in Strawberry-Grapefruit Green Smoothies, 88

in Watermelon-Mint Smoothies, 106

Mint Tea, in Chocolate-Kiwifruit Smoothies, 109

N

Nectarine-Cherry Smoothie, 159
Nectarine–Goji Berry Smoothie, 193
Nectarines
  in Nectarine-Cherry Smoothies, 159
  in Nectarine–Goji Berry Smoothies, 193
Nutmeg
  in Spiced Blueberry and Pear Smoothies, 104
  in Strawberry-Avocado Smoothies, 175
  in Sweet Potato Smoothies, 147

O

Oats, Rolled
  in Blueberry-Oat Smoothies, 132
  in Ginger-Berry-Oat Smoothies, 134
  in Happy Berry Muffin Smoothies, 146
  In Peach-Oat Smoothies, 134
Orange-Ginger Smoothie, 143
Orange-Pear Smoothie, 94
Oranges
  in Avocado-Berry Smoothies, 177
  in Banana-Cranberry Smoothies, 163
  in Banana-Orange Smoothies, 160
  in Berry-Kale Smoothies, 132
  in Blackberry-Peach Smoothies, 120
  in Blueberry-Flaxseed Smoothies, 178
  in Cherry-Banana Smoothies, 135
  in Cherry-Pomegranate Smoothies, 119
  in Cinnamon-Strawberry Smoothies, 145
  in Coconut–Goji Berry Smoothies, 158
  in Cranberry Cleanse Smoothies, 93
  in Dandelion-Orange Smoothies, 90
  in Grapefruit-Orange Smoothies, 90
  in Kiwifruit-Orange Green Smoothies, 172
  in Mango-Papaya Green Smoothies with Blueberries, 118
  in Mango-Pear Smoothies, 189
  in Orange-Ginger Smoothies, 143
  in Orange-Pear Smoothies, 94
  in Orange–Sesame Seed Smoothies, 166
  In Peach-Oat Smoothies, 134
  in Peach-Strawberry-Coconut Smoothies, 162

  in Pear-Aloe Smoothies, 164
  in Pear-Broccoli Smoothies, 144
  in Pear-Dandelion Green Smoothies, 86
  in Pineapple-Carrot Smoothies, 123
  in Pineapple-Celery Green Smoothies, 91
  in Pineapple-Citrus Smoothies, 163
  in Pineapple-Ginger Smoothies, 151
  in Pineapple-Orange Tropical Smoothies, 165
  in Raspberry-Carrot Green Smoothies, 120
  in Raspberry-Orange-Pomegranate Smoothies, 117
  in Strawberry-Orange Smoothies, 101
  in Sweet Grapefruit Smoothies, 92
  in Sweet Potato-Orange Smoothies, 158
Orange–Sesame Seed Smoothie, 166

P

Papaya
  in Cantaloupe-Papaya Smoothies, 148
  in Carrot-Papaya Smoothies, 105
  in Mango-Papaya Green Smoothies with Blueberries, 118
  in Papaya-Mint Smoothies, 143
  in Strawberry Goodness Smoothies, 173
  in Sweet Potato-Orange Smoothies, 158
  in Tropical Green Smoothies, 173
Papaya-Mint Smoothie, 143
Parsley
  in Cucumber-Parsley Smoothies, 192
  in Green Goddess Detox Smoothies, 93
  in The Green Machine, 91
  in Kale-Parsley Smoothies, 189
  in Parsley-Pear Smoothies, 191
  in Pear-Dandelion Green Smoothies, 86
  in Pineapple-Celery Green Smoothies, 91
  in Pineapple-Citrus Smoothies, 163
  in Refreshing Apple Smoothies, 188
Parsley-Pear Smoothie, 191
Peach-Cherry Smoothie, 103
Peaches
  in Avocado-Peach Green Smoothies, 174
  in Blackberry-Peach Smoothies, 120

in Cherry-Vanilla-Peach Green Smoothies, 122

in Coconut-Peach Smoothies, 165

in Coconut-Vanilla-Peach Smoothies, 202

in Ginger-Peach Smoothies, 164

in Peach-Cherry Smoothies, 103

in Peach-Mango Smoothies, 188

In Peach-Oat Smoothies, 134

in Peach-Pear Smoothies, 192

in Peach-Strawberry Green Smoothies, 107

in Peach-Strawberry-Coconut Smoothies, 162

in Peach-Vanilla Smoothies, 178

in Star Fruit–Peach Smoothies, 187

in Super Green and Peach Smoothie, 162

Peach-Mango Smoothie, 188

Peach-Oat Smoothie, 134

Peach-Pear Smoothie, 192

Peach-Strawberry Green Smoothie, 107

Peach-Strawberry-Coconut Smoothie, 162

Peach-Vanilla Smoothie, 178

Peanut Butter

in Chocolate–Peanut Butter Smoothies, 131

in Peanut Butter–Raspberry Smoothies, 137

Peanut Butter–Raspberry Smoothie, 137

Pear-Aloe Smoothie, 164

Pear-Broccoli Smoothie, 144

Pear-Dandelion Green Smoothie, 86

Pear-Grape Smoothie, 193

Pear-Kiwifruit Smoothie, 149

Pears

in Cherry-Kiwifruit Green Smoothies, 186

in Cherry-Pineapple Green Smoothies, 102

in Chocolate-Açaí Smoothies, 190

in Chocolate-Cherry Smoothies, 135

in Chocolate-Grape-Strawberry Smoothies, 106

in Cranberry Cleanse Smoothies, 93

in Goji Berry Superfood Green Smoothies, 171

in Healthy Chocolate Smoothies, 104

in Kale-Parsley Smoothies, 189

in Kiwifruit-Orange Green Smoothies, 172

in Mango-Pear Smoothies, 189

in Mesquite Cacao Smoothies, 204

in Orange-Pear Smoothies, 94

in Papaya-Mint Smoothies, 143

in Parsley-Pear Smoothies, 191

in Peach-Pear Smoothies, 192

in Pear-Aloe Smoothies, 164

in Pear-Broccoli Smoothies, 144

in Pear-Dandelion Green Smoothies, 86

in Pear-Grape Smoothies, 193

in Pear-Kiwifruit Smoothies, 149

in Pear-Tangerine Smoothies, 159

in Raspberry-Carrot Green Smoothies, 120

in Raspberry-Orange-Pomegranate Smoothies, 117

in Refreshing Lemon-Cucumber Smoothies, 150

in Spiced Blueberry and Pear Smoothies, 104

in Strawberry Goodness Smoothies, 173

Pear-Tangerine Smoothie, 159

Persimmons

in Blueberry-Persimmon Green Smoothies, 116

in Coconut-Persimmon Smoothies, 179

in Plum-Açaí Smoothies, 118

Pineapple

in Banana-Pineapple Green Smoothies, 102

in Banana-Pineapple Smoothies with Aloe and Kale, 109

in Cherry-Pineapple Green Smoothies, 102

in Cucumber-Kale Smoothies, 137

in Cucumber-Parsley Smoothies, 192

in Ginger-Carrot Smoothies, 150

in Ginger-Peach Smoothies, 164

in Kale-Parsley Smoothies, 189

in Orange-Ginger Smoothies, 143

in Pineapple-Carrot Smoothies, 123

in Pineapple-Celery Green Smoothies, 91

in Pineapple-Citrus Smoothies, 163

in Pineapple-Ginger Smoothies, 151

in Pineapple-Lime-Cilantro Smoothie, 88

in Pineapple-Mango Green Smoothies, 101

in Pineapple-Orange Tropical Smoothies, 165

in Pineapple-Plum Smoothies with Almond Milk, 119

in Spiced Pineapple Smoothies, 201

in Sweet Grapefruit Smoothies, 92

in Tropical Green Smoothies, 173

Pineapple-Carrot Smoothie, 123

Pineapple-Celery Green Smoothie, 91

Pineapple-Citrus Smoothie, 163

Pineapple-Ginger Smoothie, 151

Pineapple-Lime-Cilantro Smoothie, 88

Pineapple-Mango Green Smoothie, 101

Pineapple-Orange Tropical Smoothie, 165

Pineapple-Plum Smoothie with Almond Milk, 119

Pistachio-Banana Smoothie, 161

Pistachios, in Pistachio-Banana Smoothies, 161

Plum-Açaí Smoothie, 118

Plums

in Cherry-Plum Green Smoothies, 115

in Pineapple-Plum Smoothies with Almond Milk, 119

in Plum-Açaí Smoothies, 118

Pomegranates

in Blueberry-Cherry-Pomegranate Smoothies, 117

in Cherry-Pomegranate Smoothies, 119

in Raspberry-Orange-Pomegranate Smoothies, 117

in Super Antioxidant Blast Green Smoothies, 122

R

Rainbow Chard, in Peach-Mango Smoothies, 188

Raspberries

in Avocado-Berry Smoothies, 177

In Berry–Chia Seed Smoothies, 131

in Cantaloupe-Raspberry Green Smoothies, 174

in Chocolate-Raspberry Green Smoothies, 187

in Cucumber-Kale Smoothies, 137

in Frozen Raspberry-Lemonade Smoothies, 116

in Orange–Sesame Seed Smoothies, 166

in Peanut Butter–Raspberry Smoothies, 137

in Raspberry-Avocado Smoothies, 177

in Raspberry-Carrot Green Smoothies, 120

in Raspberry-Orange-Pomegranate Smoothies, 117

in Strawberry-Raspberry Smoothies with Avocado, 166

in Very Berry Green Smoothies, 115

Raspberry-Avocado Smoothie, 177

Raspberry-Carrot Green Smoothie, 120

Raspberry-Orange-Pomegranate Smoothie, 117

Red Delicious Apples, in Coconut-Apple-Ginger Smoothies, 175

Red Grape–Fig Smoothie, 160

Red Grapes

in Chia Seed–Red Grape Smoothies, 176

in Chocolate-Grape-Strawberry Smoothies, 106

in Pear-Grape Smoothies, 193

in Red Grape–Fig Smoothies, 160

Refreshing Apple Smoothie, 188

Refreshing Lemon-Cucumber Smoothie, 150

Romaine Lettuce

in Cherry-Vanilla-Peach Green Smoothies, 122

in Chia Seed–Red Grape Smoothies, 176

S

Sesame Seeds

in Chia Seed–Red Grape Smoothies, 176

in Nectarine-Cherry Smoothies, 159

in Orange–Sesame Seed Smoothies, 166

Spiced Blueberry and Pear Smoothie, 104
Spiced Pineapple Smoothie, 201
Spinach
    in Apple-Broccoli Smoothies, 105
    in Apple-Mango Green Smoothies, 92
    in Avocado-Peach Green Smoothies, 174
    in Banana-Pineapple Green Smoothies, 102
    in Blackberry-Almond Smoothies, 176
    in Blackberry-Peach Smoothies, 120
    in Cantaloupe-Papaya Smoothies, 148
    in Cantaloupe-Raspberry Green Smoothies, 174
    in Carrot-Papaya Smoothies, 105
    in Cherry-Apple Smoothies, 200
    in Cherry-Plum Green Smoothies, 115
    in Chocolate-Cherry Smoothies, 135
    in Chocolate-Grape-Strawberry Smoothies, 106
    in Chocolate-Kiwifruit Smoothies, 109
    in Chocolate-Mango Smoothies, 190
    in Chocolate-Raspberry Green Smoothies, 187
    in Cinnamon-Strawberry Smoothies, 145
    in Coconut-Persimmon Smoothies, 179
    in Coconut-Vanilla-Peach Smoothies, 202
    in Cranberry Cleanse Smoothies, 93
    in Cucumber-Aloe Smoothies, 194
    in Frozen Raspberry-Lemonade Smoothies, 116
    in Ginger-Berry-Oat Smoothies, 134
    in Ginger-Spinach Smoothies, 194
    in Goji Berry Superfood Green Smoothies, 171
    in Goji Berry–Maca Smoothies, 130
    in Grapefruit-Orange Smoothies, 90
    in Green Goddess Detox Smoothies, 93
    in Healthy Chocolate Smoothies, 104
    in Kiwifruit-Grape Smoothies with Broccoli, 148
    in Mango-Pear Smoothies, 189
    in Mesquite Cacao Smoothies, 204
    in Nectarine–Goji Berry Smoothies, 193
    in Orange-Ginger Smoothies, 143
    in Orange-Pear Smoothies, 94
    in Orange–Sesame Seed Smoothies, 166
    in Papaya-Mint Smoothies, 143
    In Peach-Oat Smoothies, 134
    in Peach-Vanilla Smoothies, 178
    in Peanut Butter–Raspberry Smoothies, 137
    in Pineapple-Celery Green Smoothies, 91
    in Pineapple-Mango Green Smoothies, 101
    in Pineapple-Orange Tropical Smoothies, 165
    in Spiced Pineapple Smoothies, 201
    in Star Fruit–Peach Smoothies, 187
    in Strawberry-Grapefruit Green Smoothies, 88
    in Super Antioxidant Blast Green Smoothies, 122
    in Tropical Green Smoothies, 173
    in The Veggie Green Smoothie, 186
Star Fruit–Peach Smoothie, 187
Strawberries
    in Avocado-Berry Smoothies, 177
    in Berry Cleansing Smoothies, 89
    in Berry-Banana Smoothies, 201
    In Berry–Chia Seed Smoothies, 131
    in Chocolate-Grape-Strawberry Smoothies, 106
    in Cinnamon-Strawberry Smoothies, 145
    in Ginger-Berry-Oat Smoothies, 134
    in Goji Berry Superfood Green Smoothies, 171
    in Goji Berry–Maca Smoothies, 130
    in Happy Berry Muffin Smoothies, 146
    in Mango-Maca Smoothies, 203
    in Peach-Strawberry Green Smoothies, 107
    in Peach-Strawberry-Coconut Smoothies, 162
    in Pineapple-Plum Smoothies with Almond Milk, 119
    in Strawberry Goodness Smoothies, 173

in Strawberry-Avocado Smoothies, 175

in Strawberry-Banana Smoothies, 200

in Strawberry-Grapefruit Green Smoothies, 88

in Strawberry-Lemonade Smoothies, 94

in Strawberry-Orange Smoothies, 101

in Strawberry-Raspberry Smoothies with Avocado, 166

in Watermelon-Mint Smoothies, 106

Strawberry Goodness Smoothie, 173

Strawberry-Avocado Smoothie, 175

Strawberry-Banana Smoothie, 200

Strawberry-Grapefruit Green Smoothie, 88

Strawberry-Lemonade Smoothie, 94

Strawberry-Orange Smoothie, 101

Strawberry-Raspberry Smoothie with Avocado, 166

Super Antioxidant Blast Green Smoothie, 122

Super Green and Peach Smoothie, 162

Sweet Grapefruit Smoothie, 92

Sweet Potato Smoothie, 147

Sweet Potatoes

in Cherry–Sweet Potato Smoothies, 147

in Sweet Potato Smoothies, 147

in Sweet Potato-Orange Smoothies, 158

Sweet Potato-Orange Smoothie, 158

Swiss Chard, in Vanilla-Avocado Smoothies, 136

T

Tangerines, in Pear-Tangerine Smoothies, 159

Tea, Chai, in Spiced Pineapple Smoothies, 201

Tea, Mint, in Chocolate-Kiwifruit Smoothies, 109

Tomatoes, Campari, in The Veggie Green Smoothie, 186

Tropical Green Smoothie, 173

V

Vanilla

in Avocado-Peach Green Smoothies, 174

in Banana-Pineapple Green Smoothies, 102

in Blueberry-Maca Smoothies, 133

in Cherry-Apple Smoothies, 200

in Cherry-Plum Green Smoothies, 115

in Cherry-Vanilla-Peach Green Smoothies, 122

in Chocolate-Açaí Smoothies, 190

in Chocolate-Cherry Smoothies, 135

in Chocolate–Peanut Butter Smoothies, 131

in Cinnamon-Strawberry Smoothies, 145

in Coconut-Persimmon Smoothies, 179

in Coconut-Vanilla-Peach Smoothies, 202

in Creamy Chocolate and Vanilla Smoothies, 172

in Frozen Raspberry-Lemonade Smoothies, 116

in Maca-Almond Smoothies, 203

in Peach-Mango Smoothies, 188

in Peach-Pear Smoothies, 192

in Peach-Strawberry Green Smoothies, 107

in Peach-Vanilla Smoothies, 178

in Peanut Butter–Raspberry Smoothies, 137

in Pistachio-Banana Smoothies, 161

in Raspberry-Avocado Smoothies, 177

in Sweet Grapefruit Smoothies, 92

in Vanilla-Avocado Smoothies, 136

in Vanilla-Cantaloupe Smoothies, 146

in Zucchini-Vanilla Smoothies, 145

Vanilla-Avocado Smoothie, 136

Vanilla-Cantaloupe Smoothie, 146

The Veggie Green Smoothie, 186

Very Berry Green Smoothie, 115

W

Watermelon
  in Watermelon-Blueberry Green Smooth-
    ies, 171
  in Watermelon-Mint Smoothies, 106
Watermelon-Blueberry Green Smoothie,
  171
Watermelon-Mint Smoothie, 106

Z

Zucchini
  in Black and Blue Smoothies, 121
  in Cherry-Plum Green Smoothies, 115
  in Zucchini-Vanilla Smoothies, 145
Zucchini-Vanilla Smoothie, 145

About the Author

Tracy Russell has tried just about every fad diet and expensive "superfood" supplement out there. It wasn't until she discovered the green smoothie that she lost 40 pounds, lowered her cholesterol by 50 points, and started running—marathons!

Tracy is one of the foremost experts on green smoothies and nutrition. She shares her wealth of firsthand information, research, and experiences with tens of thousands of people every day. Tracy is the author of one of the largest green smoothie websites on the Internet, Incredible Smoothies (incrediblesmoothies.com), which she launched in 2009 to help others achieve a healthy lifestyle. She is also a contributor to the Whole Pregnancy website (wholepregnancy.org). She has written guest articles for other blogs and magazines as well.

Inspired by the healthy recipes in *The Best Green Smoothies on the Planet* and want more delicious, plant-based fare?

Download a **FREE** digital copy of **BenBella's Best of Plant-Based Eating** and sign up for more exclusive offers and info at

BENBELLAVEGAN.COM

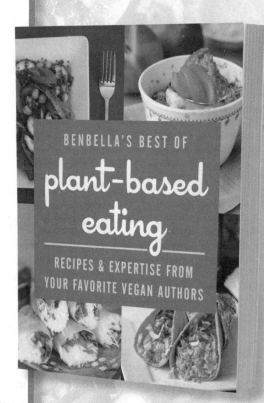

WITH NEARLY 50 RECIPES FROM

The China Study Cookbook | *The Happy Herbivore series* | *Better Than Vegan*
Blissful Bites | *The Best Green Smoothies on the Planet* | *The HappyCow Cookbook*
Jazzy Vegetarian Classics | *The PlantPure Nation Cookbook* | *YumUniverse*

AND SELECTIONS FROM

Whole | *The Low-Carb Fraud* | *Food Over Medicine* | *Healthy Eating, Healthy World*